HISTORY'S GREATEST SPEECHES

DOVER THRIFT EDITIONS

Edited by
James Daley

DOVER PUBLICATIONS, INC.
MINEOLA, NEW YORK

DOVER THRIFT EDITIONS

General Editor: Mary Carolyn Waldrep
Editor of This Volume: Janet Baine Kopito

Acknowledgments: See page vii.

Copyright

Bibliographical Note

History's Greatest Speeches is a new compilation, first published by Dover Publications, Inc., in 2013. An Introduction has been written specially for this edition by James Daley, who also has provided a biographical note for the author of each speech. Inconsistencies in spelling and capitalization occasionally have been retained in the texts to reflect their sources.

Library of Congress Cataloging-in-Publication Data

History's greatest speeches / edited by James Daley.
pages cm. — (Dover thrift editions)
ISBN-13: 978-0-486-49739-6 (pbk.) — ISBN-10: 0-486-49739-9 (pbk.)
1. Speeches, addresses, etc. 2. Speeches, addresses, etc., American. I. Daley, James, 1979–
PN6122.H55 2013
808.85—dc23

2013008804

Manufactured in the United States by RR Donnelley
49739905 2016
www.doverpublications.com

Contents

Acknowledgments

"On the Perils of Indifference," by Elie Wiesel. Originally given as a speech, April 12, 1999. Copyright © 1999 by Elie Wiesel. Reprinted by permission of Georges Borchardt, Inc., on behalf of Elie Wiesel.

Harvey Milk's "The Hope Speech" courtesy of the San Francisco Public Library.

"I Have a Dream," by Martin Luther King, Jr. Reprinted by arrangement with The Heirs to the Estate of Martin Luther King Jr., c/o Writers House as agent for the proprietor. New York, NY. Copyright © 1963 Dr. Martin Luther King, Jr; copyright renewed 1991 by Coretta Scott King.

Acknowledgments

"Ordinary [illegible]" [illegible] Elie Wiesel. Originally [illegible] speech [illegible] Copyright © [illegible] by Elie Wiesel. Reprinted by permission of [illegible] on behalf of Elie Wiesel.

[illegible] "The Hope Speech" courtesy of the San [illegible] Public Library.

[illegible] Reprinted by [illegible] [illegible] Luther King [illegible] New York, NY. Copyright © [illegible] King, Jr.; copyright renewed [illegible] by [illegible] Scott King.

Introductory Note

WHEN ABRAHAM LINCOLN ROSE to the podium in Gettysburg, Virginia, on a cold November day in 1863, he could not have known the impact that his words would have throughout history. Having only completed the writing of his speech that very morning, Lincoln offered an address as unassuming as the simple wooden platform on which he stood: a brief few words of inspiration and encouragement in the midst of a disheartening war, and in the wake of the worst battle his nation had ever known. And yet, despite Lincoln's modest intentions, the Gettysburg Address would come to define an entire period in American history, forever encapsulating a nation's struggle for equality, democracy, and unity.

That is so often how it goes with history's most memorable addresses. There is nothing that can so completely capture the feeling, mood, and meaning of a historical period like a great speech, delivered by one of its time's best orators. No amount of facts, dates, statistics, or figures—no matter how skillfully articulated—can ever hope to transport a reader to another time as effectively as the words of one addressing many.

It is with this in mind that the speeches contained in this volume were collected. Representing centuries of oration, it is the aim of this anthology to transport the reader to some of the most fascinating and important moments in history. From Pericles's "Funeral Oration" during the Peloponnesian War to Winston Churchill's declaration that "We Shall Fight Them on the Beaches" at the beginning of World War II, this collection highlights how leaders of great nations inspired their countrymen during the darkest days of battle. Through the words of Harvey Milk, Mahatma Gandhi, Martin Luther King Jr., and Sojourner Truth, it will illustrate how some of history's most courageous activists spoke truth to power in their efforts to remake the world.

Perhaps most fascinating of all, however, are the speeches whose greatest impact lies in their ability to rouse and inspire for generations past their time. In "Duties of American Citizenship," Theodore Roosevelt argues that service to one's country is not an act of selflessness or charity, but rather the absolute duty of all competent and capable citizens. Mother Theresa, in her Nobel Prize acceptance lecture, encouraged all who listened not to merely admire her life's work, but to make the needs of the poor a priority in their own lives as well. And finally, in what may be one of the most well-known inspirational speeches in this volume, there are the words of John F. Kennedy, delivered on the day of his inauguration, facing a country besieged by a faltering economy, a cultural upheaval, and a terrifying nuclear arms race:

> In the long history of the world, only a few generations have been granted the role of defending freedom in its hour of maximum danger. I do not shrink from this responsibility—I welcome it. I do not believe that any of us would exchange places with any other people or any other generation. The energy, the faith, the devotion which we bring to this endeavor will light our country and all who serve it—and the glow from that fire can truly light the world.
>
> And so, my fellow Americans: ask not what your country can do for you—ask what you can do for your country.
>
> My fellow citizens of the world: ask not what America will do for you, but what together we can do for the freedom of man.

It is with the spirit of President Kennedy's words that I hope this selection of speeches will be received. Standing before a nation during a moment of astounding and fearsome challenges, Kennedy chose not to vilify his enemies, nor to disprove his detractors, but rather to offer a vision of unity for the world and an imperative of action for his countrymen. Likewise, I hope that readers of this volume can look to the great and wise words of the past to inform and inspire their own vision of the future, no matter how trying or troublesome the present.

James Daley
Editor

History's Greatest Speeches

PERICLES

Funeral Oration (Fifth Century BCE)

Pericles (c. 495–429 BCE) was one of Ancient Greece's most renowned and powerful statesmen, leading the Athenian state for over thirty years during the Golden Age of Athens (also known as the "Age of Pericles). The following speech was delivered at a funeral ceremony in honor of the soldiers who died during the first year of the Peloponnesian War. Most noted as one of history's first great pronouncements on the importance of democracy, the "Funeral Oration" is also valued for the unique glimpse it provides into fifth century Athenian life. This speech gained its lasting notoriety after being included in Thucydides's History of the Peloponnesian War.

MOST OF MY PREDECESSORS in this place have commended him who made this speech part of the law, telling us that it is well that it should be delivered at the burial of those who fall in battle. For myself, I should have thought that the worth which had displayed itself in deeds would be sufficiently rewarded by honours also shown by deeds; such as you now see in this funeral prepared at the people's cost. And I could have wished that the reputations of many brave men were not to be imperilled in the mouth of a single individual, to stand or fall according as he spoke well or ill. For it is hard to speak properly upon a subject where it is even difficult to convince your hearers that you are speaking the truth. On the one hand, the friend who is familiar with every fact of the story may think that some point has not been set forth with that fullness which he wishes and knows it to deserve; on the other, he who is a stranger to the matter may be led by envy to suspect exaggeration if he hears anything above his own nature. For men can endure to hear others praised only so long as they can severally persuade themselves of their own ability to equal the actions recounted: when this point is passed, envy comes in and with it incredulity. However, since our ancestors have stamped this custom with their approval, it becomes my duty to obey the law and to try to satisfy your several wishes and opinions as best I may.

I shall begin with our ancestors: it is both just and proper that they should have the honour of the first mention on an occasion like the present. They dwelt in the country without break in the succession from generation to generation, and handed it down free to the present time by their valour. And if our more remote ancestors deserve praise, much more do our own fathers, who added to their inheritance the empire which we now possess, and spared no pains to be able to leave their acquisitions to us of the present generation. Lastly, there are few parts of our dominions that have not been augmented by those of us here, who are still more or less in the vigour of life; while the mother country has been furnished by us with everything that can enable her to depend on her own resources whether for war or for peace. That part of our history which tells of the military achievements which gave us our several possessions, or of the ready valour with which either we or our fathers stemmed the tide of Hellenic or foreign aggression, is a theme too familiar to my hearers for me to dilate on, and I shall therefore pass it by. But what was the road by which we reached our position, what the form of government under which our greatness grew, what the national habits out of which it sprang; these are questions which I may try to solve before I proceed to my panegyric upon these men; since I think this to be a subject upon which on the present occasion a speaker may properly dwell, and to which the whole assemblage, whether citizens or foreigners, may listen with advantage.

Our constitution does not copy the laws of neighbouring states; we are rather a pattern to others than imitators ourselves. Its administration favours the many instead of the few; this is why it is called a democracy. If we look to the laws, they afford equal justice to all in their private differences; if no social standing, advancement in public life falls to reputation for capacity, class considerations not being allowed to interfere with merit; nor again does poverty bar the way, if a man is able to serve the state, he is not hindered by the obscurity of his condition. The freedom which we enjoy in our government extends also to our ordinary life. There, far from exercising a jealous surveillance over each other, we do not feel called upon to be angry with our neighbour for doing what he likes, or even to indulge in those injurious looks which cannot fail to be offensive, although they inflict no positive penalty. But all this ease in our private relations does not make us lawless as citizens. Against this fear is our chief safeguard, teaching us to obey the magistrates and the laws, particularly such as regard the protection of the injured, whether they are actually on the statute book, or belong to that code which, although unwritten, yet cannot be broken without acknowledged disgrace.

Further, we provide plenty of means for the mind to refresh itself from business. We celebrate games and sacrifices all the year round, and the elegance of our private establishments forms a daily source of pleasure and helps to banish the spleen; while the magnitude of our city draws the produce of the world into our harbour, so that to the Athenian the fruits of other countries are as familiar a luxury as those of his own.

If we turn to our military policy, there also we differ from our antagonists. We throw open our city to the world, and never by alien acts exclude foreigners from any opportunity of learning or observing, although the eyes of an enemy may occasionally profit by our liberality; trusting less in system and policy than to the native spirit of our citizens; while in education, where our rivals from their very cradles by a painful discipline seek after manliness, at Athens we live exactly as we please, and yet are just as ready to encounter every legitimate danger. In proof of this it may be noticed that the Lacedaemonians do not invade our country alone, but bring with them all their confederates; while we Athenians advance unsupported into the territory of a neighbour, and fighting upon a foreign soil usually vanquish with ease men who are defending their homes. Our united force was never yet encountered by any enemy, because we have at once to attend to our marine and to dispatch our citizens by land upon a hundred different services; so that, wherever they engage with some such fraction of our strength, a success against a detachment is magnified into a victory over the nation, and a defeat into a reverse suffered at the hands of our entire people. And yet if with habits not of labour but of ease, and courage not of art but of nature, we are still willing to encounter danger, we have the double advantage of escaping the experience of hardships in anticipation and of facing them in the hour of need as fearlessly as those who are never free from them.

Nor are these the only points in which our city is worthy of admiration. We cultivate refinement without extravagance and knowledge without effeminacy; wealth we employ more for use than for show, and place the real disgrace of poverty not in owning to the fact but in declining the struggle against it. Our public men have, besides politics, their private affairs to attend to, and our ordinary citizens, though occupied with the pursuits of industry, are still fair judges of public matters; for, unlike any other nation, regarding him who takes no part in these duties not as unambitious but as useless, we Athenians are able to judge at all events if we cannot originate, and, instead of looking on discussion as a stumbling-block in the way of action, we think it an indispensable preliminary to any wise action at all. Again, in our enterprises we present the singular spectacle of daring and deliberation, each carried to its highest point, and both united in the same persons; although usually decision is the fruit of ignorance, hesitation of reflection. But the palm of courage will surely be adjudged most justly to those, who best know the difference between hardship and pleasure and yet are never tempted to shrink from danger. In generosity we are equally singular, acquiring our friends by conferring, not by receiving, favours. Yet, of course, the doer of the favour is the firmer friend of the two, in order by continued kindness to keep the recipient in his debt; while the debtor feels less keenly from the very consciousness that the return he makes will be a payment, not a free gift. And it is only the Athenians, who, fearless of consequences, confer their benefits not from calculations of expediency, but in the confidence of liberality.

In short, I say that as a city we are the school of Hellas, while I doubt if the world can produce a man who, where he has only himself to depend upon, is equal to so many emergencies, and graced by so happy a versatility, as the Athenian. And that this is no mere boast thrown out for the occasion, but plain matter of fact, the power of the state acquired by these habits proves. For Athens alone of her contemporaries is found when tested to be greater than her reputation, and alone gives no occasion to her assailants to blush at the antagonist by whom they have been worsted, or to her subjects to question her title by merit to rule. Rather, the admiration of the present and succeeding ages will be ours, since we have not left our power without witness, but have shown it by mighty proofs; and far from needing a Homer for our panegyrist, or other of his craft whose verses might charm for the moment only for the impression which they gave to melt at the touch of fact, we have forced every sea and land to be the highway of our daring, and everywhere, whether for evil or for good, have left imperishable monuments behind us. Such is the Athens for which these men, in the assertion of their resolve not to lose her, nobly fought and died; and well may every one of their survivors be ready to suffer in her cause.

Indeed if I have dwelt at some length upon the character of our country, it has been to show that our stake in the struggle is not the same as theirs who have no such blessings to lose, and also that the panegyric of the men over whom I am now speaking might be by definite proofs established. That panegyric is now in a great measure complete; for the Athens that I have celebrated is only what the heroism of these and their like have made her, men whose fame, unlike that of most Hellenes, will be found to be only commensurate with their deserts. And if a test of worth be wanted, it is to be found in their closing scene, and this not only in cases in which it set the final seal upon their merit, but also in those in which it gave the first intimation of their having any. For there is justice in the claim that steadfastness in his country's battles should be as a cloak to cover a man's other imperfections; since the good action has blotted out the bad, and his merit as a citizen more than outweighed his demerits as an individual. But none of these allowed either wealth with its prospect of future enjoyment to unnerve his spirit, or poverty with its hope of a day of freedom and riches to tempt him to shrink from danger. No, holding that vengeance upon their enemies was more to be desired than any personal blessings, and reckoning this to be the most glorious of hazards, they joyfully determined to accept the risk, to make sure of their vengeance, and to let their wishes wait; and while committing to hope the uncertainty of final success, in the business before them they thought fit to act boldly and trust in themselves.

Thus choosing to die resisting, rather than to live submitting, they fled only from dishonour, but met danger face to face, and after one brief moment, while at the summit of their fortune, escaped, not from their fear, but from their glory.

So died these men as became Athenians. You, their survivors, must determine to have as unfaltering a resolution in the field, though you may pray that it may have a happier issue. And not contented with ideas derived only from words of the advantages which are bound up with the defence of your country, though these would furnish a valuable text to a speaker even before an audience so alive to them as the present, you must yourselves realize the power of Athens, and feed your eyes upon her from day to day, till love of her fills your hearts; and then, when all her greatness shall break upon you, you must reflect that it was by courage, sense of duty, and a keen feeling of honour in action that men were enabled to win all this, and that no personal failure in an enterprise could make them consent to deprive their country of their valour, but they laid it at her feet as the most glorious contribution that they could offer. For this offering of their lives made in common by them all they each of them individually received that renown which never grows old, and for a sepulchre, not so much that in which their bones have been deposited, but that noblest of shrines wherein their glory is laid up to be eternally remembered upon every occasion on which deed or story shall call for its commemoration. For heroes have the whole earth for their tomb; and in lands far from their own, where the column with its epitaph declares it, there is enshrined in every breast a record unwritten with no tablet to preserve it, except that of the heart. These take as your model and, judging happiness to be the fruit of freedom and freedom of valour, never decline the dangers of war. For it is not the miserable that would most justly be unsparing of their lives; these have nothing to hope for: it is rather they to whom continued life may bring reverses as yet unknown, and to whom a fall, if it came, would be most tremendous in its consequences. And surely, to a man of spirit, the degradation of cowardice must be immeasurably more grievous than the unfelt death which strikes him in the midst of his strength and patriotism!

Comfort, therefore, not condolence, is what I have to offer to the parents of the dead who may be here. Numberless are the chances to which, as they know, the life of man is subject; but fortunate indeed are they who draw for their lot a death so glorious as that which has caused your mourning, and to whom life has been so exactly measured as to terminate in the happiness in which it has been passed. Still I know that this is a hard saying, especially when those are in question of whom you will constantly be reminded by seeing in the homes of others blessings of which once you also boasted: for grief is felt not so much for the want of what we have never known, as for the loss of that to which we have been long accustomed. Yet you who are still of an age to beget children must bear up in the hope of having others in their stead; not only will they help you to forget those whom you have lost, but will be to the state at once a reinforcement and a security; for never can a fair or just policy be expected of the citizen who does not, like his fellows, bring to the decision the interests and apprehensions of a father. While those of you who have passed your prime must congratulate yourselves with the thought that the best part of your life was fortunate, and that the brief span that remains will be cheered by the fame of the departed. For it is only the love of honour that never grows old; and honour it is, not gain, as some would have it, that rejoices the heart of age and helplessness.

Turning to the sons or brothers of the dead, I see an arduous struggle before you. When a man is gone, all are wont to praise him, and should your merit be ever so transcendent, you will still find it difficult not merely to overtake, but even to approach their renown. The living have envy to contend with, while those who are no longer in our path are honoured with a goodwill into which rivalry does not enter. On the other hand, if I must say anything on the subject of female excellence to those of you who will now be in widowhood, it will be all comprised in this brief exhortation. Great will be your glory in not falling short of your natural character; and greatest will be hers who is least talked of among the men, whether for good or for bad.

My task is now finished. I have performed it to the best of my ability, and in word, at least, the requirements of the law are now satisfied. If deeds be in question, those who are here interred have received part of their honours already, and for the rest, their children will be brought up till manhood at the public expense: the state thus offers a valuable prize, as the garland of victory in this race of valour, for the reward both of those who have fallen and their survivors. And where the rewards for merit are greatest, there are found the best citizens.

And now that you have brought to a close your lamentations for your relatives, you may depart.

Source: Thucydides (c.460/455 c.399 BCE): *Peloponnesian War, Book 2*. 34–46.

MARTIN LUTHER

"Before the Diet of Worms" (April 18, 1520)

After Pope Leo X formally excommunicated Martin Luther (1483–1546) in January of 1521, an assembly (or Diet*) was held in Worms, Germany for the purpose of addressing the Church's growing concerns about reformation. Martin Luther was summoned to this assembly, where he was asked to defend or retract his previous statements and writings against the church. In the following address, Luther responds to the assembly by explaining his teachings, and stating that he would not retract a word unless he could be convinced of a Biblical basis for his alleged errors.*

MOST SERENE EMPEROR, AND YOU ILLUSTRIOUS PRINCES AND GRACIOUS LORDS:—I this day appear before you in all humility, according to your command, and I implore your majesty and your august highnesses, by the mercies of God, to listen with favor to the defense of a cause which I am well assured is just and right. I ask pardon, if by reason of my ignorance, I am wanting in the manners that befit a court; for I have not been brought up in king's palaces, but in the seclusion of a cloister.

Two questions were yesterday put to me by his imperial majesty; the first, whether I was the author of the books whose titles were read; the second, whether I wished to revoke or defend the doctrine I have taught. I answered the first, and I adhere to that answer.

As to the second, I have composed writings on very different subjects. In some I have discussed Faith and Good Works, in a spirit at once so pure, clear, and Christian, that even my adversaries themselves, far from finding anything to censure, confess that these writings are profitable, and deserve to be perused by devout persons. The pope's bull, violent as it is, acknowledges this. What, then, should I be doing if I were now to retract these writings? Wretched man! I alone, of all men living, should be abandoning truths approved by the unanimous voice of friends and enemies, and opposing doctrines that the whole world glories in confessing!

I have composed, secondly, certain works against popery, wherein I have attacked such as by false doctrines, irregular lives, and scandalous examples, afflict the Christian world, and ruin the bodies and souls of men. And is not this confirmed by the grief of all who fear God? Is it not manifest that the laws and human doctrines of the popes entangle, vex, and distress the consciences of the faithful, while the crying and endless extortions of Rome engulf the property and wealth of Christendom, and more particularly of this illustrious nation?

If I were to revoke what I have written on that subject, what should I do . . . but strengthen this tyranny, and open a wider door to so many and flagrant impieties? Bearing down all resistance with fresh fury, we should behold these proud men swell, foam, and rage more than ever! And not merely would the yoke which now weighs down Christians be made more grinding by my retractation—it would thereby become, so to speak, lawful,—for, by my retractation, it would receive confirmation from your most serene majesty, and all the States of the Empire. Great God! I should thus be like to an infamous cloak, used to hide and cover over every kind of malice and tyranny.

In the third and last place, I have written some books against private individuals, who had undertaken to defend the tyranny of Rome by destroying the faith. I freely confess that I may have attacked such persons with more violence than was consistent with my profession as an ecclesiastic: I do not think of myself as a saint; but neither can I retract these books. because I should, by so doing, sanction the impieties of my opponents, and they would thence take occasion to crush God's people with still more cruelty.

Yet, as I am a mere man, and not God, I will defend myself after the example of Jesus Christ, who said: "If I have spoken evil, bear witness against me (John xviii:23). How much more should I, who am but dust and ashes, and so prone to error, desire that every one should bring forward what he can against my doctrine.

Therefore, most serene emperor, and you illustrious princes, and all, whether high or low, who hear me, I implore you by the mercies of God to prove to me by the writings of the prophets and apostles that I am in error. As soon as I shall be convinced, I will instantly retract all my errors, and will myself be the first to seize my writings, and commit them to the flames.

What I have just said I think will clearly show that I have well considered and weighed the dangers to which I am exposing myself; but far from being dismayed by them, I rejoice exceedingly to see the Gospel this day, as of old, a cause of disturbance and disagreement. It is the character and destiny of God's word. "I came not to send peace unto the earth, but a sword," said Jesus Christ. God is wonderful and awful in His counsels. Let us have a care, lest in our endeavors to arrest discords, we be bound to fight against the holy word of God and bring down upon our heads a frightful deluge of inextricable dangers, present disaster, and everlasting desolations.... Let us have a care lest the reign of the young and noble prince, the Emperor Charles, on whom, next to God, we build so many hopes, should not only commence, but continue and terminate its course under the most fatal auspices. I might cite examples drawn from the oracles of God. I might speak of Pharaohs, of kings of Babylon, or of Israel, who were never more contributing to their own ruin than when, by measures in appearances most prudent, they thought to establish their authority! "God removeth the mountains and they know not (Job ix: 5)."

In speaking thus, I do not suppose that such noble princes have need of my poor judgment; but I wish to acquit myself of a duty that Germany has a right to expect from her children. And so commending myself to your august majesty, and your most serene highnesses, I beseech you in all humility, not to permit the hatred of my enemies to rain upon me an indignation I have not deserved.

Since your most serene majesty and your high mightinesses require of me a simple, clear and direct answer, I will give one, and it is this: I can not submit my faith either to the pope or to the council, because it is as clear as noonday that they have fallen into error and even into glaring inconsistency with themselves.

If, then, I am not convinced by proof from Holy Scripture, or by cogent reasons, if I am not satisfied by the very text I have cited, and if my judgment is not in this way brought into subjection to God's word, I neither can nor will retract anything; for it can not be right for a Christian to speak against his country. I stand here and can say no more. God help me. Amen.

JONATHAN EDWARDS

"Sinners in the Hands of an Angry God" (July 8, 1741)

Jonathan Edwards (1703–1758) was one of early America's most noted and important Christian theologians. After the death of his grandfather in 1728, Edwards became the sole minister at his congregation in Northampton, Massachusetts, where his passionate and tenacious preaching led to the American colony's first great revivals of the eighteenth century. In the following sermon, Edwards lays out many of the theological principles that would prove central to the formation of American Christian philosophy.

THEIR FOOT SHALL SLIDE in due time. Deuteronomy 32:35.

In this verse is threatened the vengeance of God on the wicked unbelieving Israelites, that were God's visible people, and lived under means of grace; and that, notwithstanding all God's wonderful works that he had wrought towards that people, yet remained, as is expressed, ver. Deuteronomy 32:28, "void of counsel," having no understanding in them; and that, under all the cultivations of heaven, brought forth bitter and poisonous fruit; as in the two verses next preceding the text.

The expression that I have chosen for my text, "Their foot shall slide in due time," seems to imply the following things, relating to the punishment and destruction that these wicked Israelites were exposed to.

1. That they were *always* exposed to destruction, as one that stands or walks in slippery places is always exposed to fall. This is

implied in the manner of their destruction's coming upon them, being represented by their foot's sliding. The same is expressed, Psalms 73:18, "Surely thou didst set them in slippery places: thou castedst them down into destruction."

2. It implies that they were always exposed to *sudden* unexpected destruction. As he that walks in slippery places is every moment liable to fall; he can't foresee one moment whether he shall stand or fall the next; and when he does fall, he falls at once, without warning. Which is also expressed in that, Psalms 73:18–19, "Surely thou didst set them in slippery places: thou castedst them down into destruction. How are they brought into desolation as in a moment!"

3. Another thing implied is that they are liable to fall *of themselves*, without being thrown down by the hand of another. As he that stands or walks on slippery ground, needs nothing but his own weight to throw him down.

4. That the reason why they are not fallen already, and don't fall now, is only that God's appointed time is not come. For it is said, that when that due time, or appointed time comes, "their foot shall slide." Then they shall be left to fall as they are inclined by their own weight. God won't hold them up in these slippery places any longer, but will let them go; and then, at that very instant, they shall fall into destruction; as he that stands in such slippery declining ground on the edge of a pit that he can't stand alone, when he is let go he immediately falls and is lost.

The observation from the words that I would now insist upon is this:

There is nothing that keeps wicked men, at any one moment, out of hell, but the mere pleasure of God.

By "the mere pleasure of God," I mean his sovereign pleasure, his arbitrary will, restrained by no obligation, hindered by no manner of difficulty, any more than if nothing else but God's mere will had in the least degree, or in any respect whatsoever, any hand in the preservation of wicked men one moment.

The truth of this observation may appear by the following considerations.

I. There is no want of *power* in God to cast wicked men into hell at any moment. Men's hands can't be strong when God rises up: the strongest have no power to resist him, nor can any deliver out of his hands.

He is not only able to cast wicked men into hell, but he can most *easily* do it. Sometimes an earthly prince meets with a great deal of difficulty to subdue a rebel, that has found means to fortify himself, and has made himself strong by the numbers of his followers. But it is not so with God. There is no fortress that is any defense from the power of God. Though hand join in hand, and vast multitudes of God's enemies combine and associate themselves, they are easily broken in pieces: they are as great heaps of light chaff before the whirlwind; or large quantities of dry stubble before devouring flames. We find it easy to tread on and crush a worm that we see crawling on the earth; so 'tis easy for us to cut or singe a slender thread that anything hangs by; thus easy is it for God when he pleases to cast his enemies down to hell. What are we, that we should think to stand before him, at whose rebuke the earth trembles, and before whom the rocks are thrown down?

II. They *deserve* to be cast into hell; so that divine justice never stands in the way, it makes no objection against God's using his power at any moment to destroy them. Yea, on the contrary, justice calls aloud for an infinite punishment of their sins. Divine justice says of the tree that brings forth such grapes of Sodom, "Cut it down; why cumbreth it the ground" (Luke 13:7). The sword of divine justice is every moment brandished over their heads, and 'tis nothing but the hand of arbitrary mercy, and God's mere will, that holds it back.

III. They are *already* under a sentence of condemnation to hell. They don't only justly deserve to be cast down thither; but the sentence of the law of God, that eternal and immutable rule of righteousness that God has fixed between him and mankind, is gone out against them, and stands against them; so that they are bound over already to hell. John 3:18, "He that believeth not is condemned already." So that every unconverted man properly belongs to hell; that is his place; from thence he is. John 8:23, "Ye are from beneath." And thither he is bound; 'tis the place that justice, and God's Word, and the sentence of his unchangeable law assigns to him.

IV. They are now the objects of that very *same* anger and wrath of God that is expressed in the torments of hell: and the reason why they don't go down to hell at each moment, is not because God, in whose power they are, is not then very angry with them; as angry as he is with many of those miserable creatures that he is now tormenting in hell, and do there feel and bear the fierceness of his wrath. Yea, God is a great deal more angry with great numbers that are now on earth, yea, doubtless with many that are now in this congregation, that it may be are at ease and quiet, than he is with many of those that are now in the flames of hell.

So that it is not because God is unmindful of their wickedness, and don't resent it, that he don't let loose his hand and cut them off. God is not altogether such an one as themselves, though they may imagine him to be so. The wrath of God burns against them, their damnation don't slumber, the pit is prepared, the fire is made ready, the furnace is now hot, ready to receive them, the flames do now rage and glow. The glittering sword is whet, and held over them, and the pit hath opened her mouth under them.

V. The *devil* stands ready to fall upon them and seize them as his own, at what moment God shall permit him. They belong to him; he has their souls in his possession, and under his dominion. The Scripture represents them as his "goods" (Luke 11:21). The devils watch them; they are ever by them, at their right hand; they stand waiting for them, like greedy hungry lions that see their prey, and expect to have it, but are for the present kept back; if God should withdraw his hand, by which they are restrained, they would in one moment fly upon their poor souls. The old serpent is gaping for them; hell opens its mouth wide to receive them; and if God should permit it, they would be hastily swallowed up and lost.

VI. There are in the souls of wicked men those hellish *principles* reigning, that would presently kindle and flame out into hell fire, if it were not for God's restraints. There is laid in the very nature of carnal men a foundation for the torments of hell: there are those corrupt principles, in reigning power in them, and in full possession of them, that are seeds of hell fire. These principles are active and powerful, and exceeding violent in their nature, and if it were not for the restraining hand of God upon them, they would soon break out, they would flame out after the same manner as the same corruptions, the same enmity does in the hearts of damned souls, and would beget the same torments in 'em as they do in them. The souls of the wicked are in Scripture compared to the troubled sea (Isaiah 57:20). For the present God restrains their wickedness by his mighty power, as he does the raging waves of the troubled sea, saying, "Hitherto shalt thou come, and no further" [Job 38:11]; but if God should withdraw that restraining power, it would soon carry all afore it. Sin is the ruin and misery of the soul; it is destructive in its nature; and if God should leave it without restraint, there would need nothing else to make the soul perfectly miserable. The corruption of the heart of man is a thing that is immoderate and boundless in its fury; and while wicked men live here, it is like fire pent up by God's restraints, whenas if it were let loose it would set on fire the course of nature; and as the heart is now a sink of sin, so, if sin was not restrained, it would immediately turn the soul into a fiery oven, or a furnace of fire and brimstone.

VII. It is no security to wicked men for one moment, that there are no *visible means of death* at hand. 'Tis no security to a natural man, that he is now in health, and that he don't see which way he should now immediately go out of the world by any accident, and that there is no visible danger in any respect in his circumstances. The manifold and continual experience of the world in all ages, shows that this is no evidence that a man is not on the very brink of eternity, and that the next step won't be into another world. The unseen, unthought of ways and means of persons going suddenly out of the world are innumerable and inconceivable. Unconverted men walk over the pit of hell on a rotten covering, and there are innumerable places in this covering so weak that they won't bear their weight, and these places are not seen. The arrows of death fly unseen at noonday; the sharpest sight can't discern them. God has so many different unsearchable ways of taking wicked men out of the world and sending 'em to hell, that there is nothing to make it appear that God had need to be at the expense of a miracle, or go out of the ordinary course of his providence, to destroy any wicked man, at any moment. All the means that there are of sinners going out of the world, are so in God's hands, and so universally absolutely subject to his power and determination, that it don't depend at all less on the mere will of God, whether sinners shall at any moment go to hell, than if means were never made use of, or at all concerned in the case.

VIII. Natural men's *prudence* and *care* to preserve their own *lives*, or the care of others to preserve them, don't secure 'em a moment. This divine providence and universal experience does also bear testimony to. There is this clear evidence that men's own wisdom is no security to them from death: that if it were otherwise we should see some difference between the wise and politic men of the world, and others, with regard to their liableness to early and unexpected death; but how is it in fact? Ecclesiastes 2:16, "How dieth the wise man? as the fool."

IX. All wicked men's *pains* and *contrivance* they use to escape *hell*, while they continue to reject Christ, and so remain wicked men, don't secure 'em from hell one moment. Almost every natural man that hears of hell, flatters himself that he shall escape it; he depends upon himself for his own security; he flatters himself in what he has done, in what he is now doing, or what he intends to do; everyone lays out matters in his own mind how he shall avoid damnation, and flatters himself that he contrives well for himself, and that his schemes won't fail. They hear indeed that there are but few saved, and that the bigger part of men that have died heretofore are gone to hell; but each one imagines that he lays out matters better for his own escape than others have done: he don't intend to come to that place of torment; he says within himself, that he intends to take care that shall be effectual, and to order matters so for himself as not to fail.

But the foolish children of men do miserably delude themselves in their own schemes, and in their confidence in their own strength and wisdom; they trust to nothing but a shadow. The bigger part of those that heretofore have lived under the same means of grace, and are now dead, are undoubtedly gone to hell: and it was not because they were not as wise as those that are now alive; it was not because they did not lay out matters as well for themselves to secure their own escape. If it were so, that we could come to speak with them, and could inquire of them, one by one, whether they expected when alive, and when they used to hear about hell, ever to be the subjects of that misery, we doubtless should hear one and another reply, "No, I never intended to come here; I had laid out matters otherwise in my mind; I thought I should contrive well for myself; I thought my scheme good; I intended to take effectual care; but it came upon me unexpected; I did not look for it at that time, and in that manner; it came as a thief; death outwitted me; God's wrath was too quick for me; O my cursed foolishness! I was flattering myself, and pleasing myself with vain dreams of what I would do hereafter, and when I was saying, 'Peace and safety,' then sudden destruction came upon me" [1 Thessalonians 5:3].

X. God has laid himself under *no obligation* by any promise to keep any natural man out of hell one moment. God certainly has made no promises either of eternal life, or of any deliverance or preservation from eternal death, but what are contained in the covenant of grace, the promises that are given in Christ, in whom all the promises are yea and amen. But surely they have no interest in the promises of the covenant of grace that are not the children of the covenant, and that don't believe in any of the promises of the covenant, and have no interest in the *Mediator* of the covenant.

So that whatever some have imagined and pretended about promises made to natural men's earnest seeking and knocking, 'tis plain and manifest that whatever pains a natural man takes in religion, whatever prayers he makes, till he believes in Christ, God is under no manner of obligation to keep him a *moment* from eternal destruction.

So that thus it is, that natural men are held in the hand of God over the pit of hell; they have deserved the fiery pit, and are already sentenced to it; and God is dreadfully provoked, his anger is as great towards them as to those that are actually suffering the executions of the fierceness of his wrath in hell, and they have done nothing in the least to appease or abate that anger, neither is God in the least bound by any promise to hold 'em up one moment; the devil is waiting for them, hell is gaping for them, the flames gather and flash about them, and would fain lay hold on them, and swallow them up; the fire pent up in their own hearts is struggling to break out; and they have no interest in any mediator, there are no means within reach that can be any security to them. In short, they have no refuge, nothing to take hold of, all that preserves them every moment is the mere arbitrary will, and uncovenanted unobliged forbearance of an incensed God.

Application.

The *Use* may be of *Awakening* to unconverted persons in this congregation. This that you have heard is the case of everyone of you that are out of Christ. That world of misery, that lake of burning brimstone is extended abroad under you. *There* is the dreadful pit of the glowing flames of the wrath of God; there is hell's wide gaping mouth open; and you have nothing to stand upon, nor anything to take hold of: there is nothing between you and hell but the air; 'tis only the power and mere pleasure of God that holds you up.

You probably are not sensible of this; you find you are kept out of hell, but don't see the hand of God in it, but look at other things, as the good state of your bodily constitution, your care of your own life, and the means you use for your own preservation. But indeed these things are nothing; if God should withdraw his hand, they would avail no more to keep you from falling, than the thin air to hold up a person that is suspended in it.

Your wickedness makes you as it were heavy as lead, and to tend downwards with great weight and pressure towards hell; and if God should let you go, you would immediately sink and swiftly descend and plunge into the bottomless gulf, and your healthy constitution, and your own care and prudence, and best contrivance, and all your righteousness, would have no more influence to uphold you and keep you out of hell, than a spider's web would have to stop a falling rock. Were it not that so is the sovereign pleasure of God, the earth would not bear you one moment; for you are a burden to it; the creation groans with you; the creature is made subject to the bondage of your corruption, not willingly; the sun don't willingly shine upon you to give you light to serve sin and Satan; the earth don't willingly yield her increase to satisfy your lusts; nor is it willingly a stage for your wickedness to be acted upon; the air don't willingly serve you for breath to maintain the flame of life in your vitals, while you spend your life in the service of God's enemies. God's creatures are good, and were made for men to serve God with, and don't willingly subserve to any other purpose, and groan when they are abused to purposes so directly contrary to their nature and end. And the world would spew you out, were it not for the sovereign hand of him who hath subjected it in hope. There are the black clouds of God's wrath now hanging directly over your heads, full of the dreadful storm, and big with thunder; and were it not for the restraining hand of God it would immediately burst forth upon you. The sovereign pleasure of God for the present stays his rough wind; otherwise it would come with fury, and your destruction would come like a whirlwind, and you would be like the chaff of the summer threshing floor.

The wrath of God is like great waters that are dammed for the present; they increase more and more, and rise higher and higher, till an outlet is given, and the longer the stream is stopped, the more rapid and mighty is its course, when once it is let loose. 'Tis true, that judgment against your evil works has not been executed hitherto; the floods of God's vengeance have been withheld; but your guilt in the meantime is constantly increasing, and you are every day treasuring up more wrath; the waters are continually rising and waxing more and more mighty; and there is nothing but the mere pleasure of God that holds the waters back that are unwilling to be stopped, and press hard to go forward; if God should only withdraw his hand from the floodgate, it would immediately fly open, and the fiery floods of the fierceness and wrath of God would rush forth with inconceivable fury, and would come upon you with omnipotent power; and if your strength were ten thousand times greater than it is, yea, ten thousand times greater than the strength of the stoutest, sturdiest devil in hell, it would be nothing to withstand or endure it.

The bow of God's wrath is bent, and the arrow made ready on the string, and Justice bends the arrow at your heart, and strains the bow, and it is nothing but the mere pleasure of God, and that of an angry God, without any promise or obligation at all, that keeps the arrow one moment from being made drunk with your blood.

Thus are all you that never passed under a great change of heart, by the mighty power of the Spirit of God upon your souls; all that were never born again, and made new creatures, and raised from being dead in sin, to a state of new, and before altogether unexperienced light and life (however you may have reformed your life in many things, and may have had religious affections, and may keep up a form of religion in your families and closets, and in the house of God, and may be strict in it), you are thus in the hands of an angry God; 'tis nothing but his mere pleasure that keeps you from being this moment swallowed up in everlasting destruction.

However unconvinced you may now be of the truth of what you hear, by and by you will be fully convinced of it. Those that are gone from being in the like circumstances with you, see that it was so with them; for destruction came suddenly upon most of them, when they expected nothing of it, and while they were saying, "Peace and safety": now they see, that those things that they depended on for peace and safety, were nothing but thin air and empty shadows.

The God that holds you over the pit of hell, much as one holds a spider, or some loathsome insect, over the fire, abhors you, and is dreadfully provoked; his wrath towards you burns like fire; he looks upon you as worthy of nothing else, but to be cast into the fire; he is of purer eyes than to bear to have you in his sight; you are ten thousand times so abominable in his eyes as the most hateful venomous serpent is in ours. You have offended him infinitely more than ever a stubborn rebel did his prince: and yet 'tis nothing but his hand that holds you from falling into the fire every moment; 'tis to be ascribed to nothing else, that you did not go to hell the last night; that you was suffered to awake again in this world, after you closed your eyes to sleep: and there is no other reason to be given why you have not dropped into hell since you arose in the morning, but that God's hand has held you up; there is no other reason to be given why you han't gone to hell since you have sat here in the house of God, provoking his pure eyes by your sinful wicked manner of attending his solemn worship: yea, there is nothing else that is to be given as a reason why you don't this very moment drop down into hell.

O sinner! Consider the fearful danger you are in: 'tis a great furnace of wrath, a wide and bottomless pit, full of the fire of wrath, that you are held over in the hand of that God, whose wrath is provoked and incensed as much against you as against many of the damned in hell; you hang by a slender thread, with the flames of divine wrath flashing about it, and ready every moment to singe it, and burn it asunder; and you have no interest in any mediator, and nothing to lay hold of to save yourself, nothing to keep off the flames of wrath, nothing of your own, nothing that you ever have done, nothing that you can do, to induce God to spare you one moment.

And consider here more particularly several things concerning that wrath that you are in such danger of.

First. Whose wrath it is: it is the wrath of the infinite God. If it were only the wrath of man, though it were of the most potent prince, it would be comparatively little to be regarded. The wrath of kings is very much dreaded, especially of absolute monarchs, that have the possessions and lives of their subjects wholly in their power, to be disposed of at their mere will. Proverbs 20:2, "The fear of a king is as the roaring of a lion: whoso provoketh him to anger, sinneth against his own soul." The subject that very much enrages an arbitrary prince, is liable to suffer the most extreme torments, that human art can invent or human power can inflict. But the greatest earthly potentates, in their greatest majesty and strength, and when clothed in their greatest terrors, are but feeble despicable worms of the dust, in comparison of the great and almighty Creator and King of heaven and earth: it is but little that they can do, when most enraged, and when they have exerted the utmost of their fury. All the kings of the earth before God are as grasshoppers, they are nothing and less than nothing: both their love and their hatred is to be despised. The wrath of the great King of kings is as much more terrible than theirs as his majesty is greater. Luke 12:4-05, "And I say unto you my friends, Be not afraid of them that kill the body, and after that have no more that they can do. But I will forewarn you whom ye shall fear: Fear him which after he hath killed hath power to cast into hell; yea, I say unto you, fear him."

Second. 'Tis the *fierceness* of his wrath that you are exposed to. We often read of the *fury* of God; as in Isaiah 59:18, "According to their deeds, accordingly he will repay fury to his adversaries." So Isaiah 66:15, "For, behold, the Lord will come with fire, and with chariots like a whirlwind, to render his anger with fury, and his rebukes with flames of fire." And so in many other places. So we read of God's *fierceness*. Revelation 19:15, there we read of "the winepress of the fierceness and wrath of almighty God." The words are exceeding terrible: if it had only been said, "the wrath of God," the words would have implied that which is infinitely dreadful; but 'tis not only said so, but "the fierceness and wrath of God": the fury of God! the fierceness of Jehovah! Oh how dreadful must that be! Who can utter or conceive what such expressions carry in them! But it is not only said so, but "the fierceness and wrath of *almighty God*." As though there would be a very great manifestation of his almighty power, in what the fierceness of his wrath should inflict, as though omnipotence should be as it were enraged, and exerted, as men are wont to exert their strength in the fierceness of their wrath. Oh! then what will be consequence! What will become of the poor worm that shall suffer it! Whose hands can be strong? and whose heart endure? To what a dreadful, inexpressible, inconceivable depth of misery must the poor creature be sunk, who shall be the subject of this!

Consider this, you that are here present, that yet remain in an unregenerate state. That God will execute the fierceness of his anger, implies that he will inflict wrath without any pity: when God beholds the ineffable extremity of your case, and sees your torment to be so vastly disproportioned to your strength, and sees how your poor soul is crushed and sinks down, as it were into an infinite gloom, he will have no compassion upon you, he will not forbear the executions of his wrath, or in the least lighten his hand; there shall be no moderation or mercy, nor will God then at all stay his rough wind; he will have no regard to your welfare, nor be at all careful lest you should suffer too much, in any other sense than only that you shall not suffer beyond what strict justice requires: nothing shall be withheld, because it's so hard for you to bear. Ezekiel 8:18, "Therefore will I also deal in fury: mine eye shall not spare, neither will I have pity; and though they cry in mine ears with a loud voice, yet I will not hear them." Now God stands ready to pity you; this is a day of mercy; you may cry now with some encouragement of obtaining mercy: but when once the day of mercy is past, your most lamentable and dolorous cries and shrieks will be in vain; you will be wholly lost and thrown away of God as to any regard to your welfare; God will have no other use to put you to but only to suffer misery; you shall be continued in being to no other end; for you will be a vessel of wrath fitted to destruction; and there will be no other use of this vessel but only to be filled full of wrath: God will be so far from pitying you when you cry to him, that 'tis said he will only laugh and mock (Proverbs 1:25–32).

How awful are those words, Isaiah 63:3, which are the words of the great God, "I will tread them in mine anger, and will trample them in my fury, and their blood shall be sprinkled upon my garments, and I will stain all my raiment." 'Tis perhaps impossible to conceive of words that carry in them greater manifestations of these three things, viz. contempt, and hatred, and fierceness of indignation. If you cry to God to pity you, he will be so far from pitying you in your doleful case, or showing you the least regard or favor, that instead of that he'll only tread you under foot: and though he will know that you can't bear the weight of omnipotence treading upon you, yet he won't regard that, but he will crush you under his feet without mercy; he'll crush out your blood, and make it fly, and it shall be sprinkled on his garments, so as to stain all his raiment.

He will not only hate you, but he will have you in the utmost contempt; no place shall be thought fit for you, but under his feet, to be trodden down as the mire of the streets.

Third. The misery you are exposed to is that which God will inflict to that end, that he might *show* what that *wrath* of Jehovah is. God hath had it on his heart to show to angels and men, both how excellent his love is, and also how terrible his wrath is. Sometimes earthly kings have a mind to show how terrible *their* wrath is, by the extreme punishments they would execute on those that provoke 'em. Nebuchadnezzar, that mighty and haughty monarch of the Chaldean empire, was willing to show *his* wrath, when enraged with Shadrach, Meshach, and Abednego; and accordingly gave order that the burning fiery furnace should be het seven times hotter than it was before; doubtless it was raised to the utmost degree of fierceness that human art could raise it: but the great God is also willing to show *his wrath*, and magnify his awful majesty and mighty power in the extreme sufferings of his enemies. Romans 9:22, "What if God, willing to show *his* wrath, and to make his power known, endured with much longsuffering the vessels of wrath fitted to destruction?" And seeing this is his design, and what he has determined, to show how terrible the unmixed, unrestrained wrath, the fury and fierceness of Jehovah is, he will do it to effect. There will be something accomplished and brought to pass, that will be dreadful with a witness. When the great and angry God hath risen up and executed his awful vengeance on the poor sinner; and the wretch is actually suffering the infinite weight and power of his indignation, then will God call upon the whole universe to behold that awful majesty, and mighty power that is to be seen in it. Isaiah 33:12–14, "And the people shall be as the burning of lime: as thorns cut up shall they be burnt in the fire. Hear, ye that are far off, what I have done; and ye that are near, acknowledge my might. The sinners in Zion are afraid; fearfulness hath surprised the hypocrites. Who among us shall dwell with the devouring fire? who among us shall dwell with everlasting burnings?"

Thus it will be with you that are in an unconverted state, if you continue in it; the infinite might, and majesty and terribleness of the omnipotent God shall be magnified upon you, in the ineffable strength of your torments: you shall be tormented in the presence of the holy angels, and in the presence of the Lamb; and when you shall be in this state of suffering, the glorious inhabitants of heaven shall go forth and look on the awful spectacle, that they may see what the wrath and fierceness of the Almighty is, and when they have seen it, they will fall down and adore that great power and majesty. Isaiah 66:23–24, "And it shall come to pass, that from one new moon to another, and from one sabbath to another, shall all flesh come to worship before me, saith the Lord. And they shall go forth, and look upon the carcasses of the men that have transgressed against me: for their worm shall not die, neither shall their fire be quenched; and they shall be an abhorring unto all flesh."

Fourth. 'Tis *everlasting* wrath. It would be dreadful to suffer this fierceness and wrath of almighty God one moment; but you must suffer it to all eternity: there will be no end to this exquisite horrible misery. When you look forward, you shall see a long forever, a boundless duration before you, which will swallow up your thoughts, and amaze your soul; and you will absolutely despair of ever having any deliverance, any end, any mitigation, any rest at all; you will know certainly that you must wear out long ages, millions of millions of ages, in wrestling and conflicting with this almighty merciless vengeance; and then when you have so done, when so many ages have actually been spent by you in this manner, you will know that all is but a point to what remains. So that your punishment will indeed be infinite. Oh who can express what the state of a soul in such circumstances is! All that we can possibly say about it, gives but a very feeble faint representation of it; 'tis inexpressible and inconceivable: for "who knows the power of God's anger?" [Psalms 90:11].

How dreadful is the state of those that are daily and hourly in danger of this great wrath, and infinite misery! But this is the dismal case of every soul in this congregation, that has not been born again, however moral and strict, sober and religious they may otherwise be. Oh that you would consider it, whether you be young or old. There is reason to think, that there are many in this congregation now hearing this discourse, that will actually be the subjects of this very misery to all eternity. We know not who they are, or in what seats they sit, or what thoughts they now have: it may be they are now at ease, and hear all these things without much disturbance, and are now flattering themselves that they are not the persons, promising themselves that they shall escape. If we knew that there was one person, and but one, in the whole congregation that was to be the subject of this misery, what an awful thing would it be to think of! If we knew who it was, what an awful sight would it be to see such a person! How might all the rest of the congregation lift up a lamentable and bitter cry over him! But alas! instead of one, how many is it likely will remember this discourse in hell? And it would be a wonder if some that are now present, should not be in hell in a very short time, before this year is out. And it would be no wonder if some person that now sits here in some seat of this meeting house in health, and quiet and secure, should be there before tomorrow morning. Those of you that finally continue in a natural condition, that shall keep out of hell longest, will be there in a little time! your damnation don't slumber; it will come swiftly, and in all probability very suddenly upon many of you. You have reason to wonder, that you are not already in hell. 'Tis doubtless the case of some that heretofore you have seen and known, that never deserved hell more than you, and that heretofore appeared as likely to have been now alive as you: their case is past all hope; they are crying in extreme misery and perfect despair; but here you are in the land of the living, and in the house of God, and have an opportunity to obtain salvation. What would not those poor damned, hopeless souls give for one day's such opportunity as you now enjoy!

And now you have an extraordinary opportunity, a day wherein Christ has flung the door of mercy wide open, and stands in the door calling and crying with a loud voice to poor sinners; a day wherein many are flocking to him, and pressing into the kingdom of God; many are daily coming from the east, west, north and south; many that were very lately in the same miserable condition that you are in, are in now an happy state, with their hearts filled with love to him that has loved them and washed them from their sins in his own blood, and rejoicing in hope of the glory of God. How awful is it to be left behind at such a day! To see so many others feasting, while you are pining and perishing! To see so many rejoicing and singing for joy of heart, while you have cause to mourn for sorrow of heart, and howl for vexation of spirit! How can you rest one moment in such a condition? Are not your souls as precious as the souls of the people at Suffield, where they are flocking from day to day to Christ?

Are there not many here that have lived *long* in the world, that are not to this day born again, and so are aliens from the commonwealth of Israel, and have done nothing ever since they have lived, but treasure up wrath against the day of wrath? Oh sirs, your case in an especial manner is extremely dangerous; your guilt and hardness of heart is extremely great. Don't you see how generally persons of your years are passed over and left, in the present remarkable and wonderful dispensation of God's mercy? You had need to consider yourselves, and wake thoroughly out of sleep; you cannot bear the fierceness and wrath of the infinite God.

And you that are *young men*, and *young women*, will you neglect this precious season that you now enjoy, when so many others of your age are renouncing all youthful vanities, and flocking to Christ? You especially have now an extraordinary opportunity; but if you neglect it, it will soon be with you as it is with those persons that spent away all the precious days of youth in sin, and are now come to such a dreadful pass in blindness and hardness.

And you *children* that are unconverted, don't you know that you are going down to hell, to bear the dreadful wrath of that God that is now angry with you every day, and every night? Will you be content to be the children of the devil, when so many other children in the land are converted, and are become the holy and happy children of the King of kings?

And let everyone that is yet out of Christ, and hanging over the pit of hell, whether they be old men and women, or middle aged, or young people, or little children, now hearken to the loud calls of God's Word and providence. This acceptable year of the Lord, that is a day of such great favor to some, will doubtless be a day of as remarkable vengeance to others. Men's hearts harden, and their guilt increases apace at such a day as this, if they neglect their souls: and never was there so great danger of such persons being given up to hardness of heart, and blindness of mind. God seems now to be hastily gathering in his elect in all parts of the land; and probably the bigger part of adult persons that ever shall be saved, will be brought in now in a little time, and that it will be as it was on that great outpouring of the Spirit upon the Jews in the apostles' days, the election will obtain, and the rest will be blinded. If this should be the case with you you will eternally curse this day, and will curse the day that ever you was born, to see such a season of the pouring out of God's Spirit; and will wish that you had died and gone to hell before you had seen it. Now undoubtedly it is, as it was in the days of John the Baptist, the ax is in an extraordinary manner laid at the root of the trees, that every tree that brings not forth good fruit, may be hewn down, and cast into the fire.

Therefore let everyone that is out of Christ, now awake and fly from the wrath to come. The wrath of almighty God is now undoubtedly hanging over great part of this congregation: let everyone fly out of Sodom. Haste and escape for your lives, look not behind you, escape to the mountain, lest you be consumed [Genesis 19:17].

PATRICK HENRY

"Give Me Liberty or Give Me Death!" (March 23, 1775)

Although he spent most of his life as a planter and an attorney, Patrick Henry (1736–1799) was best known for the role he played as an advocate for armed rebellion during the lead-up to the American Revolution. After representing Virginia at the Continental Congress in 1774, Henry attended the Virginia House of Burgesses at St. John Church in Richmond, Virginia, in 1775. When the convention became embroiled in a debate about whether or not to mobilize American forces against the British, Henry delivered the following impassioned appeal.

No man thinks more highly than I do of the patriotism, as well as abilities, of the very worthy gentlemen who have just addressed the House. But different men often see the same subject in different lights; and, therefore, I hope that it will not be thought disrespectful to those gentlemen, if entertaining, as I do, opinions of a character very opposite to theirs, I shall speak forth *my* sentiments freely, and without reserve. This is no time for ceremony. The question before the House is one of awful moment to this country. For my own part, I consider it as nothing less than a question of freedom or slavery. And in proportion to the magnitude of the subject, ought to be the freedom of the debate. It is only in this way that we can hope to arrive at truth and fulfill the great responsibility which we hold to God and our country. Should I keep back my opinions at such a time, through fear of giving offense, I should consider myself as guilty of treason towards my country and of an act of disloyalty towards the majesty of Heaven which I revere above all earthly kings.

Mr. President, it is natural to man to indulge in the illusions of hope. We are apt to shut our eyes against a painful truth—and listen to the song of the siren till she transforms us into beasts. Is this the part of wise men engaged in a great and arduous struggle for liberty? Are we disposed to be of the number of those who, having eyes, see not, and having ears, hear not, the things which so nearly concern their temporal salvation? For my part, whatever anguish of spirit it may cost, *I* am willing to know the whole truth; to know the worst and to provide for it.

I have but one lamp by which my feet are guided; and that is the lamp of experience. I know of no way of judging of the future but by the past. And judging by the past, I wish to know what there has been in the conduct of the British ministry for the last ten years to justify those hopes with which gentlemen have been pleased to solace themselves and the house? Is it that insidious smile with which our petition has been lately received? Trust it not, sir; it will prove a snare to your feet. Suffer not yourselves to be betrayed with a kiss. Ask yourselves how this gracious reception of our petition comports with these warlike preparations which cover our waters and darken our land. Are fleets and armies necessary to a work of love and reconciliation? Have we shown ourselves so unwilling to be reconciled that force must be called in to win back our love? Let us not deceive ourselves, sir. These are the implements of war and subjugation—the last arguments to which kings resort.

I ask gentlemen, sir, what means this martial array if its purpose be not to force us to submission? Can gentlemen assign any other possible motives for it? Has Great Britain any enemy, in this quarter of the world to call for all this accumulation of navies and armies? No, sir, she has none. They are meant for us: they can be meant for no other. They are sent over to bind and rivet upon us those chains which the British ministry have been so long forging.

And what have we to oppose to them? Shall we try argument? Sir, we have been trying that for the last ten years. Have we anything new to offer on the subject? Nothing. We have held the subject up in every light of which it is capable; but it has been all in vain. Shall we resort to entreaty and humble supplication? What terms shall we find which have not been already exhausted?

Let us not, I beseech you, sir, deceive ourselves longer. Sir, we have done everything that could be done to avert the storm which is now coming on. We have petitioned—we have remonstrated—we have supplicated—we have prostrated ourselves before the throne, and have implored its interposition to arrest the tyrannical hands of the ministry and Parliament. Our petitions have been slighted; our remonstrances have produced additional violence and insult; our supplications have been disregarded; and we have been spurned, with contempt, from the foot of the throne.

In vain, after these things, may we indulge the fond hope of peace and reconciliation. *There is no longer any room for hope.* If we wish to be free—if we mean to preserve inviolate those inestimable privileges for which we have been so long contending—if we mean not basely to abandon the noble struggle in which we have been so long engaged, and which we have pledged ourselves never to abandon until the glorious object of our contest shall be obtained—we must fight! I repeat it, sir, we must fight! An appeal to arms and to the God of Hosts is all that is left us!

They tell us, sir, that we are weak—unable to cope with so formidable an adversary. But when shall we be stronger? Will it be the next week, or the next year? Will it be when we are totally disarmed, and when a British guard shall be stationed in every house? Shall we gather strength by irresolution and inaction? Shall we acquire the means of effectual resistance by lying supinely on our backs, and hugging the delusive phantom of Hope, until our enemies shall have bound us hand and foot?

Sir, we are not weak, if we make a proper use of the means which the God of nature hath placed in our power. Three millions of people, armed in the holy cause of liberty, and in such a country as that which we possess, are invincible by any force which our enemy can send against us.

Besides, sir, we shall not fight our battles alone. There is a just God who presides over the destinies of nations, and who will raise up friends to fight our battles for us. The battle, sir, is not to the strong alone; it is to the vigilant, the active, the brave. Besides, sir, we have no election. If we were base enough to desire it, it is now too late to retire from the contest. There is no retreat, but in submission and slavery! Our chains are forged, their clanking may be heard on the plains of Boston! The war is inevitable—and let it come! I repeat it, sir, let it come!

It is in vain, sir, to extenuate the matter. Gentlemen may cry, peace, peace—but there is no peace. The war is actually begun. The next gale that sweeps from the north will bring to our ears the clash of resounding arms! Our brethren are already in the field! Why stand we here idle? What is it that gentlemen wish? What would they have? Is life so dear, or peace so sweet, as to be purchased at the price of chains and slavery? Forbid it, Almighty God! I know not what course others may take; but as for me, give me liberty, or give me death!

GEORGE WASHINGTON

"Resignation Speech" (December 23, 1783)

While many of his countrymen were clamoring to crown him as king of the new nation, General George Washington (1732–1799) appeared before Congress in Annapolis, Maryland, to resign his commission as commander-in-chief of the Continental Army. Washington's decision to voluntarily give up power was unprecedented in modern history, and this single act of statesmanship would help to cement the democratic ideals on which the United States and its constitution were soon to be founded. Upon delivering the following address, Washington returned to his home in Mount Vernon, where he lived as a private citizen until the Constitutional Convention of 1787; the election of 1789 led to his ascendency as the first president of the United States.

[To the Continental Congress]

[Annapolis, Md. 23 December 1783]

Mr President,

The great events on which my resignation depended having at length taken place; I have now the honor of offering my sincere Congratulations to Congress & of presenting myself before them to surrender into their hands the trust committed to me, and to claim the indulgence of retiring from the Service of my Country.

Happy in the confirmation of our Independence and Sovereignty, and pleased with the oppertunity afforded the United States of becoming a respectable Nation, I resign with satisfaction the Appointment I accepted with diffidence—A diffidence in my abilities to accomplish so arduous a task, which however was superseded by a confidence in the rectitude of our Cause, the support of the Supreme Power of the Union, and the patronage of Heaven.

The Successful termination of the War has verified the more sanguine expectations—and my gratitude for the interposition of Providence, and the assistance I have received from my Countrymen encreases with every review of the momentous Contest.

While I repeat my obligations to the Army in general, I should do injustice to my own feelings not to acknowledge in this place the peculiar Services and distinguished merits of the Gentlemen who have been attached to my person during the War. It was impossible the choice of confidential Officers to compose my family should have been more fortunate. Permit me Sir, to recommend in particular those, who have continued in Service to the present moment, as worthy of the favorable notice & patronage of Congress.

I consider it an indispensable duty to close this last solemn act of my Official life, by commanding the Interests of our dearest Country to the protection of Almighty God, and those Who have the superintendence of them, to his holy keeping.

Having now finished the work assigned me, I retire from the great theatre of Action—and bidding an Affectionate farewell to this August body under whose orders I have so long acted, I here offer my Commission, and take my leave of all the employments of public life.

Notes

1. Washington's letter is kept in the National Archives, Washington, D.C., Papers of the Continental Congress, item 152; a contemporary copy of the letter is in the same repository, item 169 (see also Worthington C. Ford et al., eds., *Journals of the Continental Congress*, vol. 25:818).
2. Ibid., 837–38.

ADf copy (facsimile), New York Public Libary, New York, Emmet Collection. The original draft was given to James McHenry and is now at the Maryland State Archives (MdAA, 2007).

DANIEL WEBSTER

The Plymouth Oration, (December 22, 1820)

Regarded as one of the nation's finest orators, Daniel Webster (1782–1852) served five terms in the House of Representatives, three terms in the Senate, and was Secretary of State under three presidents. In the following address, delivered at the bicentennial celebration of the Pilgrims' landing at Plymouth Rock, Webster pays homage to the country's forebears, using their plight to make a passionate argument in favor of progress, individual rights, and the abolition of slavery.

LET US REJOICE that we behold this day. Let us be thankful that we have lived to see the bright and happy breaking of the auspicious morn, which commences the third century of the history of New England. Auspicious, indeed—bringing a happiness beyond the common allotment of Providence to men—full of present joy, and gilding with bright beams the prospect of futurity, is the dawn that awakens us to the commemoration of the landing of the Pilgrims.

Living at an epoch which naturally marks the progress of the history of our native land, we have come hither to celebrate the great event with which that history commenced. For ever honored be this, the place of our fathers' refuge! For ever remembered the day which saw them, weary and distressed, broken in every thing but spirit, poor in all but faith and courage, at last secure from the dangers of wintry seas, and impressing this shore with the first footsteps of civilized man!

It is a noble faculty of our nature which enables us to connect our thoughts, our sympathies, and our happiness with what is distant in place or time; and looking before and after, to hold communion at once with our ancestors and our posterity. Human and mortal although we are, we are nevertheless not mere insulated beings, without relation to the past or the future. Neither the point of time, nor the spot of earth, in which we physically live, bounds our rational and intellectual enjoyments. We live in the past by a knowledge of its history; and in the future by hope and anticipation. By ascending to an association with our ancestors; by contemplating their example and studying their character; by partaking their sentiments, and imbibing their spirit; by accompanying them in their toils, by sympathizing in their sufferings, and rejoicing in their successes and their triumphs; we seem to belong to their age, and to mingle our existence with theirs. We become their contemporaries, live the lives which they lived, endure what they endured, and partake in the rewards which they enjoyed. And in like manner, by running along the line of future time, by contemplating the probable fortunes of those who are coming after us, by attempting something which may promote their happiness, and leave some not dishonorable memorial of ourselves for their regard, when we shall sleep with the fathers, we protract our own earthly being, and seem to crowd whatever is future, as well as all that is past, into the narrow compass of our earthly existence. As it is not a vain and false, but an exhalted and religious imagination, which leads us to raise our thoughts from the orb, which, amidst this universe of worlds, the Creator has given us to inhabit, and to send them with something of the feeling which nature prompts, and teaches to be proper among children of the same Eternal Parent, to the contemplation of the myriads of fellow-beings, with which his goodness has peopled the infinite of space; so neither is it false or vain to consider ourselves as interested and connected with our whole race, through all time; allied to our ancestors; allied to our posterity; closely compacted on all sides with others; ourselves being but links in the great chain of being, which begins with the origin of our race, runs onward through its successive generations, binding together the past, the present, and the future, and terminating at last, with the consummation of all things earthly, at the throne of God.

There may be, and there often is, indeed, a regard for ancestry, which nourishes only a weak pride; as there is also a care for posterity, which only disguises an habitual avarice, or hides the workings of a low and grovelling vanity. But there is also a moral and philosophical respect for our ancestors, which elevates the character and improves the heart. Next to the sense of religious duty and moral feeling, I hardly know what should bear with stronger obligation on a liberal and enlightened mind, than a consciousness of alliance with excellence which is departed; and a consciousness, too, that in its acts and conduct, and even in its sentiments and thoughts, it may be actively operating on the happiness of those who come after it. Poetry is found to have few stronger conceptions by which it would affect or overwhelm the mind, than those in which it presents the moving and speaking image of the departed dead to the senses of the living. This belongs to poetry, only because it is congenial to our nature. Poetry, is, in this respect, but the hand-maid of true philosophy and morality; it deals with us as human beings, naturally reverencing those whose visible connection with this state of existence is severed, and who may yet exercise we know not what sympathy with ourselves; and when it carries us forward, also, and shows us the long-continued result of all the good we do, in the prosperity of those who follow us, till it bears us from ourselves, and absorbs us in an intense interest for what shall happen to the generations after us, it speaks only in the language of our nature, and affects us with sentiments which belong to us as human beings.

Standing in this relation to our ancestors and our posterity, we are assembled on this memorable spot, to perform the duties which that relation and the present occasion impose upon us. We have come to this Rock, to record here our homage for our Pilgrim Fathers; our sympathy in their sufferings; our gratitude for their labors; our admiration of their virtues; our veneration for their piety; and our attachment to those principles of civil and religious liberty, which they encountered the dangers of the ocean, the storms of heaven, the violence of savages, disease, exile and famine, to enjoy and to establish. And we would leave here, also, for the generations which are rising up rapidly to fill our places, some proof that we have endeavored to transmit the great inheritance unimpaired; that in our estimate of public principles and private virtue, in our veneration of religion and piety, in our devotion to civil and religious liberty, in our regard for whatever advances human knowledge or improves human happiness, we are not altogether unworthy of our origin.

There is a local feeling connected with this occasion, too strong to be resisted; a sort of *genius of the place*, which inspires and awes us.

We feel that we are on the spot where the first scene of our history was laid; where the hearths and altars of New England were first placed; where Christianity, and civilization, and letters made their first lodgement, in a vast extent of country, covered with a wilderness, and peopled by roving barbarians. We are here, at the season of the year at which the event took place. The imagination irresistibly and rapidly draws around us the principal features and the leading characters in the original scene. We cast our eyes abroad on the ocean, and we see where the little bark, with the interesting group upon its deck, made its slow progress to the shore. We look around us, and behold the hills and promontories where the anxious eyes of our fathers first saw the places of habitation and of rest. We feel the cold which benumbed, and listen to the winds which pierced them. Beneath us is the Rock, on which New England received the feet of the Pilgrims. We seem even to behold them, as they struggle with the elements, and with toilsome efforts, gain the shore. We listen to the chiefs in council; we see the unexampled exhibition of female fortitude and resignation; we hear the whisperings of youthful impatience; and we see, what a painter of our own has also represented by his pencil, chilled and shivering childhood—houseless, but for a mother's arms—couchless, but for a mother's breast, till our own blood almost freezes. The mild dignity of CARVER and of BRADFORD; the decisive and soldier-like air and manner of STANDISH; the devout BREWSTER; the enterprising ALLERTON; the general firmness and thoughtfulness of the whole band; their conscious joy for dangers escaped; their deep solicitude about dangers to come; their trust in Heaven; their high religious faith, full of confidence and anticipation; all of these seem to belong to this place, and to be present upon this occasion, to fill us with reverence and admiration.

The settlement of New England by the colony which landed here on the twenty-second of December, sixteen hundred and twenty, although not the first European establishment in what now constitutes the United States, was yet so peculiar in its causes and character, and has been followed and must still be followed by such consequences, as to give it a high claim to lasting commemoration. On these causes and consequences, more than on its immediate attendant circumstances, its importance, as an historical event, depends. Great actions and striking occurrences, having excited a temporary admiration, often pass away and are forgotten, because they leave no lasting results, affecting the prosperity and happiness of communities. Such is frequently the fortune of the most brilliant military achievements. Of the ten thousand battles which have been fought, of all the fields fertilized with carnage, of the banners which have been bathed in blood, of the warriors who have hoped that they had risen from the field of conquest to a glory as bright and as durable as the stars, how few that continue long to interest mankind! The victory of yesterday is reversed by the defeat of to-day; the star of military glory, rising like a meteor, like a meteor has fallen; disgrace and disaster hang on the heels of conquest and renown; victor and vanquished presently pass away to oblivion, and the world goes on in its course, with the loss only of so many lives and so much treasure.

But if this be frequently, or generally, the fortune of military achievements, it is not always so. There are enterprises, military as well as civil, which sometimes check the current of events, give a new turn to human affairs, and transmit their consequences through ages. We see their importance in their results, and call them great, because great things follow. There have been battles which have fixed the fate of nations. These come down to us in history with a solid and permanent interest, not created by a display of glittering armor, the rush of adverse battalions, the sinking and rising of pennons, the flight, the pursuit, and the victory; but by their effect in advancing or retarding human knowledge, in overthrowing or establishing despotism, in extending or destroying human happiness. When the traveller pauses on the plain of Marathon, what are the emotions which strongly agitate his breast? What is that glorious recollection, which thrills through his frame, and suffuses his eyes? Not, I imagine, that Grecian skill and Grecian valor were here most signally displayed; but that Greece herself was saved. It is because to this spot, and to the event which has rendered it immortal, he refers all the succeeding glories of the republic. It is because, if that day had gone otherwise, Greece had perished. It is because he perceives that her philosophers and orators, her poets and painters, her sculptors and architects, her governments and free institutions, point backward to Marathon, and that their future existence seems to have been suspended on the contingency, whether the Persian or the Grecian banner should wave victorious in the beams of that day's setting sun. And, as his imagination kindles at the retrospect, he is transported back to the interesting moment; he counts the fearful odds of the contending hosts; his interest for the result overwhelms him; he trembles, as if it were still uncertain, and seems to doubt whether he may consider Socrates and Plato, Demosthenes, Sophocles, and Phidias, as secure, yet, to himself and to the world.

"If we conquer," said the Athenian commander on the approach of that decisive day, "if we conquer, we shall make Athens the greatest city of Greece." A prophecy, how well fulfilled! "If God prosper us," might have been the more appropriate language of our fathers, when they landed upon this Rock, "if God prosper us, we shall here begin a work which shall last for ages; we shall plant here a new society, in the principle of the fullest liberty and the purest religion; we shall subdue this wilderness which is before us; we shall fill this region of the great continent, which stretches almost from pole to pole, with civilization and Christianity; the temples of the true God shall rise, where now ascends the smoke of idolatrous sacrifice; fields and gardens, the flowers of summer, and the waving and golden harvest of autumn shall spread over a thousand hills, and stretch along a thousand valleys, never yet, since the creation, reclaimed to the use of civilized man. We shall whiten the coast with the canvass of a prosperous commerce; we shall stud the long and winding shore with a hundred cities. That which we sow in weakness shall be raised in strength. From our sincere, but houseless worship, there shall spring splendid temples to record God's goodness; from the simplicity of our social union, there shall arise wise and politic constitutions of government, full of the liberty which we ourselves bring and breathe; from our zeal for learning, institutions shall spring which shall scatter the light of knowledge throughout the land, and, in time, paying back where they have borrowed, shall contribute their part to the great aggregate of human knowledge; and our descendants, through all generations, shall look back to this spot, and to this hour, with unabated affection and regard."

A brief remembrance of the causes which led to the settlement of this place; some account of the peculiarities and charcteristic qualities of that settlement, as distinguished from other instances of colonization; a short notice of the progress of New England in the great interests of society, during the century which is now elapsed; with a few observations on the principles upon which society and government are established in this country; comprise all that can be attempted, and much more than can be satisfactorily performed, on the present occasion.

Of the motives which influenced the first settlers to a voluntary exile, induced them to relinquish their native country, and to seek an asylum in this then unexplored wilderness, the first and principal, no doubt, were connected with religion. They sought to enjoy a higher degree of religious freedom, and what they esteemed a purer form of religious worship, than was allowed to their choice, or presented to their imitation, in the Old World. The love of religious liberty is a stronger sentiment, when fully excited, than an attachment to civil or political freedom. That freedom which the conscience demands, and which men feel bound by their hope of salvation to contend for, can hardly fail to be attained. Conscience, in the cause of religion and the worship of the Deity, prepares the mind to act and to suffer beyond almost all other causes. It sometimes gives an impulse so irresistible, that no fetters of power or of opinion can withstand it. History instructs us that this love of religious liberty, a compound sentiment in the breast of man, made up of the clearest sense of right and the highest conviction of duty, is able to look the sternest despotism in the face, and, with means apparently most inadequate, to shake principalities and powers. There is a boldness, a spirit of daring, in religious reformers, not to be measured by the general rules which control men's purposes and actions. If the hand of power be laid upon it, this only seems to augment its force and its elasticity, and to cause its action to be more formidable and violent. Human invention has devised nothing, human power has compassed nothing, that can forcibly restrain it, when it breaks forth. Nothing can stop it, but to give way to it; nothing can check it, but to give way to indulgence. It loses its power only when it has gained its object. The principle of toleration, to which the world has come so slowly, is at once the most just and the most wise of all principles. Even when religous feeling takes a character of extravagance and enthusiasm, and seems to threaten the order of society and shake the columns of the social edifice, its principal danger is in its restraint. If it be allowed indulgence and expansion, like the elemental fires, it only agitates, and perhaps purifies the atmosphere; whilst its efforts to throw off restraint would burst the world asunder.

It is certain that, although many of them were republicans in principle, we have no evidence that our New England ancestors would have emigrated, as they did, from their own native country, would have become wanderers in Europe, and finally would have undertaken the establishment of a colony here, merely from their dislike of the political systems of Europe. They fled not so much from the civil government, as from the hierarchy, and the laws which enforced conformity to the church establishment. Mr. Robinson had left England as early as 1608, on account of the persecutions for non-conformity, and had retired to Holland. He left England, from no disappointed ambition in affairs of state, from no regrets at the want of preferment in the church, nor from any motive of distinction or of gain. Uniformity in matters of religion was pressed with such extreme rigor, that a voluntary exile seemed the most eligible mode of escaping from the penalties of noncompliance. The accession of Elizabeth had, it is true, quenched the fires of Smithfield, and put an end to the easy acquisition of the crown of martyrdom. Her long reign had established the Reformation, but toleration was a virtue beyond her conception, and beyond the age. She left no example of it to her successor; and he was not of a character which rendered it probable that a sentiment either so wise or so liberal would originate with him. At the present period, it seems incredible that the learned, accomplished, unassuming, and inoffensive Robinson, should neither be tolerated in his peaceable mode of worship in his own country, nor suffered quietly to depart from it. Yet such was the fact. He left his country by stealth, that he might elsewhere enjoy those rights which ought to belong to men in all countries. The departure of the Pilgrims for Holland is deeply interesting, from its circumstances, and also as it marks the character of the times, independently of its connection with names now incorporated with the history of empire. The embarkation was intended to be made in such a manner, that it might escape the notice of the officers of government. Great pains had been taken to secure boats, which should come undiscovered to the shore, and receive the fugitives; and frequent disappointments had been experienced in this respect.

At length the appointed time came, bringing with it unusual severity of cold and rain. An unfrequented and barren heath, on the shores of Lincolnshire, was the selected spot, where the feet of the Pilgrims were to tread, for the last time, the land of their fathers. The vessel which was to receive them did not come until the next day, and in the meantime the little band was collected, and men and women and children and baggage were crowded together, in melancholy and distressed confusion. The sea was rough, and the women and children were already sick, from their passage down the river to the place of embarkation on the sea. At length the wished-for boat silently and fearfully approaches the shore, and men and women and children, shaking with fear and with cold, as many as the small vessel could bear, venture off on a dangerous sea. Immediately the advance of horses is heard from behind, armed men appear, and those not yet embarked are seized, and taken into custody. In the hurry of the moment, the first parties had been sent on board without any attempt to keep members of the same family together, and on account of the appearance of the horsemen, the boat never returned for the residue. Those who had got away, and those who had not, were in equal distress. A storm, of great violence and long duration, arose at sea, which not only protracted the voyage, rendered distressing by the want of all those accommodations which the interruption of the embarkation had occasioned, but also forced the vessel out of her course, and menaced immediate shipwreck; while those on shore, when they were dismissed from the custody of the officers of justice, having no longer homes or houses to retire to, and their friends and protectors being already gone, became objects of necessary charity, as well as of deep commiseration.

As this scene passes before us, we can hardly forbear asking, whether this be a band of malefactors and felons, flying from justice. What are their crimes, that they hide themselves in darkness? To what punishment are they exposed, that, to avoid it, men, and women, and children, thus encounter the surf of the North Sea, and the terrors of a night storm? What induces this armed pursuit, and this arrest of fugitives, of all ages and both sexes? Truth does not allow us to answer these inquiries in a manner that does credit to the wisdom or the justice of the times. This was not the flight of guilt, but of virtue. It was an humble and peaceable religion, flying from causeless oppression. It was conscience, attempting to escape from the arbitrary rule of the Stuarts. It was Robinson and Brewster, leading off their little band from their native soil, at first to find shelter on the shore of the neighboring continent, but ultimately to come hither; and having surmounted all difficulties and braved a thousand dangers, to find here a place of refuge and of rest. Thanks be to God, that this spot was honored as the asylum of religious liberty! May its standard, reared here, remain for ever! May it rise up as high as heaven, till its banner shall fan the air of both continents, and wave as a glorious ensign of peace and security to the nations!

The peculiar character, condition, and circumstances of the colonies which introduced civilization and an English race into New England, afford a most interesting and extensive topic of discussion. On these, much of our subsequent character and fortune has depended. Their influence has essentially affected our whole history, through the two centuries which have elapsed; and as they have become intimately connected with government, laws, and property, as well as our opinions on the subjects of religion and civil liberty, that influence is likely to continue to be felt through the centuries which shall succeed. Emigration from one region to another, and the emission of colonies to people countries more or less distant from the residence of the parent stock, are common incidents in the history of mankind; but it has not often, perhaps never happened, that the establishment of colonies should be attempted under circumstances, however beset with present difficulties and dangers, yet so favorable to ultimate success, and so conducive to magnificent results, as those which attended the first settlements on this part of the American continent. In other instances, emigration has proceeded from a less exalted purpose, in periods of less general intelligence, or more without plan and by accident; or under circumstances, physical and moral, less favorable to the expectation of laying a foundation for great public prosperity and future empire.

A great resemblance exists, obviously, between all the English colonies established within the present limits of the United States; but the occasion attracts our attention more immediately to those which took possession of New England, and the peculiarities of these furnish a strong contrast with most other instances of colonization.

Among the ancient nations, the Greeks, no doubt, sent forth from their territories the greatest number of colonies. So numerous, indeed, were they, and so great the extent of space over which they were spread, that the parent country fondly and naturally persuaded herself that by means of them she had laid a sure foundation for the universal civilization of the world. These establishments, from obvious causes, were most numerous in places most contiguous; yet they were found on the coasts of France, on the shores of the Euxine Sea, in Africa, and even, as is alleged, on the borders of India. These emigrations appear to have been sometimes voluntary and sometimes compulsory; arising from the spontaneous enterprise of individuals, or the order and regulation of government. It was a common opinion with ancient writers, that they were undertaken in religious obedience to the commands of oracles, and it is probable that impressions of this sort might have had more or less influence; but it is probable, also, that on these occasions the oracles did not speak a language dissonant from the views and purposes of the state.

Political science among the Greeks seems never to have extended to the comprehension of a system which should be adequate to the government of a great nation upon principles of liberty. They were accustomed only to the contemplation of small republics, and were led to consider an augmented population as incompatible with free institutions. The desire of a remedy for this supposed evil, and the wish to establish marts for trade, led the governments often to undertake the establishment of colonies as an affair of state expediency. Colonization and commerce, indeed, would naturally become objects of interest to an ingenious and enterprising people, inhabiting a territory closely circumscribed in its limits, and in no small part mountainous and sterile; while the islands of the adjacent seas, and the promontories and coasts of the neighboring continents, by their mere proximity, strongly solicited the excited spirit of emigration. Such was this proximity, in many instances, that the new settlements appeared rather to be the mere extension of population over contiguous territory, than the establishment of distant colonies. In proportion as they were near to the parent state, they would be under its authority, and partake of its fortunes. The colony at Marseilles might perceive lightly, or not at all, the sway of Phocis; while the islands in the Ægean Sea could hardly attain to independence of their Athenian origin. Many of these establishments took place at an early age; and if there were defects in the governments of the parent states, the colonists did not possess philosophy or experience sufficient to correct such evils in their own institutions, even if they had not been, by other causes, deprived of the power. An immediate necessity, connected with the support of life, was the main and direct inducement to these undertakings, and there could hardly exist more than the hope of a successful imitation of institutions with which they were already acquainted, and of holding an equality with their neighbors in the course of improvement. The laws and customs, both political and municipal, as well as the religious worship of the parent city, were transferred to the colony; and the parent city herself, with all such of her colonies as were not too far remote for frequent intercourse and common sentiments, would appear like a family of cities, more or less dependent, and more or less connected. We know how imperfect this system was, as a system of general politics, and what scope it gave to those mutual dissensions and conflicts which proved so fatal to Greece.

But it is more pertinent to our present purpose to observe, that nothing existed in the character of Grecian emigrations, or in the spirit and intelligence of the emigrants, likely to give a new and important direction to human affairs, or a new impulse to the human mind. Their motives were not high enough, their views were not sufficiently large and prospective. They went not forth, like our ancestors, to erect systems of more perfect civil liberty, or to enjoy a higher degree of religious freedom. Above all, there was nothing in the religion and learning of the age, that could either inspire high purposes, or give the ability to execute them. Whatever restraints on civil liberty, or whatever abuses in religious worship, existed at the time of our fathers' emigration, yet even then all was light in the moral and mental world, in comparison with its condition in most periods of the ancient states. The settlement of a new continent, in an age of progressive knowledge and improvement, could not but do more than merely enlarge the natural boundaries of the habitable world. It could not but do much more even than extend commerce and increase wealth among the human race. We see how this event has acted, how it must have acted, and wonder only why it did not act sooner, in the production of moral effects, on the state of human knowledge, the general tone of human sentiments, and the prospects of human happiness. It gave to civilized man not only a new continent to be inhabited and cultivated, and new seas to be explored; but it it gave him also a new range for his thoughts, new objects for curiosity, and new excitements to knowledge and improvement.

Roman colonization resembled, far less than that of the Greeks, the original settlements of this country. Power and dominion were the objects of Rome, even in her colonial establishments. Her whole exterior aspect was for centuries hostile and terrific. She grasped at dominion, from India to Britain, and her measures of colonization partook of the character of her general system. Her policy was military, because her objects were power, ascendency and subjugation. Detachments of emigrants from Rome incorporated themselves with, and governed, the original inhabitants of conquered countries. She sent citizens where she had first sent soldiers; her law followed her sword. Her colonies were a sort of military establishment; so many advanced posts in the career of her dominion. A governor from Rome ruled the new colony with absolute sway, and often with unbounded rapacity. In Sicily, in Gaul, in Spain, and in Asia, the power of Rome prevailed, not nominally only, but really and effectually. Those who immediately exercised it were Roman; the tone and tendency of its administration, Roman. Rome herself continued to be the heart and centre of the great system which she had established. Extortion and rapacity, finding a wide and often rich field of action in the provinces, looked nevertheless to the banks of the Tiber, as the scene in which their ill-gotten treasures should be displayed; or, if a spirit of more honest acquisition prevailed, the object, nevertheless, was ultimate enjoyment in Rome itself. If our own history and our own times did not sufficiently expose the inherent and incurable evils of provincial government, we might see them portrayed, to our amazement, in the desolated and ruined provinces of the Roman empire. We might hear them, in a voice that terrifies us, in those strains of complaint and accusation, which the advocates of the provinces poured forth in the Roman Forum:—"Quas res luxuries in flagitiis, crudelitas in suppliciis, avaritia in rapinis, superbia in contumeliis, efficere potuisset, eas omnes sese pertulisse."

As was to be expected, the Roman provinces partook of the fortunes, as well as of the sentiments and general character, of the seat of empire. They lived together with her, they flourished with her, and fell with her. The branches were lopped away even before the vast and venerable trunk itself fell prostrate to the earth. Nothing had proceeded from her which could support itself, and bear up the name of its origin, when her own sustaining arm should be enfeebled or withdrawn. It was not given to Rome to see, either at her zenith or in her decline, a child of her own, distant, indeed, and independent of her control, yet speaking her language and inheriting her blood, springing forward to a competition with her own power, and a comparison with her own great renown. She saw not a vast region of the earth peopled from her stock, full of states and political communities, improving upon the models of her institutions, and breathing in fuller measure the spirit which she had breathed in the best periods of her existence; enjoying and extending her arts and her literature; rising rapidly from political childhood to manly strength and independence; her offspring, yet now her equal; unconnected with the causes which might affect the duration of her own power and greatness; of common origin, but not linked to a common fate; giving ample pledge, that her name should not be forgotten; that her language should not cease to be used among men; that whatsoever she had done for human knowledge and human happiness should be treasured up and preserved; that the record of her existence and her achievements should not be obscured, although, in the inscrutable purposes of Providence, it might be her destiny to fall from opulence and splendor; although the time might come when darkness should settle on all her hills; when foreign or domestic violence should overturn her altars and her temples; when ignorance and despotism should fill the places where Laws, and Arts, and Liberty had flourished; when the feet of barbarism should trample on the tombs of her consuls, and the walls of her senate-house and forum echo only to the voice of savage triumph. She saw not this glorious vision, to inspire and fortify her against the possible decay or downfall of her power. Happy are they who in our day may behold it, if they shall contemplate it with the sentiments which it ought to inspire!

The New England colonies differ quite as widely from the Asiatic establishments of the modern European nations, as from the models of the ancient states. The sole objects of those establishments was originally trade; although we have seen, in one of them, the anomaly of a mere trading company attaining a political character, disbursing revenues, and maintaining armies and fortresses, until it has extended its control over seventy millions of people. Differing from these, and still more from the New England and North American colonies, are the European settlements in the West India Islands. It is not strange that, when men's minds were turned to the settlement of America, different objects should be proposed by those who emigrated to the different regions of so vast a country. Climate, soil and condition were not all equally favorable to all pursuits. In the West Indies, the purpose of those who went thither was to engage in that species of agriculture, suited to the soil and climate, which seems to bear more resemblance to commerce, than to the hard and plain tillage of New England. The great staples of these countries, being partly an agricultural and partly a manufactured product, and not being of the necessaries of life, become the object of calculation, with respect to a profitable investment of capital, like any other enterprise of trade or manufacture. The more especially, as, requiring, by necessity or habit, slave labor for their production, the capital necessary to carry on the work of this production is very considerable. The West Indies are resorted to, therefore, rather for the investment of capital, than for the purpose of sustaining life by personal labor. Such as possess a considerable amount of capital, or such as choose to adventure in commercial speculations without capital, can alone be fitted to be emigrants to the islands. The agriculture of these regions, as before observed, is a sort of commerce; and it is a species of employment in which labor seems to form an inconsiderable ingredient in the productive causes, since the portion of white labor is exceedingly small, and slave labor is rather more like profit on stock or capital, than *labor* properly so called. The individual who undertakes an establishment of this kind, takes into the account the cost of the necessary number of slaves, in the same manner as he calculates the cost of the land. The uncertainty, too, of this species of employment, affords another ground of resemblance to commerce. Although gainful on the whole, and in a series of years, it is often very disastrous for a single year, and, as the capital is not readily invested in other pursuits, bad crops or bad markets not only affect the profits, but the capital itself. Hence the sudden depressions which take place in the value of such estates.

But the great and leading observation, relative to these establishments, remains to be made. It is, that the owners of the soil and of the capital seldom consider themselves *at home* in the colony. A very great portion of the soil itself is usually owned in the mother country; a still greater is mortgaged for capital obtained there; and, in general, those who are to derive an interest from the products look to the parent country as the place for enjoyment of their wealth. The population is therefore constantly fluctuating. Nobody comes but to return. A constant succession of owners, agents and factors takes place. Whatsoever the soil, forced by the unmitigated toil of slavery, can yield, is sent home to defray rents, and interest, and agencies, or to give the means of living in a better society. In such a state, it is evident that no spirit of permanent improvement is likely to spring up. Profits will not be invested with a distant view of benefiting posterity. Roads and canals will hardly be built; schools will not be founded; colleges will not be endowed. There will be few fixtures in society, no principles of utility or of elegance, planted now, with the hope of being developed and expanded hereafter. Profit, immediate profit, must be the principal active spring in the social system. There may be many particular exceptions to these general remarks, but the outline of the whole is such as is here drawn.

Another most important consequence of such a state of things is, that no idea of independence of the parent country is likely to arise; unless, indeed, it should spring up in a form that would threaten universal desolation. The inhabitants have no strong attachment to the place which they inhabit. The hope of a great portion of them is to leave it; and their great desire, to leave it soon. However useful they may be to the parent state, how much soever they may add to the conveniencies and luxuries of life, these colonies are not favored spots for the expansion of the human mind, for the progress of permanent improvement, or for sowing the seeds of future independent empire.

Different, indeed, most widely different, from all these instances of emigration and plantation, were the condition, the purposes, and the prospects of our fathers, when they established their infant colony upon this spot. They came hither from a land to which they were never to return. Hither they had brought, and here they were to fix their hopes, their attachments, and their objects in life. Some natural tears they shed, as they left the pleasant abodes of their fathers, and some emotions they suppressed, when the white cliffs of their native country, now seen for the last time, grew dim to their sight. They were acting, however, on a resolution not to be daunted. With whatever stifled regrets, with whatever occasional hesitation, with whatever appalling apprehensions, which might sometimes arise with force to shake the firmest purpose, they had yet committed themselves to Heaven and the elements; and a thousand leagues of water soon interposed to separate them for ever from the region which gave them birth. A new existence awaited them here; and when they saw these shores, rough, cold, barbarous, and barren, as then they were, they beheld their country. That mixed and strong feeling, which we call love of country, and which is, in general, never extinguished in the heart of man, grasped and embraced its proper object here. Whatever constitutes country, except the earth and the sun, all the moral causes of affection and attachment which operate upon the heart, they had brought with them to their new abode. Here were now their families and friends, their homes, and their property. Before they reached the shore, they had established the elements of a social system, and at a much earlier period had settled their forms of religious worship. At the moment of their landing, therefore, they possessed institutions of government, and institutions of religion; and friends and families, and social and religious institutions, framed by consent, founded on choice and preference, how nearly do these fill up our whole idea of country! The morning that beamed on the first night of their repose saw the Pilgrims already *at home* in their country. There were political institutions, and civil liberty, and religious worship. Poetry has fancied nothing, in the wanderings of heroes, so distinct and characteristic. Here was man, indeed, unprotected, and unprovided for, on the shore of a rude and fearful wilderness; but it was politic, intelligent, and educated man. Every thing was civilized but the physical world. Institutions, containing in substance all that ages had done for human government, were organized in a forest. Cultivated mind was to act on uncultivated nature; and, more than all, a government and a country were to commence, with the very first foundations laid under the divine right of the Christian religion. Happy auspices of a happy futurity! Who would wish that his country's existence had otherwise begun? Who would desire the power of going back to the ages of fable? Who would wish for an origin obscured in the darkness of antiquity! Who would wish for other emblazoning of his country's heraldry, or other ornaments of her genealogy, than to be able to say, that her first existence was with intelligence, her first breath the inspiration of liberty, her first principle the truth of divine religion?

Local attachments and sympathies would ere long spring up in the breasts of our ancestors, endearing to them the place of their refuge. Whatever natural objects are associated with interesting scenes and high efforts obtain a hold on human feeling, and demand from the heart a sort of recognition and regard. This Rock soon became hallowed in the esteem of the Pilgrims, and these hills grateful to their sight. Neither they nor their children were again to till the soil of England, nor again to traverse the seas which surround her. But here was a new sea, now open to their enterprise, and a new soil, which had not failed to respond gratefully to their laborious industry, and which was already assuming a robe of verdure. Hardly had they provided shelter for the living, ere they were summoned to erect sepulchres for the dead. The ground had become sacred, by inclosing the remains of some of their companions and connections. A parent, a child, a husband, or a wife, had gone the way of all flesh, and mingled with the dust of New England. We naturally look with strong emotions to the spot, though it be a wilderness, where the ashes of those we have loved repose. Where the heart has laid down what it loved most, there it is desirous of laying itself down. No sculptured marble, no enduring monument, no honorable inscription, no ever-burning taper that would drive away the darkness of the tomb, can soften our sense of the reality of death, and hallow to our feelings the ground which is to cover us, like the consciousness that we shall sleep, dust to dust, with the objects of our affections.

In a short time other causes sprung up to bind the Pilgrims with new cords to their chosen land. Children were born, and the hopes of future generations arose, in the spot of their new habitation. The second generation found this the land of their nativity, and saw that they were bound to its fortunes. They beheld their fathers' graves around them, and while they read the memorials of their toils and labors, they rejoiced in the inheritance which they found bequeathed to them.

Under the influence of these causes, it was to be expected that an interest and a feeling should arise here, entirely different from the interest and feeling of mere Englishmen; and all the subsequent history of the colonies proves this to have actually and gradually taken place. With a general acknowledgment of the supremacy of the British crown, there was, from the first, a repugnance to an entire submission to the control of British legislation. The colonies stood upon their charters, which, as they contended, exempted them from the ordinary power of the British Parliament, and authorized them to conduct their own concerns by their own counsels. They utterly resisted the notion that they were to be ruled by the mere authority of the government at home, and would not endure even that their own charter governments should be established on the other side of the Atlantic. It was not a controlling or protecting board in England, but a government of their own, and existing immediately within their limits, which could satisfy their wishes. It was easy to foresee, what we know also to have happened, that the first great cause of collision and jealousy would be, under the notion of political economy then and still prevalent in Europe, an attempt on the part of the mother country to monopolize the trade of the colonies. Whoever has looked deeply into the causes which produced our Revolution, has found, if I mistake not, the original principal far back in this claim, on the part of England, to monopolize our trade, and a continued effort on the part of the colonies to resist or evade that monopoly; if, indeed, it be not still more just and philosophical to go farther back, and to consider it decided, that an independent government must arise here, the moment it was ascertained that an English colony, such as landed in this place, could sustain itself against the dangers which surrounded it, and, with other similar establishments, overspread the land with an English population. Accidental causes retarded at times, and at times accelerated the progress of the controversy. The colonies wanted strength and time to give it to them. They required measures of strong and palpable injustice, on the part of the mother country, to justify resistance; the early part of the late king's reign furnished them. They needed spirits of high order, of great daring, of long foresight, and of commanding power, to seize the favoring occasion to strike a blow, which should sever, for all time, the tie of colonial dependence; and these spirits were found, in all the extent which that or any crisis could demand, in Otis, Adams, Hancock, and the other immediate authors of our independence.

Still, it is true that, for a century, causes had been in operation tending to prepare things for this great result. In the year 1660, the English Act of Navigation was passed; the first and grand object of which seems to have been to secure to England the whole trade with her plantations. It was provided by that act that none but English ships should transport American produce over the ocean, and that the principal articles of that produce should be allowed to be sold only in the markets of the mother country. Three years afterwards another law was passed, which enacted that such commodities as the colonies might wish to purchase should be bought only in the markets of the mother country. Severe rules were prescribed to enforce the provisions of these laws, and heavy penalties imposed on all who should violate them. In the subsequent years of the same reign, other statutes were enacted to re-enforce these statutes, and other rules prescribed to secure a compliance with these rules. In this manner was the trade to and from the colonies restricted, almost to the exclusive advantage of the parent country. But laws, which rendered the interest of a whole people subordinate to that of another people, were not likely to execute themselves; nor was it easy to find many on the spot, who could be depended upon for carrying them into execution. In fact, these laws were more or less evaded or resisted, in all the colonies. To enforce them was the constant endeavor of the government at home; to prevent or elude their operation, the perpetual object here. "The laws of navigation," says a living British writer, "were nowhere so openly disobeyed and contemned as in New England." "The people of Massachusetts Bay," he adds, "were from the first disposed to act as if independent of the mother country; and having a governor and magistrates of their own choice, it was difficult to enforce any regulation which came from the English Parliament, adverse to their interests." To provide more effectually for the execution of these laws, we know that courts of admiralty were afterwards established by the crown, with power to try revenue causes, as questions of admiralty, upon the construction given by the crown lawyers to an act of Parliament; a great departure from the ordinary principles of English jurisprudence, but which has been maintained, nevertheless, by the force of habit and precedent, and is adopted in our own existing forms of government.

"There lie," says another English writer, whose connection with the Board of Trade has enabled him to ascertain many facts connected with colonial history, "There lie among the documents in the Board of Trade and State-paper office, the most satisfactory proofs, from the epoch of the English Revolution in 1688, throughout every reign, and during every administration, of the settled purpose of the colonies to acquire direct independence and positive sovereignty." Perhaps this may be stated somewhat too strongly; but it cannot be denied that, from the very nature of the establishments here, and from the general character of the measures respecting their concerns early adopted and steadily pursued by the English government, a division of the empire was the natural and necessary result to which every thing tended.

I have dwelt on this topic, because it seems to me that the peculiar original character of the New England colonies, and certain causes coeval with their existence, have had a strong and decided influence on all their subsequent history, and especially on the great event of the Revolution. Whoever would write our history, and would understand and explain early transactions, should comprehend the nature and force of the feeling which I have endeavored to describe. As a son, leaving the house of his father for his own, finds, by the order of nature, and the very law of his being, nearer and dearer objects around which his affections circle, while his attachment to the parental roof becomes moderated, by degrees, to a composed regard and an affectionate remembrance; so our ancestors, leaving their native land, not without some violence to the feelings of nature and affection, yet, in time, found here a new circle of engagements, interests and affections; a feeling, which more and more encroached upon the old, till an undivided sentiment, *that this was their country*, occupied the heart; and patriotism, shutting out from its embraces the parent realm, became *local* to America.

Some retrospect of the century which has now elapsed is among the duties of the occasion. It must, however, necessarily be imperfect, to be compressed within the limits of a single discourse. I shall content myself, therefore, with taking notice of a few of the leading and most important occurrences which have distinguished the period.

When the first century closed, the progress of the country appeared to have been considerable; notwithstanding that, in comparison with its subsequent advancement, it now seems otherwise. A broad and lasting foundation had been laid; excellent institutions had been established; many of the prejudices of former times had been removed; a more liberal and catholic spirit on subjects of religious concern had begun to extend itself, and many things conspired to give promise of increasing future prosperity. Great men had arisen in public life, and the liberal professions. The Mathers, father and son, were then sinking low in the western horizon; Leverett, the learned, the accomplished, the excellent Leverett, was about to withdraw his brilliant and useful light. In Pemberton great hopes had been suddenly extinguished, but Prince and Colman were in our sky; and along the east had begun to flash the crepuscular light of a great luminary which was about to appear, and which was to stamp the age with his own name, as the age of Franklin.

The bloody Indian wars, which harrassed the people for a part of the first century; the restrictions on the trade of the colonies, added to the discouragements inherently belonging to all forms of colonial government; the distance from Europe, and the small hope of immediate profit to adventurers, are among the causes which had contributed to retard the progress of population. Perhaps it may be added, also, that during the period of the civil wars in England, and the reign of Cromwell, many persons, whose religious opinions and religious temper might, under other circumstances, have induced them to join the New England colonists, found reasons to remain in England; either on account of active occupation in the scenes which were passing, or of an anticipation of the enjoyment, in their own country, of a form of government, civil and religious, accommodated to their views and principles. The violent measures, too, pursued against the colonies in the reign of Charles the Second, the mockery of a trial, and the forfeiture of the charters, were serious evils. And during the open violence of the short reign of James the Second, and the tyranny of Andros, as the venerable historian of Connecticut observes, "All the motives to great actions, to industry, economy, enterprise, wealth, and population, were in a manner annihilated. A general inactivity and languishment pervaded the public body. Liberty, property, and every thing which ought to be dear to men, every day grew more and more insecure."

With the Revolution in England, a better prospect had opened on this country, as well as on that. The joy had been as great at that event, and far more universal, in New England than in Old England. A new charter had been granted to Massachusetts, which, although it did not confirm to her inhabitants all their former privileges, yet relieved them from great evils and embarrassments, and promised future security. More than all, perhaps, the Revolution in England had done good to the general cause of liberty and justice. A blow had been struck in favor of the rights and liberties, not of England alone, but of descendants and kinsmen of England all over the world. Great political truths had been established. The champions of liberty had been successful in a fearful and perilous conflict. Somers, and Cavendish, and Jekyl, and Howard, had triumphed in one of the most noble causes ever undertaken by men. A revolution had been made upon principle. A monarch had been dethroned for violating the original compact between king and people. The rights of the people to partake in the government, and to limit the monarch by fundamental rules of government, had been maintained; and however unjust the government of England might afterwards be towards other governments or towards her colonies, she had ceased to be governed herself by the arbitrary maxims of the Stuarts.

New England had submitted to the violence of James the Second not longer than Old England. Not only was it reserved to Massachusetts, that on her soil should be acted the first scene of that great revolutionary drama, which was to take place near a century afterwards, but the English Revolution itself, as far as the colonies were concerned, commenced in Boston. The seizure and imprisonment of Andros, in April, 1689, were acts of direct and forcible resistance to the authority of James the Second. The pulse of liberty beat as high in the extremities as at the heart. The vigorous feeling of the colony burst out before it was known how the parent country would finally conduct herself. The king's representative, Sir Edmund Andros, was a prisoner in the castle at Boston, before it was or could be known that the king himself had ceased to exercise his full dominion on the English throne.

Before it was known here, whether the invasion of the Prince of Orange would or could prove successful; as soon only as it was known that it had been undertaken, the people of Massachusetts, at the imminent hazards of their lives and fortunes, had accomplished the revolution as far as respected themselves. It is probable, that, reasoning on general principles, and the known attachment of the English people to their constitution and liberties, and their deep and fixed dislike of the king's religion and politics, the people of New England expected a catastrophe fatal to the power of the reigning Prince. Yet, it was not either certain enough, or near enough, to come to their aid against the authority of the crown, in that crisis which had arrived, and in which they trusted to put themselves, relying on God, and their own courage. There were spirits in Massachusetts, congenial with the spirits of the distinguished friends of the revolution in England. There were those, who were fit to associate with the boldest asserters of civil liberty; and Mather himself, then in England, was not unworthy to be ranked with those sons of the church, whose firmness and spirit in resisting kingly encroachment in religion, entitled them to the gratitude of their own and succeeding ages.

The second century opened upon New England under circumstances which evinced that much had already been accomplished, and that still better prospects, and brighter hopes, were before her. She had laid, deep and strong, the foundations of her society. Her religious principles were firm, and her moral habits exemplary. Her public schools had begun to diffuse widely the elements of knowledge; and the College, under the excellent and acceptable administration of Leverett, had been raised to a high degree of credit and usefulness.

The commercial character of the country, notwithstanding all discouragement, had begun to display itself, and *five hundred vessels*, then belonging to Massachusetts, placed her in relation to commerce, thus early, at the head of the colonies. An author who wrote very near the close of the first century says: "New England is almost deserving that *noble name*, so mightily hath it increased; and from a small settlement, at first, is now become a very *populous* and *flourishing* government. The *capital city*, Boston, is a place of *great wealth and trade;* and by much the largest of any in the English empire of America; and not exceeded but by few cities, perhaps two or three, in all the American world."

But, if our ancestors at the close of the first century, could look back with joy, and even admiration at the progress of the country; what emotions must we not feel, when, from the point in which we stand, we look back and run along the events of the century which has now closed? The country, which then, as we have seen was thought deserving of a "noble name;" which then had "mightily increased," and become "very populous;" what was it, in comparison with what our eyes behold it? At that period, a very great proportion of its inhabitants lived in the eastern section of Massachusetts proper, and in this colony. In Connecticut, there were towns along the coast, some of them respectable, but in the interior, all was a wilderness beyond Hartford.—On Connecticut river, settlements had proceeded as far up as Deerfield, and Fort Dummer had been built, near where is now the south line of New Hampshire. In New Hampshire, no settlement was then begun thirty miles from the mouth of Piscataqua river, and, in what is now Maine, the inhabitants were confined to the coast. The aggregate of the whole population of New England did not exceed one hundred and sixty thousand. Its present amount is probably one million seven hundred thousand. Instead of being confined to its former limits, her population has rolled backward and filled up the spaces included within her actual local boundaries. Not this only, but it has overflowed those boundaries, and the waves of emigration have pressed further and further toward the west. The Alleghany has not checked it; the banks of the Ohio have been covered with it. New England farms, houses, villages, and churches spread over, and adorn the immense extent from the Ohio to Lake Erie; and stretch along, from the Alleghany onwards, beyond the Miamis, and toward the Falls of St. Anthony. Two thousand miles westward from the rock where their fathers landed, may now be found the sons of the Pilgrims; cultivating smiling fields, rearing towns and villages, and cherishing, we trust, the patrimonial blessings of wise institutions, of liberty and religion. The world has seen nothing like this. Regions large enough to be empires, and which, half a century ago, were known only as remote and unexplored wildernesses, are now teeming with population, and prosperous in all the great concerns of life; in good governments, the means of subsistence, and social happiness. It may be safely asserted, that there are now more than a million of people, descendants of New England ancestry, living free and happy, in regions, which hardily sixty years ago were tracts of unpenetrated forest. Nor do rivers, or mountains, or seas resist the progress of industry and enterprise. Ere long, the sons of the Pilgrims will be on the shores of the Pacific. The imagination hardily keeps up with the progress of population, improvement, and civilization.

It is now five and forty years, since the growth and rising glory of America were portrayed in the English parliament, with inimitable beauty, by the most consummate orator of modern times. Going back somewhat more than half a century, and describing our progress as foreseen from that point, by his amiable friend Lord Bathurst, then living, he spoke of the wonderful progress which America had made during the period of a single human life. There is no American heart, I imagine, that does not glow, both with conscious patriotic pride, and admiration for one of the happiest efforts of eloquence, so often as the vision, of "that little speck, scarce visible in the mass of national interest, a small seminal principle, rather than a formed body," and the progress of its astonishing development and growth, are recalled to the recollection. But a stronger feeling might be produced, if we were able to take up this prophetic description where he left it; and placing ourselves at the point of time in which he was speaking, to set forth with equal felicity the subsequent progress of the country. There is yet among the living a most distinguished and venerable name, a descendant of the Pilgrims; one who has been attended through life by a great and fortunate genius; a man illustrious by his own great merits, and favored of Heaven in the long continuation of his years. The time when the English orator was thus speaking of America, preceded, by a few days, the actual opening of the revolutionary drama at Lexington. He to whom I have alluded. then at the age of forty, was among the most zealous and able defenders of the violated rights of his country.—He seemed already to have filled a full measure of public service, and attained an honorable fame. The moment was full of difficulty and danger, and big with events of immeasurable importance. The country was on the very brink of a civil war, of which no man could foretell the duration or the result. Something more than a courageous hope, or characteristic ardor, would have been necessary to impress the glorious prospect on his belief, if, at that moment, before the sound of the first shock of actual war had reached his ears, some attendant spirit had opened to him the vision of the future; if it had said to him, "The blow is struck, and America is severed from England forever!" if it had informed him, that he himself, the next annual revolution of the sun, should put his own hand to the great instrument of Independence, and write his name where all nations should behold it, and all time should not efface it; that ere long he himself should maintain the interest and represent the sovereignty of his new-born country, in the proudest courts of Europe; that he should one day exercise her supreme magistracy; that he should yet live to behold ten millions of fellow citizens paying him the homage of their deepest gratitude and kindest affections; that he should see distinguished talent and high public trust resting where his name rested; and that he should even see with his own unclouded eyes, the close of the second century of New England, who had begun life almost with its commencement, and lived through nearly half the whole history of his country; and that on the morning of this auspicious day, he should be found in the political councils of his native state, revising by the light of experience, that system of government, which forty years before he had assisted to frame and establish; and great and happy as he should then behold his country, there should be nothing in prospect to cloud the scene, nothing to check the ardor of that confident and patriotic hope, which should glow in his bosom to the end of his long protracted and happy life.

It would far exceed the limits of this discourse, even to mention the principal events even in the civil and political history of New England during the century; the more so, as for the last half of the period, that history has been most happily, closely interwoven with the general history of the United States. New England bore an honorable part in the wars which took place between England and France. The capture of Louisburg gave her a character for military achievement; and in the war which terminated with the peace of 1763, her exertions on the frontiers were of most essential service as well to the mother country as to all the colonies.

In New England the war of the revolution commenced. I address those who remember the memorable 19th of April, 1775; who shortly after saw the burning spires of Charlestown; who beheld the deeds of Prescott, and heard the voice of Putnam, amidst the storm of war, and saw the generous Warren fall, the first distinguished victim in the cause of liberty. It would be superfluous to say, that no portion of the country did more than the states of New England, to bring the revolutionary struggle to a successful issue.—It is scarcely less to her credit, that she saw early the necessity of a closer union of the states, and gave an efficient and indispensable aid to the establishment and organization of the federal government.

Perhaps we might safely say, that a new spirit, and a new excitement began to exist here, about the middle of the last century. To whatever causes it may be imputed, there seems then to have commenced a more rapid improvement. The colonies had attracted more of the attention of the mother country, and some renown in arms had been acquired. Lord Chatham was the first English minister who attached high importance to these possessions of the crown, and who foresaw anything of their future growth and extension. His opinion was, that the great rival of England was chiefly to be feared as a maritime and commercial power, and to drive her out of North America, and deprive her of her West India possessions was a leading object in his policy. He dwelt often on the fisheries, as nurseries of British seamen, and the colonial trade, as furnishing them employment. The war, conducted by him with vigor, terminated in a peace, by which Canada was ceded to England. The effect of this was immediately visible in the New England colonies; for the fear of Indian hostilities on the frontiers being now happily removed, settlements went on with an activity before that time altogether unprecedented, and public affairs wore a new and encouraging aspect. Shortly after this fortunate termination of the French war, the interesting topics connected with the taxation of America by the British Parliament began to be discussed, and the attention and all the faculties of the people drawn towards them. There is perhaps no portion of our history more full of interest than the period from 1760 to the actual commencement of the war. The progress of opinion, in this period, though less known, is not less important, than the progress of arms afterwards. Nothing deserves more consideration than those events and discussions which affected the public sentiment, and settled the revolution in men's minds, before hostilities openly broke out.

Internal improvement followed the establishment, and prosperous commencement, of the present government. More has been done for roads, canals, and other public works, within the last thirty years, than in all our former history. In the first of these particulars, few countries excel the New England States. The astonishing increase of the navigation and trade is known to every one, and now belongs to the history of our national wealth.

We may flatter ourselves, too, that literature and taste have not been stationary, and that some advancement has been made in the elegant, as well as in the useful arts.

The nature and constitution of society and government in this country are interesting topics, to which I would devote what remains of the time allowed to this occasion. Of our system of government the first thing to be said is, that it is really and practically a free system. It originates entirely with the people, and rests on no other foundation than their assent. To judge of its actual operation, it is not enough to look merely at the form of its construction. The practical character of government depends often on a variety of considerations, besides the abstract frame of its constitutional organization. Among these are the condition and tenure of property; the laws regulating its alienation and descent; the presence or absence of a military power; an armed or unarmed yeomanry; the spirit of the age, and the degree of general intelligence. In these respects it cannot be denied that the circumstances of this country are most favorable to the hope of maintaining the government of a great nation on principles entirely popular. In the absence of military power, the nature of government must essentially depend on the manner in which property is holden and distributed. There is a natural influence belonging to property, whether it exists in many hands or few; and it is on the right of property that both despotism and unrestrained popular violence ordinarily commence their attacks. Our ancestors began their system of government here under a condition of comparative equality in regard to wealth, and their early laws were of a nature to favor and continue this equality.

A republican form of government rests not more on political constitutions, than on those laws which regulate the descent and transmission of property. Governments like ours could not have been maintained, where property was holden according to the principles of the feudal system; nor, on the other hand, could the feudal constitution possibly exist with us. Our New England ancestors brought hither no great capitals from Europe; and if they had, there was nothing productive in which they could have been invested. They left behind them the whole feudal policy of the other continent. They broke away at once from the system of military service established in the Dark Ages, and which continues, down even to the present time, more or less to affect the condition of property all over Europe. They came to a new country. There were, as yet, no lands yielding rent, and no tenants rendering service. The whole soil was unreclaimed from barbarism. They were themselves, either from their original condition, or from the necessity of their common interest, nearly on a general level in respect to property. Their situation demanded a parcelling out and division of the lands, and it may be fairly said that this necessary act *fixed the future frame and form of their government.* The character of their political institutions was determined by the fundamental laws respecting property. The laws rendered estates divisible among sons and daughters. The right of primogeniture, at first limited and curtailed, was afterwards abolished. The property was all freehold. The entailment of estates, long trusts, and the other processes for fettering and tying up inheritances, were not applicable to the condition of society, and seldom made use of. On the contrary, alienation of the land was every way facilitated, even to the subjecting of it to every species of debt. The establishment of public registries, and the simplicity of our forms of conveyance, have greatly facilitated the change of real estate from one proprietor to another. The consequence of all these causes has been, a great subdivision of the soil, and a great equality of condition; the true basis, most certainly, of a popular government. "If the people," says Harrington, "hold three parts in four of the territory, it is plain there can neither be any single person nor nobility able to dispute the government with them; in this case, therefore, *except force be interposed*, they govern themselves."

The history of other nations may teach us how favorable to public liberty are the division of the soil into small freeholds, and a system of laws, of which the tendency is, without violence or injustice, to produce and to preserve a degree of equality of property. It has been estimated, if I mistake not, that about the time of Henry the Seventh four-fifths of the land in England was holden by the great barons and ecclesiastics. The effects of a growing commerce soon afterwards began to break in on this state of things, and before the Revolution, in 1688, a vast change had been wrought. It may be thought probable that, for the last half century, the process of subdivision in England has been retarded, if not reversed; that the great weight of taxation has compelled many of the lesser freeholders to dispose of their estates, and to seek employment in the army and navy, in the professions of civil life, in commerce, or in the colonies. The effect of this on the British constitution cannot but be most unfavorable. A few large estates grow larger; but the number of those who have no estates also increases; and there may be danger, lest the inequality of property become so great, that those who possess it may be dispossessed by force; in other words, that the government may be overturned.

A most interesting experiment of the effect of a subdivision of property on government is now making in France. It is understood, that the law regulating the transmission of property in that country, now divides it, real and personal, among all the children equally, both sons and daughters; and that there is, also, a very great restraint on the power of making dispositions of property by will. It has been supposed, that the effects of this might probably be, in time, to break up the soil into such small subdivisions, that the proprietors would be too poor to resist the encroachments of executive power. I think far otherwise. What is lost in individual wealth will be more than gained in numbers, in intelligence, and in a sympathy of sentiment. If, indeed, only one or a few landholders were to resist the crown, like the barons of England, they must, of course, be great and powerful landholders, with multitudes of retainers, to promise success. But if the proprietors of a given extent of territory are summoned to resistance, there is no reason to believe that such resistance would be less forcible, or less successful, because the number of such proprietors happened to be great. Each would perceive his own importance, and his own interest, and would feel that natural elevation of character which the consciousness of property inspires. A common sentiment would unite all, and numbers would not only add strength, but excite enthusiasm. It is true, that France possesses a vast military force, under the direction of an hereditary executive government; and military power, it is possible, may overthrow any government. It is in vain, however, in this period of the world, to look for security against military power to the arm of the great landholders. That notion is derived from a state of things long since past; a state in which a feudal baron, with his retainers, might stand against the sovereign and his retainers, himself but the greatest baron. But at present, what could the richest landholder do, against one regiment of disciplined troops? Other securities, therefore, against the prevalence of military power must be provided. Happily for us, we are not so situated as that any purpose of national defence requires, ordinarily and constantly, such a military force as might seriously endanger our liberties.

In respect, however, to the recent law of succession in France, to which I have alluded, I would, presumptiously perhaps, hazard a conjecture, that, if the government do not change the law, the law in half a century will change the government; and that this change will be, not in favor of the power of the crown, as some European writers have supposed, but against it. Those writers only reason upon what they think correct general principles, in relation to this subject. They acknowledge a want of experience. Here we have had that experience; and we know that a multitude of small proprietors, acting with intelligence, and that enthusiasm which a common cause inspires, constitute not only a formidable, but an invincible power.

The true principle of a free and popular government would seem to be, so to construct it as to give to all, or at least to a very great majority, an interest in its preservation; to found it, as other things are founded, on men's interest. The stability of government demands that those who desire its continuance should be more powerful than those who desire its dissolution. This power, of course, is not always to be measured by mere numbers. Education, wealth, talents, are all parts and elements of the general aggregate of power; but numbers, nevertheless, constitute ordinarily the most important consideration, unless, indeed, there be a military force in the hands of the few, by which they can control the many. In this country we have actually existing systems of government, in the maintenance of which, it should seem, a great majority, both in numbers and in other means of power and influence, must see their interest. But this state of things is not brought about solely by written political constitutions, or the mere manner of organizing the government; but also by the laws which regulate the descent and transmission of property. The freest government, if it could exist, would not be long acceptable, if the tendency of the laws were to create a rapid accumulation of property in few hands, and to render the great mass of the population dependent and penniless. In such a case, the popular power would be likely to break in upon the rights of property, or else the influence of property to limit and control the exercise of popular power. Universal suffrage, for example, could not long exist in a community where there was great inequality of property. The holders of estates would be obliged, in such case, in some way to restrain the right of suffrage, or else such right of suffrage would, before long, divide the property. In the nature of things, those who have not property, and see their neighbors possess much more than they think them to need, cannot be favorable to laws made for the protection of property. When this class becomes numerous, it grows clamorous. It looks on property as its prey and plunder, and is naturally ready, at all times, for violence and revolution.

It would seem, then, to be the part of political wisdom to found government on property; and to establish such distribution of property, by the laws which regulate its transmission and alienation, as to interest the great majority of society in the support of the government. This is, I imagine, the true theory and the actual practice of our republican institutions. With property divided as we have it, no other government than that of a republic could be maintained even were we foolish enough to desire it. There is reason, therefore, to expect a long continuance of our system. Party and passion, doubtless, may prevail at times, and much temporary mischief be done. Even modes and forms may be changed, and perhaps for the worse. But a great revolution in regard to property must take place, before our governments can be moved from their republican basis, unless they be violently struck off by military power. The people possess the property, more emphatically than it could ever be said of the people of any other country, and they can have no interest to overturn a government which protects that property by equal laws.

Let it not be supposed, that this state of things possesses too strong tendencies towards the production of a dead and uninteresting level in society. Such tendencies are sufficiently counteracted by the infinite diversities in the characters and fortunes of individuals. Talent, activity, industry, and enterprise tend at all times to produce inequality and distinction; and there is room still for the accumulation of wealth, with its great advantages, to all reasonable and useful extent. It has been often urged against the state of society in America, that it furnishes no class of fortune and leisure. This may be partly true, but it is not entirely so, and the evil, if it be one, would affect rather the progress of taste and literature, than the general prosperity of the people. But the promotion of taste and literature cannot be primary objects of political institutions; and if they could, it might be doubted whether, in the long course of things, as much is not gained by a wide diffusion of general knowledge, as is lost by diminishing the number of those who are enabled by fortune and leisure to devote themselves exclusively to scientific and literary pursuits. However this may be, it is to be considered that it is the spirit of our system to be equal and general, and if there be particular disadvantages incident to this, they are far more than counterbalanced by the benefits which weigh against them. The important concerns of society are generally conducted, in all countries, by the men of business and practical ability; and even in matters of taste and literature, the advantages of mere leisure are liable to be overrated. If there exist adequate means of education and a love of letters be excited, that love will find a way to the object of its desire, through the crowd and pressure of the most busy society.

Connected with this division of property, and the consequent participation of the great mass of people in its possession and enjoyments, is the system of representation, which is admirably accommodated to our condition, better understood among us, and more familiarly and extensively practiced, in the higher and in the lower departments of government, than it has been by any other people. Great facility has been given to this in New England by the early division of the country into townships or small districts, in which all concerns of local police are regulated, and in which representatives to the legislature are elected. Nothing can exceed the utility of these little bodies. They are so many councils or parliaments, in which common interests are discussed, and useful knowledge acquired and communicated.

The division of governments into departments, and the division, again, of the legislative department into two chambers, are essential provisions in our system. This last, although not new in itself, yet seems to be new in its application to governments wholly popular. The Grecian republics, it is plain, knew nothing of it; and in Rome, the check and balance of legislative power, such as it was, lay between the people and the senate. Indeed, few things are more difficult than to ascertain accurately the true nature and construction of the Roman commonwealth. The relative power of the senate and the people of the consuls and the tribunes, appears not to have been at all times the same, nor at any time accurately defined or strictly observed. Cicero, indeed, describes to us an admirable arrangement of political power, and a balance of the constitution, in that beautiful passage, in which he compares the democracies of Greece with the Roman commonwealth." "O morem preclarum, disciplinamque, quam a majoribus accepimus, si quidem teneremus! sed nescio quo pacto jam de manibus elabitur. Nullam enim illi nostri sapientissimi et sanctissimi viri vim concionis esse voluerunt, quæ scisseret plebs, aut quæ populus juberet; summota conscione, distributis partibus, tributim et centuriatim descriptis ordinibus, classibus, ætatibus, auditus auctoribus, re multos dies promulgata et cognita, juberi vetarique voluerunt. Græcorum autem totæ respublicæ sedentis concionis temeritate administrantur."

But at what time this wise system existed in this perfection at Rome, no proofs remain to show. Her constitution, originally framed for a monarchy, never seemed to be adjusted in its several parts after the expulsion of the kings. Liberty there was, but it was a disputatious, an uncertain, an ill-secured liberty. The patrician and plebian orders, instead of being matched and joined, each in its just place and proportion, to sustain the fabric of the state, were rather like hostile powers, in perpetual conflict. With us, an attempt has been made, and so far not without success, to divide representation into chambers, and, by difference of age, character, qualification, or mode of election, to establish salutary checks, in governments altogether elective.

Having detained you so long with these observations, I must yet advent to another most interesting topic,—the Free Schools. In this particular, New England may be allowed to claim, I think, a merit of a peculiar character, She early adopted, and has constantly maintained the principle, that it is the undoubted right and the

bounden duty of government to provide for the instruction of all youth. That which is elsewhere left to chance or charity, we secure by law. For the purpose of public instruction, we hold every man subject to taxation in proportion to his property, and we look not to the question, whether he himself have, or have not, children to be benefitted by the education for which he pays. We regard it as a wise and liberal system of police, by which property, and life, and the peace of society are secured. We seek to prevent in some measure the extension of the penal code, by inspiring a salutary and conservative principle of virtue and of knowledge in an early age. We strive to excite a feeling of respectability, and a sense of character, by enlarging the capacity and increasing the sphere of intellectual enjoyment. By general instruction, we seek, as far possible, to purify the whole moral atmosphere; to keep good sentiments uppermost, and to turn the strong current of feeling and opinion, as well as the censures of the law and the denunciations of religion, against immorality and crime. We hope for a security beyond the law, and above the law, in the prevalence of an enlightened and well-principled moral sentiment. We hope to continue and prolong the time, when, in the villages and farm-houses of New England, there may be undisturbed sleep within unbarred doors. And knowing that our government rests directly on the public will, in order that we may preserve it, we endeavor to give a safe and proper director that public will. We do not, indeed, expect all men to be philosophers or statesmen; but we confidently trust, and our expectation of the duration of our system of government rests on that trust, that, by the diffusion of general knowledge and good and virtuous sentiments, the political fabric may be secure, as well against open violence and overthrow, as against the slow, but sure, undermining of licentiousness.

We know that, at the present time, an attempt is making in the English Parliament to provide by law for the education of the poor, and that a gentleman of distinguished character (Mr. Brougham) has taken the lead in presenting a plan to government for carrying that purpose into effect. And yet, although the representatives of the three kingdoms listened to him with astonishment as well as delight, we hear no principles with which we ourselves have not been familiar from youth; we see nothing in the plan but an approach towards that system which has been established in New England for more than a century and a half. It is said that

in England not more than *one child in fifteen* possesses the means of being taught to read and write; in Wales, *one in twenty*; in France, until lately, when some improvement was made, not more than *one in thirty-five*. Now, it is hardly too strong to say, that in New England *every child possesses* such means. It would be difficult to find an instance to the contrary, unless where it should be owing to the negligence of the parent; and, in truth, the means are actually used and enjoyed by nearly every one. A youth of fifteen, of either sex, who cannot both read and write, is very seldom to be found. Who can make this comparison, or contemplate this spectacle, without delight and a feeling of just pride? Does any history show property more beneficently applied? Did any government ever subject the property of those who have estates to a burden, for a purpose more favorable to the poor, or more useful to the whole community?

A conviction of importance of public instruction was one of the earliest sentiments of our ancestors. No lawgiver of ancient or modern times has expressed more just opinions, or adopted wiser measures, than the early records of the Colony of Plymouth show to have prevailed here. Assembled on this very spot, a hundred and fifty three years ago, the legislature of this Colony declared, "Forasmuch as the maintenance of good literature doth much tend to the advancement of the weal and flourishing state of societies and republics, this Court doth therefore order, that in whatever township in this government, consisting of fifty families or upwards, any meet man shall be obtained to teach a grammar school, such township shall allow at least twelve pounds, to be raised by rate on all the inhabitants."

Having provided that all youth should be instructed in the elements of learning by the institution of free schools, our ancestors had yet another duty to perform. Men were to be educated for the professions and the public. For this purpose they founded the University, and with incredible zeal and perseverance they cherished and supported it, through all trials and discouragements. On the subject of the University, it is not possible for a son of New England to think without pleasure, or to speak without emotion. Nothing confers more honor on the State where it it is established, or more utility on the country at large. A respectable university is an establishment which must be the work of time. If pecuniary means were not wanting, no new institution could possess character and respectability at once. We owe deep obligation to our ancestors, who began, almost on the moment of their arrival the work of building up the institution.

Although established in a different government, the Colony of Plymouth manifested warm friendship for Harvard College. At an early period, its government took measures to promote a general subscription throughout all the towns in this Colony, in aid of its small funds. Other colleges were subsequently founded and endowed, in other places, as the ability of the people allowed; and we may flatter ourselves, that the means of education at present enjoyed in New England are not only adequate to the diffusion of the elements of knowledge among all classes, but sufficient also for respectable attainments in literature and the sciences.

Lastly, our ancestors established their system of government on morality and religious sentiment. Moral habits, they believed, cannot safely be trusted on any other foundation than religious principle, nor any government be secure which is not supported by moral habits. Living under the heavenly light of revelation, they hoped to find all the social dispositions, all the duties which men owe to each other and to society, enforced and performed. Whatever makes men good Christians, makes them good citizens. Our fathers came here to enjoy their religion free and unmolested; and, at the end of two centuries, there is nothing upon which we can pronounce more confidently, nothing of which we can express a more deep and earnest conviction, than of the inestimable importance of that religion to man, both in regard to this life and that which is to come.

If the blessings of our political and social condition have not been too highly estimated, we cannot well overrate the responsibility and duty which they impose upon us. We hold these institutions of government, religion, and learning, to be transmitted, as well as enjoyed. We are in the line of conveyance, through which whatever has been obtained by the spirit and efforts of our ancestors is to be communicated to our children.

We are bound to maintain public liberty, and, by the example of our own systems, to convince the world that order and law, religion and morality, the rights of conscience, the rights of persons, and the rights of property, may all be preserved and secured, in the most perfect manner, by a government entirely and purely elective. If we fail in this, our disaster will be signal, and will furnish an argument, stronger than has yet been found, in support of those opinions which maintain that government can rest safely on nothing but power and coercion. As far as experience may show errors in our establishments, we are bound to correct them; and if any practices exist contrary to the principles of justice and humanity within the reach of our laws or our influence, we are inexcusable if we do not exert ourselves to restrain and abolish them.

I deem it my duty on this occasion to suggest, that the land is not yet wholly free from the contamination of a traffic, at which every feeling of humanity must for ever revolt,—I mean the African slave-trade. At the moment when God in his mercy has blessed the Christian world with a universal peace, there is reason to fear, that, to the disgrace of the Christian name and character, new efforts are making for the extension of this trade by subjects and citizens of Christian states, in whose hearts there dwell no sentiments of humanity or of justice, and over whom neither the fear of God nor the fear of man exercises a control. In the sight of our law, the African slave-trader is a pirate and a felon; and in the sight of Heaven, an offender far beyond the ordinary depth of human guilt. There is no brighter page of our history, than that which records the measures which have been adopted by the government at an early day, and at different times since, for the suppression of this traffic; and I would call on all the true sons of New England to co-operate with the laws of man, and the justice of Heaven. If then be, within the extent of our knowledge or influence, any participation in this traffic, let us pledge ourselves here, upon the rock of Plymouth, to extirpate and destroy it. It is not fit that the land of the Pilgrims should bear the shame longer. I hear the sound of the hammer, I see the smoke of the furnaces where manacles and fetters are still forged for human limbs. I see the visages of those who by stealth and at midnight labor in this work of hell, foul and dark, as may become the artificers of such instruments of misery and torture. Let that spot be purified, or let it cease to be of New England. Let it be purified, or let it be set aside from the Christian world; let it be put out of the circle of human sympathies and human regards, and let civilized man henceforth have no communion with it.

I would invoke those who fill the seats of justice, and all who minister at her altar, that they execute the wholesome and necessary severity of the law. I invoke the ministers of our religion, that they proclaim its denunciation of these crimes, and add the solemn sanctions to the authority of human laws. If the pulpit be silent, whenever, or wherever, there may be a sinner bloody with this guilt, within the hearing of its voice, the pulpit is false to its trust. I call on the fair merchant, who have reaped his harvest upon the seas, that he assist in scourging from those seas the worst pirates which ever infested them. That ocean, which seems to wave with a gentle magnificence to waft the burden of an honest commerce, and to roll along its treasures with a conscious pride; that ocean, which hardy industry regards, even when the winds have ruffled its surface, as a field of grateful toil, what is it to be the victim of this oppression, when he is brought to its shores, and looks forth upon it, for the first time, from beneath chains, and bleeding with stripes? What is it to him, but a wide spread prospect of suffering, anguish and death? Nor do the skies smile longer, nor is the air longer fragrant to him. The sun is cast down from heaven. An inhuman and accursed traffic has cut him off in his manhood, or in his youth, from every enjoyment belonging to his being, and every blessing which his Creator intended for him.

The Christian communities send forth their emissaries of religion and letters, who stop, here and there, along the coast of the vast continent of Africa, and with painful and tedious efforts, make some almost imperceptible progress in the communication of knowledge, and in the general improvement of the natives who are immediately about them. Not thus slow and imperceptible is the transmission of the vices and bad passions which the subjects of Christian states carry to the land. The slave trade having touched the coast, its influence and its evils spread, like a pestilence, over the whole continent, making savage wars more savage, and more frequent, and adding new and fierce passions to the contests of barbarians.

I pursue this topic no further; except again to say, that all Christendom being now blessed with peace, is bound by everything which belongs to its character, and to the character of the present age, to put a stop to this inhuman and disgraceful traffic.

We are bound not only to maintain the general principles of public liberty, but to support also those existing forms of government, which have so well secured its enjoyment, and so highly promoted the public prosperity. It is now more than thirty years that these states have been united under the Federal constitution, and whatever fortune may await them hereafter, it is impossible that this period of their history should not be regarded as distinguished by signal prosperity and success. They must be sanguine, indeed, who can hope for benefit from change. Whatever divisions of the public judgment may have existed in relation to particular measures of the government, all must agree, one should think, in the opinion, that in its general course it has been eminently productive of public happiness. Its most ardent friends could not well have hoped from it more than it has accomplished; and those who disbelieved or doubted ought to feel less concern about predictions, which the event has not verified, than pleasure in the good which has been obtained. Whoever shall hereafter write this part of our history, although he may see occasional errors or defects, will be able to record no great failure in the ends and objects of government. Still less will he be able to record any series of lawless and despotic acts, or any successful usurpation. His page will contain no exhibition of provinces depopulated, of civil authority habitually trampled down by military power, or of a community crushed by the burden of taxation. He will speak, rather, of public liberty protected, and public happiness advanced; of increased revenue, and population augmented beyond all example; of the growth of commerce, manufactures, and the arts; and of that happy condition, in which the restraint and coercion of government are almost invisible and imperceptible, and its influence felt only in the benefits which it confers. We can entertain no better wish for our country than that this government may be preserved; nor have a clearer duty than to maintain and support it in the full exercise of all its just constitutional powers.

The cause of science and literature also imposes upon us an important and delicate trust. The wealth and population of the country are now so far advanced, as to authorize the expectation of a correct literature, and a well formed taste, as well as respectable progress in the abstruse sciences. The country has risen from a state of colonial dependency; it has established an independent government, and is now in the undisturbed enjoyment of peace and political security. The elements of knowledge are universally diffused, and the reading portion of the community large. Let us hope that the present may be an auspicious era of literature. If, almost on the day of their landing, our ancestors founded schools and endowed colleges, what obligations do not rest upon us, living under circumstances so much more favorable both for providing and for using the means of education? Literature becomes free institutions.

It is the graceful ornament of civil liberty, and a happy restraint on the asperities, which political controversy sometimes occasions. Just taste is not only an embellishment of society, but it rises almost to the rank of the virtues, and diffuses positive good throughout the whole extent of its influence. There is a connexion between right feeling and right principles, and truth in taste is allied with truth in morality. With nothing in our past history to discourage us, and with something in our present condition and prospects to animate us, let us hope, that as it is our fortune to live in an age when we may behold a wonderful advancement of the country in all its other great interests, we may see also equal progress and success attend the cause of letters.

Finally, let us not forget the religious character of our origin. Our fathers were brought hither by their high veneration for the Christian religion. They journeyed by the light, and labored in its hope. They sought to incorporate its principles with the elements of their society, and to diffuse its influence through all their institutions, civil, political, or literary. Let us cherish these sentiments, and extend this influence still more widely; in the full conviction, that that is the happiest society, which partakes in the highest degree of the mild and peaceable spirit of Christianity.

The hours of this day are rapidly flying, and this occasion will soon be passed. Neither we nor our children can expect to behold its return. They are in the distant regions of futurity, they exist only in the all-creating power of God, who shall stand here, a hundred years hence, to trace, through us, their descent from the Pilgrims, and to survey, as we have now surveyed, the progress of their country, during the lapse of a century. We would anticipate their concurrence with us in our sentiments of deep regard for our common ancestors. We would anticipate and partake the pleasure with which they will then recount the steps of New England's advancement. On the morning of that day, although it will not disturb us in our repose, the voice of acclamation and gratitude, commencing on the Rock of Plymouth, shall be transmitted through millions of the sons of the Pilgrims, till it lose itself in the murmurs of the Pacific seas.

We would leave for the consideration of those who shall then occupy our places some proof that we hold the blessings transmitted from our fathers in just estimation; some proof of our attachment to the cause of good government, and of civil and religious liberty; some proof of a sincere and ardent desire to promote everything which may enlarge the understandings and improve the hearts of men. And when from the long distance of an hundred years, they shall look back upon us, they shall know, at least, that we possessed affections, which running backward, and warming with gratitude for what our ancestors have done for our happiness, run forward also to our posterity, and meet them with cordial salutation, ere yet they have arrived on the shore of being.

Advance, then, ye future generations! We would hail you, as you rise in your long succession, to fill the places which we now fill, and to taste the blessings of existence, where we are passing, and soon shall have passed, our own human duration. We bid you welcome to this pleasant land of the fathers. We bid you welcome to the healthful skies and the verdant fields of New England. We greet your accession to the great inheritance which we have enjoyed. We welcome you to the blessings of good government, and religious liberty. We welcome you to the treasures of science, and the delights of learning. We welcome you to the transcendent sweets of domestic life, to the happiness of kindred, and parents, and children. We welcome you to the immeasurable blessings of rational existence, the immortal hope of Christianity and the light of everlasting truth!

SOJOURNER TRUTH

"Ain't I A Woman?" (May 29, 1851)

Sojourner Truth (1797–1883), born Isabella Baumfree, was a slave in Ulster County, New York, until gaining her freedom in 1827. In 1843 she took the name Sojourner Truth and began her lauded career as an abolitionist and feminist. The following speech was given by Truth at a women's rights convention in Akron, Ohio. It was offered largely in response to a clergyman who had previously argued that women were too weak and helpless to be given the right to vote.

WELL, CHILDREN, where there is so much racket there must be something out of kilter. I think that 'twixt the negroes of the South and the women at the North, all talking about rights, the white men will be in a fix pretty soon. But what's all this here talking about?

That man over there says that women need to be helped into carriages, and lifted over ditches, and to have the best place everywhere. Nobody ever helps me into carriages, or over mud-puddles, or gives me any best place! And ain't I a woman? Look at me! Look at my arm! I have ploughed and planted, and gathered into barns, and no man could head me! And ain't I a woman? I could work as much and eat as much as a man—when I could get it—and bear the lash as well! And ain't I a woman? I have borne thirteen children, and seen most all sold off to slavery, and when I cried out with my mother's grief, none but Jesus heard me! And ain't I a woman?

Then they talk about this thing in the head; what's this they call it? [member of audience whispers, "intellect"] That's it, honey.

What's that got to do with women's rights or negroes' rights? If my cup won't hold but a pint, and yours holds a quart, wouldn't you be mean not to let me have my little half measure full?

Then that little man in black there, he says women can't have as much rights as men, 'cause Christ wasn't a woman! Where did your Christ come from? Where did your Christ come from? From God and a woman! Man had nothing to do with Him.

If the first woman God ever made was strong enough to turn the world upside down all alone, these women together ought to be able to turn it back, and get it right side up again! And now they is asking to do it, the men better let them.

Obliged to you for hearing me, and now old Sojourner ain't got nothing more to say.

FREDERICK DOUGLASS

"What to the Slave is the Fourth of July?" (July 5, 1852)

Born to a slave mother and a white father, Frederick Douglass (1818–1895) spent most of his childhood as a house servant in Baltimore, where he was taught to read by his master's wife. Douglass escaped slavery in 1838 and was given the position of agent for the Massachusetts Anti-Slavery Society in 1841—thus beginning his long career as an abolitionist. Douglass delivered this speech in Rochester, New York, at the city's annual Fourth of July celebration. He chose not to deliver a patriotic address, but rather a scathing rebuke of the hypocrisy inherent in asking a former slave to present a speech on such an occasion.

MR. PRESIDENT, Friends and Fellow Citizens: He who could address this audience without a quailing sensation, has stronger nerves than I have. I do not remember ever to have appeared as a speaker before any assembly more shrinkingly, nor with greater distrust of my ability, than I do this day. A feeling has crept over me, quite unfavorable to the exercise of my limited powers of speech. The task before me is one which requires much previous thought and study for its proper performance. I know that apologies of this sort are generally considered flat and unmeaning. I trust, however, that mine will not be so considered. Should I seem at ease, my appearance would much misrepresent me. The little experience I have had in addressing public meetings, in country schoolhouses, avails me nothing on the present occasion.

The papers and placards say, that I am to deliver a 4th [of] July oration. This certainly sounds large, and out of the common way, for it is true that I have often had the privilege to speak in this beautiful Hall, and to address many who now honor me with their presence. But neither their familiar faces, nor the perfect gage I think I have of Corinthian Hall, seems to free me from embarrassment.

The fact is, ladies and gentlemen, the distance between this platform and the slave plantation, from which I escaped, is considerable—and the difficulties to be overcome in getting from the latter to the former, are by no means slight. That I am here to-day is, to me, a matter of astonishment as well as of gratitude. You will not, therefore, be surprised, if in what I have to say I evince no elaborate preparation, nor grace my speech with any high sounding exordium. With little experience and with less learning, I have been able to throw my thoughts hastily and imperfectly together; and trusting to your patient and generous indulgence, I will proceed to lay them before you.

This, for the purpose of this celebration, is the 4th of July. It is the birthday of your National Independence, and of your political freedom. This, to you, is what the Passover was to the emancipated people of God. It carries your minds back to the day, and to the act of your great deliverance; and to the signs, and to the wonders, associated with that act, and that day. This celebration also marks the beginning of another year of your national life; and reminds you that the Republic of America is now 76 years old. I am glad, fellow-citizens, that your nation is so young. Seventy-six years, though a good old age for a man, is but a mere speck in the life of a nation. Three score years and ten is the allotted time for individual men; but nations number their years by thousands. According to this fact, you are, even now, only in the beginning of your national career, still lingering in the period of childhood. I repeat, I am glad this is so. There is hope in the thought, and hope is much needed, under the dark clouds which lower above the horizon. The eye of the reformer is met with angry flashes, portending disastrous times; but his heart may well beat lighter at the thought that America is young, and that she is still in the impressible stage of her existence. May he not hope that high lessons of wisdom, of justice and of truth, will yet give direction to her destiny? Were the nation older, the patriot's heart might be sadder, and the reformer's brow heavier. Its future might be shrouded in gloom, and the hope of its prophets go out in sorrow. There is consolation in the thought that America is young. Great streams are not easily turned from channels, worn deep in the course of ages. They may sometimes rise in quiet and stately majesty, and inundate the land, refreshing and fertilizing the earth with their mysterious properties. They may also rise in wrath and fury, and bear away, on their angry waves, the accumulated wealth of years of toil and hardship. They, however, gradually flow back to the same old channel, and flow on as serenely as ever. But, while the river may not be turned aside, it may dry up, and leave nothing behind but the withered branch, and the unsightly rock, to howl in the abyss-sweeping wind, the sad tale of departed glory. As with rivers so with nations.

Fellow-citizens, I shall not presume to dwell at length on the associations that cluster about this day. The simple story of it is that, 76 years ago, the people of this country were British subjects. The style and title of your "sovereign people" (in which you now glory) was not then born. You were under the British Crown. Your fathers esteemed the English Government as the home government; and England as the fatherland. This home government, you know, although a considerable distance from your home, did, in the exercise of its parental prerogatives, impose upon its colonial children, such restraints, burdens and limitations, as, in its mature judgment, it deemed wise, right and proper.

But, your fathers, who had not adopted the fashionable idea of this day, of the infallibility of government, and the absolute character of its acts, presumed to differ from the home government in respect to the wisdom and the justice of some of those burdens and restraints. They went so far in their excitement as to pronounce the measures of government unjust, unreasonable, and oppressive, and altogether such as ought not to be quietly submitted to. I scarcely need say, fellow-citizens, that my opinion of those measures fully accords with that of your fathers. Such a declaration of agreement on my part would not be worth much to anybody. It would, certainly, prove nothing, as to what part I might have taken, had I lived during the great controversy of 1776. To say now that America was right, and England wrong, is exceedingly easy. Everybody can say it; the dastard, not less than the noble brave, can flippantly discant on the tyranny of England towards the American Colonies. It is fashionable to do so; but there was a time when to pronounce against England, and in favor of the cause of the colonies, tried men's souls. They who did so were accounted in their day, plotters of mischief, agitators and rebels, dangerous men. To side with the right, against the wrong, with the weak against the strong, and with the oppressed against the oppressor! here lies the merit, and the one which, of all others, seems unfashionable in our day. The cause of liberty may be stabbed by the men who glory in the deeds of your fathers. But, to proceed.

Feeling themselves harshly and unjustly treated by the home government, your fathers, like men of honesty, and men of spirit, earnestly sought redress. They petitioned and remonstrated; they did so in a decorous, respectful, and loyal manner. Their conduct was wholly unexceptionable. This, however, did not answer the purpose. They saw themselves treated with sovereign indifference, coldness and scorn. Yet they persevered. They were not the men to look back.

As the sheet anchor takes a firmer hold, when the ship is tossed by the storm, so did the cause of your fathers grow stronger, as it breasted the chilling blasts of kingly displeasure. The greatest and best of British statesmen admitted its justice, and the loftiest eloquence of the British Senate came to its support. But, with that blindness which seems to be the unvarying characteristic of tyrants, since Pharaoh and his hosts were drowned in the Red Sea, the British Government persisted in the exactions complained of.

The madness of this course, we believe, is admitted now, even by England; but we fear the lesson is wholly lost on our present ruler.

Oppression makes a wise man mad. Your fathers were wise men, and if they did not go mad, they became restive under this treatment. They felt themselves the victims of grievous wrongs, wholly incurable in their colonial capacity. With brave men there is always a remedy for oppression. Just here, the idea of a total separation of the colonies from the crown was born! It was a startling idea, much more so, than we, at this distance of time, regard it. The timid and the prudent (as has been intimated) of that day, were, of course, shocked and alarmed by it.

Such people lived then, had lived before, and will, probably, ever have a place on this planet; and their course, in respect to any great change, (no matter how great the good to be attained, or the wrong to be redressed by it), may be calculated with as much precision as can be the course of the stars. They hate all changes, but silver, gold and copper change! Of this sort of change they are always strongly in favor.

These people were called Tories in the days of your fathers; and the appellation, probably, conveyed the same idea that is meant by a more modern, though a somewhat less euphonious term, which we often find in our papers, applied to some of our old politicians.

Their opposition to the then dangerous thought was earnest and powerful; but, amid all their terror and affrighted vociferations against it, the alarming and revolutionary idea moved on, and the country with it.

On the 2d of July, 1776, the old Continental Congress, to the dismay of the lovers of ease, and the worshipers of property, clothed that dreadful idea with all the authority of national sanction. They did so in the form of a resolution; and as we seldom hit upon resolutions, drawn up in our day whose transparency is at all equal to this, it may refresh your minds and help my story if I read it. "Resolved, That these united colonies are, and of right, ought to be free and Independent States; that they are absolved from all allegiance to the British Crown; and that all political connection between them and the State of Great Britain is, and ought to be, dissolved."

Citizens, your fathers made good that resolution. They succeeded; and to-day you reap the fruits of their success. The freedom gained is yours; and you, therefore, may properly celebrate this anniversary. The 4th of July is the first great fact in your nation's history—the very ring-bolt in the chain of your yet undeveloped destiny.

Pride and patriotism, not less than gratitude, prompt you to celebrate and to hold it in perpetual remembrance. I have said that the Declaration of Independence is the ring-bolt to the chain of your nation's destiny; so, indeed, I regard it. The principles contained in that instrument are saving principles. Stand by those principles, be true to them on all occasions, in all places, against all foes, and at whatever cost.

From the round top of your ship of state, dark and threatening clouds may be seen. Heavy billows, like mountains in the distance, disclose to the leeward huge forms of flinty rocks! That bolt drawn, that chain broken, and all is lost. Cling to this day—cling to it, and to its principles, with the grasp of a storm-tossed mariner to a spar at midnight.

The coming into being of a nation, in any circumstances, is an interesting event. But, besides general considerations, there were peculiar circumstances which make the advent of this republic an event of special attractiveness.

The whole scene, as I look back to it, was simple, dignified and sublime.

The population of the country, at the time, stood at the insignificant number of three millions. The country was poor in the munitions of war. The population was weak and scattered, and the country a wilderness unsubdued. There were then no means of concert and combination, such as exist now. Neither steam nor lightning had then been reduced to order and discipline. From the Potomac to the Delaware was a journey of many days. Under these, and innumerable other disadvantages, your fathers declared for liberty and independence and triumphed.

Fellow Citizens, I am not wanting in respect for the fathers of this republic. The signers of the Declaration of Independence were brave men. They were great men too—great enough to give fame to a great age. It does not often happen to a nation to raise, at one time, such a number of truly great men. The point from which I am compelled to view them is not, certainly, the most favorable; and yet I cannot contemplate their great deeds with less than admiration. They were statesmen, patriots and heroes, and for the good they did, and the principles they contended for, I will unite with you to honor their memory.

They loved their country better than their own private interests; and, though this is not the highest form of human excellence, all will concede that it is a rare virtue, and that when it is exhibited, it ought to command respect. He who will, intelligently, lay down his life for his country, is a man whom it is not in human nature to despise. Your fathers staked their lives, their fortunes, and their sacred honor, on the cause of their country. In their admiration of liberty, they lost sight of all other interests.

They were peace men; but they preferred revolution to peaceful submission to bondage. They were quiet men; but they did not shrink from agitating against oppression. They showed forbearance; but that they knew its limits. They believed in order; but not in the order of tyranny. With them, nothing was "settled" that was not right. With them, justice, liberty and humanity were "final;" not slavery and oppression. You may well cherish the memory of such men. They were great in their day and generation. Their solid manhood stands out the more as we contrast it with these degenerate times.

How circumspect, exact and proportionate were all their movements! How unlike the politicians of an hour! Their statesmanship looked beyond the passing moment, and stretched away in strength into the distant future. They seized upon eternal principles, and set a glorious example in their defense. Mark them!

Fully appreciating the hardship to be encountered, firmly believing in the right of their cause, honorably inviting the scrutiny of an on-looking world, reverently appealing to heaven to attest their sincerity, soundly comprehending the solemn responsibility they were about to assume, wisely measuring the terrible odds against them, your fathers, the fathers of this republic, did, most deliberately, under the inspiration of a glorious patriotism, and with a sublime faith in the great principles of justice and freedom, lay deep the corner-stone of the national superstructure, which has risen and still rises in grandeur around you.

Of this fundamental work, this day is the anniversary. Our eyes are met with demonstrations of joyous enthusiasm. Banners and pennants wave exultingly on the breeze. The din of business, too, is hushed. Even Mammon seems to have quitted his grasp on this day. The ear-piercing fife and the stirring drum unite their accents with the ascending peal of a thousand church bells. Prayers are made, hymns are sung, and sermons are preached in honor of this day; while the quick martial tramp of a great and multitudinous nation, echoed back by all the hills, valleys and mountains of a vast continent, bespeak the occasion one of thrilling and universal interests nation's jubilee.

Friends and citizens, I need not enter further into the causes which led to this anniversary. Many of you understand them better than I do. You could instruct me in regard to them. That is a branch of knowledge in which you feel, perhaps, a much deeper interest than your speaker. The causes which led to the separation of the colonies from the British crown have never lacked for a tongue. They have all been taught in your common schools, narrated at your firesides, unfolded from your pulpits, and thundered from your legislative halls, and are as familiar to you as household words. They form the staple of your national poetry and eloquence.

I remember, also, that, as a people, Americans are remarkably familiar with all facts which make in their own favor. This is esteemed by some as a national trait—perhaps a national weakness. It is a fact, that whatever makes for the wealth or for the reputation of Americans, and can be had cheap! will be found by Americans. I shall not be charged with slandering Americans, if I say I think the American side of any question may be safely left in American hands.

I leave, therefore, the great deeds of your fathers to other gentlemen whose claim to have been regularly descended will be less likely to be disputed than mine!

THE PRESENT

My business, if I have any here to-day, is with the present. The accepted time with God and his cause is the ever-living now.

> *"Trust no future, however pleasant,*
> *Let the dead past bury its dead;*
> *Act, act in the living present,*
> *Heart within, and God overhead."*

We have to do with the past only as we can make it useful to the present and to the future. To all inspiring motives, to noble deeds which can be gained from the past, we are welcome. But now is the time, the important time. Your fathers have lived, died, and have done their work, and have done much of it well. You live and must die, and you must do your work. You have no right to enjoy a child's share in the labor of your fathers, unless your children are to be blest by your labors. You have no right to wear out and waste the hard-earned fame of your fathers to cover your indolence. Sydney Smith tells us that men seldom eulogize the wisdom and virtues of their fathers, but to excuse some folly or wickedness of their own. This truth is not a doubtful one. There are illustrations of it near and remote, ancient and modern. It was fashionable, hundreds of years ago, for the children of Jacob to boast, we have "Abraham to our father," when they had long lost Abraham's faith and spirit. That people contented themselves under the shadow of Abraham's great name, while they repudiated the deeds which made his name great. Need I remind you that a similar thing is being done all over this country to-day? Need I tell you that the Jews are not the only people who built the tombs of the prophets, and garnished the sepulchres of the righteous? Washington could not die till he had broken the chains of his slaves. Yet his monument is built up by the price of human blood, and the traders in the bodies and souls of men, shout—"We have Washington to our father." Alas! that it should be so; yet so it is.

"The evil that men do, lives after them,
The good is oft-interred with their bones."

What have I, or those I represent, to do with your national independence?

Fellow-citizens, pardon me, allow me to ask, why am I called upon to speak here to-day? What have I, or those I represent, to do with your national independence? Are the great principles of political freedom and of natural justice, embodied in that Declaration of Independence, extended to us? and am I, therefore, called upon to bring our humble offering to the national altar, and to confess the benefits and express devout gratitude for the blessings resulting from your independence to us?

Would to God, both for your sakes and ours, that an affirmative answer could be truthfully returned to these questions! Then would my task be light, and my burden easy and delightful. For who is there so cold, that a nation's sympathy could not warm him? Who so obdurate and dead to the claims of gratitude, that would not thankfully acknowledge such priceless benefits? Who so stolid and selfish, that would not give his voice to swell the hallelujahs of a nation's jubilee, when the chains of servitude had been torn from his limbs? I am not that man. In a case like that, the dumb might eloquently speak, and the "lame man leap as an hart."

But, such is not the state of the case. I say it with a sad sense of the disparity between us. I am not included within the pale of this glorious anniversary! Your high independence only reveals the immeasurable distance between us. The blessings in which you, this day, rejoice, are not enjoyed in common. The rich inheritance of justice, liberty, prosperity and independence, bequeathed by your fathers, is shared by you, not by me. The sunlight that brought life and healing to you, has brought stripes and death to me. This Fourth [of] July is yours, not mine. You may rejoice, I must mourn. To drag a man in fetters into the grand illuminated temple of liberty, and call upon him to join you in joyous anthems, were inhuman mockery and sacrilegious irony. Do you mean, citizens, to mock me, by asking me to speak to-day? If so, there is a parallel to your conduct. And let me warn you that it is dangerous to copy the example of a nation whose crimes, lowering up to heaven, were thrown down by the breath of the Almighty, burying that nation in irrecoverable ruin! I can to-day take up the plaintive lament of a peeled and woe-smitten people!

"By the rivers of Babylon, there we sat down. Yea! we wept when we remembered Zion. We hanged our harps upon the willows in the midst thereof. For there, they that carried us away captive, required of us a song; and they who wasted us required of us mirth, saying, Sing us one of the songs of Zion. How can we sing the Lord's song in a strange land? If I forget thee, O Jerusalem, let my right hand forget her cunning. If I do not remember thee, let my tongue cleave to the roof of my mouth."

Fellow-citizens; above your national, tumultuous joy, I hear the mournful wail of millions! whose chains, heavy and grievous yesterday, are, to-day, rendered more intolerable by the jubilee shouts that reach them. If I do forget, if I do not faithfully remember those bleeding children of sorrow this day, "may my right hand forget her cunning, and may my tongue cleave to the roof of my mouth!" To forget them, to pass lightly over their wrongs, and to chime in with the popular theme, would be treason most scandalous and shocking, and would make me a reproach before God and the world. My subject, then fellow-citizens, is AMERICAN SLAVERY. I shall see, this day, and its popular characteristics, from the slave's point of view. Standing, there, identified with the American bondman, making his wrongs mine, I do not hesitate to declare, with all my soul, that the character and conduct of this nation never looked blacker to me than on this 4th of July! Whether we turn to the declarations of the past, or to the professions of the present, the conduct of the nation seems equally hideous and revolting. America is false to the past, false to the present, and solemnly binds herself to be false to the future. Standing with God and the crushed and bleeding slave on this occasion, I will, in the name of humanity which is outraged, in the name of liberty which is fettered, in the name of the constitution and the Bible, which are disregarded and trampled upon, dare to call in question and to denounce, with all the emphasis I can command, everything that serves to perpetuate slavery—the great sin and shame of America! "I will not equivocate; I will not excuse;" I will use the severest language I can command; and yet not one word shall escape me that any man, whose judgment is not blinded by prejudice, or who is not at heart a slaveholder, shall not confess to be right and just.

But I fancy I hear some one of my audience say, it is just in this circumstance that you and your brother abolitionists fail to make a favorable impression on the public mind. Would you argue more, and denounce less, would you persuade more, and rebuke less, your cause would be much more likely to succeed. But, I submit, where all is plain there is nothing to be argued. What point in the anti-slavery creed would you have me argue? On what branch of the subject do the people of this country need light? Must I undertake to prove that the slave is a man? That point is conceded already. Nobody doubts it. The slaveholders themselves acknowledge it in the enactment of laws for their government. They acknowledge it when they punish disobedience on the part of the slave. There are seventy-two crimes in the State of Virginia, which, if committed by a black man, (no matter how ignorant he be), subject him to the punishment of death; while only two of the same crimes will subject a white man to the like punishment. What is this but the acknowledgement that the slave is a moral, intellectual and responsible being? The manhood of the slave is conceded. It is admitted in the fact that Southern statute books are covered with enactments forbidding, under severe fines and penalties, the teaching of the slave to read or to write. When you can point to any such laws, in reference to the beasts of the field, then I may consent to argue the manhood of the slave. When the dogs in your streets, when the fowls of the air, when the cattle on your hills, when the fish of the sea, and the reptiles that crawl, shall be unable to distinguish the slave from a brute, there will I argue with you that the slave is a man!

For the present, it is enough to affirm the equal manhood of the Negro race. Is it not astonishing that, while we are ploughing, planting and reaping, using all kinds of mechanical tools, erecting houses, constructing bridges, building ships, working in metals of brass, iron, copper, silver and gold; that, while we are reading, writing and cyphering, acting as clerks, merchants and secretaries, having among us lawyers, doctors, ministers, poets, authors, editors, orators and teachers; that, while we are engaged in all manner of enterprises common to other men, digging gold in California, capturing the whale in the Pacific, feeding sheep and cattle on the hill-side, living, moving, acting, thinking, planning, living in families as husbands, wives and children, and, above all, confessing and worshipping the Christian's God, and looking hopefully for life and immortality beyond the grave, we are called upon to prove that we are men!

Would you have me argue that man is entitled to liberty? that he is the rightful owner of his own body? You have already declared it. Must I argue the wrongfulness of slavery? Is that a question for Republicans? Is it to be settled by the rules of logic and argumentation, as a matter beset with great difficulty, involving a doubtful application of the principle of justice, hard to be understood? How should I look to-day, in the presence of Americans, dividing, and subdividing a discourse, to show that men have a natural right to freedom? speaking of it relatively, and positively, negatively, and affirmatively. To do so, would be to make myself ridiculous, and to offer an insult to your understanding. There is not a man beneath the canopy of heaven, that does not know that slavery is wrong for him.

What, am I to argue that it is wrong to make men brutes, to rob them of their liberty, to work them without wages, to keep them ignorant of their relations to their fellow men, to beat them with sticks, to flay their flesh with the lash, to load their limbs with irons, to hunt them with dogs, to sell them at auction, to sunder their families, to knock out their teeth, to burn their flesh, to starve them into obedience and submission to their masters? Must I argue that a system thus marked with blood, and stained with pollution, is wrong? No! I will not. I have better employments for my time and strength than such arguments would imply.

What, then, remains to be argued? Is it that slavery is not divine; that God did not establish it; that our doctors of divinity are mistaken? There is blasphemy in the thought. That which is inhuman, cannot be divine! Who can reason on such a proposition? They that can, may; I cannot. The time for such argument is past.

At a time like this, scorching irony, not convincing argument, is needed. O! had I the ability, and could I reach the nation's ear, I would, to-day, pour out a fiery stream of biting ridicule, blasting reproach, withering sarcasm, and stern rebuke. For it is not light that is needed, but fire; it is not the gentle shower, but thunder. We need the storm, the whirlwind, and the earthquake. The feeling of the nation must be quickened; the conscience of the nation must be roused; the propriety of the nation must be startled; the hypocrisy of the nation must be exposed; and its crimes against God and man must be proclaimed and denounced.

What, to the American slave, is your 4th of July? I answer: a day that reveals to him, more than all other days in the year, the gross injustice and cruelty to which he is the constant victim. To him, your celebration is a sham; your boasted liberty, an unholy license; your national greatness, swelling vanity; your sounds of rejoicing are empty and heartless; your denunciations of tyrants, brass fronted impudence; your shouts of liberty and equality, hollow mockery; your prayers and hymns, your sermons and thanksgivings, with all your religious parade, and solemnity, are, to him, mere bombast, fraud, deception, impiety, and hypocrisy—a thin veil to cover up crimes which would disgrace a nation of savages. There is not a nation on the earth guilty of practices, more shocking and bloody, than are the people of these United States, at this very hour.

Go where you may, search where you will, roam through all the monarchies and despotisms of the old world, travel through South America, search out every abuse, and when you have found the last, lay your facts by the side of the everyday practices of this nation, and you will say with me, that, for revolting barbarity and shameless hypocrisy, America reigns without a rival.

Take the American slave-trade, which, we are told by the papers, is especially prosperous just now. Ex-Senator Benton tells us that the price of men was never higher than now. He mentions the fact to show that slavery is in no danger. This trade is one of the peculiarities of American institutions. It is carried on in all the large towns and cities in one-half of this confederacy; and millions are pocketed every year, by dealers in this horrid traffic. In several states, this trade is a chief source of wealth. It is called (in contradistinction to the foreign slave-trade) "the internal slave trade." It is, probably, called so, too, in order to divert from it the horror with which the foreign slave-trade is contemplated. That trade has long since been denounced by this government, as piracy. It has been denounced with burning words, from the high places of the nation, as an execrable traffic. To arrest it, to put an end to it, this nation keeps a squadron, at immense cost, on the coast of Africa. Everywhere, in this country, it is safe to speak of this foreign slave-trade, as a most inhuman traffic, opposed alike to the laws of God and of man. The duty to extirpate and destroy it, is admitted even by our doctors of divinity. In order to put an end to it, some of these last have consented that their colored brethren (nominally free) should leave this country, and establish themselves on the western coast of Africa! It is, however, a notable fact that, while so much execration is poured out by Americans upon those engaged in the foreign slave-trade, the men engaged in the slave-trade between the states pass without condemnation, and their business is deemed honorable.

Behold the practical operation of this internal slave-trade, the American slave-trade, sustained by American politics and American religion. Here you will see men and women reared like swine for the market. You know what is a swine-drover? I will show you a man-drover. They inhabit all our Southern States. They perambulate the country, and crowd the highways of the nation, with droves of human stock. You will see one of these human flesh-jobbers, armed with pistol, whip and bowie-knife, driving a company of a hundred men, women, and children, from the Potomac to the slave market at New Orleans. These wretched people are to be sold singly, or in lots, to suit purchasers. They are food for the cotton-field, and the deadly sugar-mill. Mark the sad procession, as it moves wearily along, and the inhuman wretch who drives them. Hear his savage yells and his blood-chilling oaths, as he hurries on his affrighted captives! There, see the old man, with locks thinned and gray. Cast one glance, if you please, upon that young mother, whose shoulders are bare to the scorching sun, her briny tears falling on the brow of the babe in her arms. See, too, that girl of thirteen, weeping, yes! weeping, as she thinks of the mother from whom she has been torn! The drove moves tardily. Heat and sorrow have nearly consumed their strength; suddenly you hear a quick snap, like the discharge of a rifle; the fetters clank, and the chain rattles simultaneously; your ears are saluted with a scream, that seems to have torn its way to the center of your soul! The crack you heard, was the sound of the slave-whip; the scream you heard, was from the woman you saw with the babe. Her speed had faltered under the weight of her child and her chains! that gash on her shoulder tells her to move on. Follow the drove to New Orleans. Attend the auction; see men examined like horses; see the forms of women rudely and brutally exposed to the shocking gaze of American slave-buyers. See this drove sold and separated forever; and never forget the deep, sad sobs that arose from that scattered multitude. Tell me citizens, WHERE, under the sun, you can witness a spectacle more fiendish and shocking. Yet this is but a glance at the American slave-trade, as it exists, at this moment, in the ruling part of the United States.

I was born amid such sights and scenes. To me the American slave-trade is a terrible reality. When a child, my soul was often pierced with a sense of its horrors. I lived on Philpot Street, Fell's Point, Baltimore, and have watched from the wharves, the slave ships in the Basin, anchored from the shore, with their cargoes of human flesh, waiting for favorable winds to waft them down the Chesapeake. There was, at that time, a grand slave mart kept at the head of Pratt Street, by Austin Woldfolk. His agents were sent into every town and county in Maryland, announcing their arrival, through the papers, and on flaming "hand-bills," headed CASH FOR NEGROES. These men were generally well dressed men, and very captivating in their manners. Ever ready to drink, to treat, and to gamble. The fate of many a slave has depended upon the turn of a single card; and many a child has been snatched from the arms of its mother by bargains arranged in a state of brutal drunkenness.

The flesh-mongers gather up their victims by dozens, and drive them, chained, to the general depot at Baltimore. When a sufficient number have been collected here, a ship is chartered, for the purpose of conveying the forlorn crew to Mobile, or to New Orleans. From the slave prison to the ship, they are usually driven in the darkness of night; for since the antislavery agitation, a certain caution is observed.

In the deep still darkness of midnight, I have been often aroused by the dead heavy footsteps, and the piteous cries of the chained gangs that passed our door. The anguish of my boyish heart was intense; and I was often consoled, when speaking to my mistress in the morning, to hear her say that the custom was very wicked; that she hated to hear the rattle of the chains, and the heart-rending cries. I was glad to find one who sympathized with me in my horror.

Fellow-citizens, this murderous traffic is, to-day, in active operation in this boasted republic. In the solitude of my spirit, I see clouds of dust raised on the highways of the South; I see the bleeding footsteps; I hear the doleful wail of fettered humanity, on the way to the slave-markets, where the victims are to be sold like horses, sheep, and swine, knocked off to the highest bidder. There I see the tenderest ties ruthlessly broken, to gratify the lust, caprice and rapacity of the buyers and sellers of men. My soul sickens at the sight.

"Is this the land your Fathers loved,
The freedom which they toiled to win?
Is this the earth whereon they moved?
Are these the graves they slumber in?"

But a still more inhuman, disgraceful, and scandalous state of things remains to be presented.

By an act of the American Congress, not yet two years old, slavery has been nationalized in its most horrible and revolting form. By that act, Mason & Dixon's line has been obliterated; New York has become as Virginia; and the power to hold, hunt, and sell men, women, and children as slaves remains no longer a mere state institution, but is now an institution of the whole United States. The power is co-extensive with the Star-Spangled Banner and American Christianity. Where these go, may also go the merciless slave-hunter. Where these are, man is not sacred. He is a bird for the sportsman's gun. By that most foul and fiendish of all human decrees, the liberty and person of every man are put in peril. Your broad republican domain is hunting ground for men. Not for thieves and robbers, enemies of society, merely, but for men guilty of no crime. Your lawmakers have commanded all good citizens to engage in this hellish sport. Your President, your Secretary of State, your lords, nobles, and ecclesiastics, enforce, as a duty you owe to your free and glorious country, and to your God, that you do this accursed thing. Not fewer than forty Americans have, within the past two years, been hunted down and, without a moment's warning, hurried away in chains, and consigned to slavery and excruciating torture. Some of these have had wives and children, dependent on them for bread; but of this, no account was made. The right of the hunter to his prey stands superior to the right of marriage, and to all rights in this republic, the rights of God included! For black men there are neither law, justice, humanity, not religion. The Fugitive Slave Law makes MERCY TO THEM, A CRIME; and bribes the judge who tries them. An American JUDGE GETS TEN DOLLARS FOR EVERY VICTIM HE CONSIGNS to slavery, and five, when he fails to do so. The oath of any two villains is sufficient, under this hell-black enactment, to send the most pious and exemplary black man into the remorseless jaws of slavery! His own testimony is nothing. He can bring no witnesses for himself. The minister of American justice is bound by the law to hear but one side; and that side, is the side of the oppressor. Let this damning fact be perpetually told. Let it be thundered around the world, that, in tyrant-killing, king-hating, people-loving, democratic, Christian America, the seats of justice are filled with judges, who hold their offices under an open and palpable bribe, and are bound, in deciding in the case of a man's liberty, hear only his accusers!

In glaring violation of justice, in shameless disregard of the forms of administering law, in cunning arrangement to entrap the defenseless, and in diabolical intent, this Fugitive Slave Law stands alone in the annals of tyrannical legislation. I doubt if there be another nation on the globe, having the brass and the baseness to put such a law on the statute-book. If any man in this assembly thinks differently from me in this matter, and feels able to disprove my statements, I will gladly confront him at any suitable time and place he may select.

I take this law to be one of the grossest infringements of Christian Liberty, and, if the churches and ministers of our country were not stupidly blind, or most wickedly indifferent, they, too, would so regard it.

At the very moment that they are thanking God for the enjoyment of civil and religious liberty, and for the right to worship God according to the dictates of their own consciences, they are utterly silent in respect to a law which robs religion of its chief significance, and makes it utterly worthless to a world lying in wickedness. Did this law concern the "mint, anise and cummin"—abridge the right to sing psalms, to partake of the sacrament, or to engage in any of the ceremonies of religion, it would be smitten by the thunder of a thousand pulpits. A general shout would go up from the church, demanding repeal, repeal, instant repeal! And it would go hard with that politician who presumed to solicit the votes of the people without inscribing this motto on his banner. Further, if this demand were not complied with, another Scotland would be added to the history of religious liberty, and the stern old Covenanters would be thrown into the shade. A John Knox would be seen at every church door, and heard from every pulpit, and Fillmore would have no more quarter than was shown by Knox, to the beautiful, but treacherous queen Mary of Scotland. The fact that the church of our country, (with fractional exceptions), does not esteem "the Fugitive Slave Law" as a declaration of war against religious liberty, implies that that church regards religion simply as a form of worship, an empty ceremony, and not a vital principle, requiring active benevolence, justice, love and good will towards man. It esteems sacrifice above mercy; psalm-singing above right doing; solemn meetings above practical righteousness. A worship that can be conducted by persons who refuse to give shelter to the houseless, to give bread to the hungry, clothing to the naked, and who enjoin obedience to a law forbidding these acts of mercy, is a curse, not a blessing to mankind. The Bible addresses all such persons as "scribes, Pharisees, hypocrites, who pay tithe of mint, anise, and cummin, and have omitted the weightier matters of the law, judgment, mercy and faith."

But the church of this country is not only indifferent to the wrongs of the slave, it actually takes sides with the oppressors. It has made itself the bulwark of American slavery, and the shield of American slave-hunters. Many of its most eloquent Divines, who stand as the very lights of the church, have shamelessly given the sanction of religion and the Bible to the whole slave system. They have taught that man may, properly, be a slave; that the relation of master and slave is ordained of God; that to send back an escaped bondman to his master is clearly the duty of all the followers of the Lord Jesus Christ; and this horrible blasphemy is palmed off upon the world for Christianity.

For my part, I would say, welcome infidelity! welcome atheism! welcome anything! in preference to the gospel, as preached by those Divines! They convert the very name of religion into an engine of tyranny, and barbarous cruelty, and serve to confirm more infidels, in this age, than all the infidel writings of Thomas Paine, Voltaire, and Bolingbroke, put together, have done! These ministers make religion a cold and flinty-hearted thing, having neither principles of right action, nor bowels of compassion. They strip the love of God of its beauty, and leave the throng of religion a huge, horrible, repulsive form. It is a religion for oppressors, tyrants, man-stealers, and thugs. It is not that "pure and undefiled religion" which is from above, and which is "first pure, then peaceable, easy to be entreated, full of mercy and good fruits, without partiality, and without hypocrisy." But a religion which favors the rich against the poor; which exalts the proud above the humble; which divides mankind into two classes, tyrants and slaves; which says to the man in chains, stay there; and to the oppressor, oppress on; it is a religion which may be professed and enjoyed by all the robbers and enslavers of mankind; it makes God a respecter of persons, denies his fatherhood of the race, and tramples in the dust the great truth of the brotherhood of man. All this we affirm to be true of the popular church, and the popular worship of our land and nation—a religion, a church, and a worship which, on the authority of inspired wisdom, we pronounce to be an abomination in the sight of God. In the language of Isaiah, the American church might be well addressed, "Bring no more vain ablations; incense is an abomination unto me: the new moons and Sabbaths, the calling of assemblies, I cannot away with; it is iniquity even the solemn meeting. Your new moons and your appointed feasts my soul hateth. They are a trouble to me; I am weary to bear them; and when ye spread forth your hands I will hide mine eyes from you. Yea! when ye make many prayers, I will not hear. YOUR HANDS ARE FULL OF BLOOD; cease to do evil, learn to do well; seek judgment; relieve the oppressed; judge for the fatherless; plead for the widow."

The American church is guilty, when viewed in connection with what it is doing to uphold slavery; but it is superlatively guilty when viewed in connection with its ability to abolish slavery. The sin of which it is guilty is one of omission as well as of commission. Albert Barnes but uttered what the common sense of every man at all observant of the actual state of the case will receive as truth, when he declared that "There is no power out of the church that could sustain slavery an hour, if it were not sustained in it."

Let the religious press, the pulpit, the Sunday school, the conference meeting, the great ecclesiastical, missionary, Bible and tract associations of the land array their immense powers against slavery and slave-holding; and the whole system of crime and blood would be scattered to the winds; and that they do not do this involves them in the most awful responsibility of which the mind can conceive.

In prosecuting the anti-slavery enterprise, we have been asked to spare the church, to spare the ministry; but how, we ask, could such a thing be done? We are met on the threshold of our efforts for the redemption of the slave, by the church and ministry of the country, in battle arrayed against us; and we are compelled to fight or flee. From what quarter, I beg to know, has proceeded a fire so deadly upon our ranks, during the last two years, as from the Northern pulpit? As the champions of oppressors, the chosen men of American theology have appeared—men, honored for their so-called piety, and their real learning. The LORDS of Buffalo, the SPRINGS of New York, the LATHROPS of Auburn, the COXES and SPENCERS of Brooklyn, the GANNETS and SHARPS of Boston, the DEWEYS of Washington, and other great religious lights of the land, have, in utter denial of the authority of Him, by whom they professed to be called to the ministry, deliberately taught us, against the example of the Hebrews and against the remonstrance of the Apostles, they teach "that we ought to obey man's law before the law of God."

My spirit wearies of such blasphemy; and how such men can be supported, as the "standing types and representatives of Jesus Christ," is a mystery which I leave others to penetrate. In speaking of the American church, however, let it be distinctly understood that I mean the great mass of the religious organizations of our land. There are exceptions, and I thank God that there are. Noble men may be found, scattered all over these Northern States, of whom Henry Ward Beecher of Brooklyn, Samuel J. May of Syracuse, and my esteemed friend on the platform, are shining examples; and let me say further, that upon these men lies the duty to inspire our ranks with high religious faith and zeal, and to cheer us on in the great mission of the slave's redemption from his chains.

One is struck with the difference between the attitude of the American church towards the anti-slavery movement, and that occupied by the churches in England towards a similar movement in that country. There, the church, true to its mission of ameliorating, elevating, and improving the condition of mankind, came forward promptly, bound up the wounds of the West Indian slave, and restored him to his liberty. There, the question of emancipation was a high[ly] religious question. It was demanded, in the name of humanity, and according to the law of the living God. The Sharps, the Clarksons, the Wilberforces, the Buxtons, and Burchells and the Knibbs, were alike famous for their piety, and for their philanthropy. The anti-slavery movement there was not an anti-church movement, for the reason that the church took its full share in prosecuting that movement: and the anti-slavery movement in this country will cease to be an anti-church movement, when the church of this country shall assume a favorable, instead or a hostile position towards that movement. Americans! your republican politics, not less than your republican religion, are flagrantly inconsistent. You boast of your love of liberty, your superior civilization, and your pure Christianity, while the whole political power of the nation (as embodied in the two great political parties), is solemnly pledged to support and perpetuate the enslavement of three millions of your countrymen. You hurl your anathemas at the crowned headed tyrants of Russia and Austria, and pride yourselves on your Democratic institutions, while you yourselves consent to be the mere tools and bodyguards of the tyrants of Virginia and Carolina. You invite to your shores fugitives of oppression from abroad, honor them with banquets, greet them with ovations, cheer them, toast them, salute them, protect them, and pour out your money to them like water; but the fugitives from your own land you advertise, hunt, arrest, shoot and kill. You glory in your refinement and your universal education yet you maintain a system as barbarous and dreadful as ever stained the character of a nation—a system begun in avarice, supported in pride, and perpetuated in cruelty. You shed tears over fallen Hungary, and make the sad story of her wrongs the theme of your poets, statesmen and orators, till your gallant sons are ready to fly to arms to vindicate her cause against her oppressors; but, in regard to the ten thousand wrongs of the American slave, you would enforce the strictest silence, and would hail him as an enemy of the nation who dares to make those wrongs the subject of public discourse! You are all on fire at the mention of liberty for France or for Ireland; but are as cold as an iceberg at the thought of liberty for the enslaved of America. You discourse eloquently on the dignity of labor; yet, you sustain a system which, in its very essence, casts a stigma upon labor. You can bare your bosom to the storm of British artillery to throw off a three-penny tax on tea; and yet wring the last hard-earned farthing from the grasp of the black laborers of your country. You profess to believe "that, of one blood, God made all nations of men to dwell on the face of all the earth," and hath commanded all men, everywhere to love one another; yet you notoriously hate, (and glory in your hatred), all men whose skins are not colored like your own. You declare, before the world, and are understood by the world to declare, that you "hold these truths to be self evident, that all men are created equal; and are endowed by their Creator with certain inalienable rights; and that, among these are, life, liberty, and the pursuit of happiness;" and yet, you hold securely, in a bondage which, according to your own Thomas Jefferson, "is worse than ages of that which your fathers rose in rebellion to oppose," a seventh part of the inhabitants of your country.

Fellow-citizens! I will not enlarge further on your national inconsistencies. The existence of slavery in this country brands your republicanism as a sham, your humanity as a base pretence, and your Christianity as a lie. It destroys your moral power abroad; it corrupts your politicians at home. It saps the foundation of religion; it makes your name a hissing, and a by word to a mocking earth. It is the antagonistic force in your government, the only thing that seriously disturbs and endangers your Union. It fetters your progress; it is the enemy of improvement, the deadly foe of education; it fosters pride; it breeds insolence; it promotes vice; it shelters crime; it is a curse to the earth that supports it; and yet, you cling to it, as if it were the sheet anchor of all your hopes. Oh! be warned! be warned! a horrible reptile is coiled up in your nation's bosom; the venomous creature is nursing at the tender breast of your youthful republic; for the love of God, tear away, and fling from you the hideous monster, and let the weight of twenty millions crush and destroy it forever!

But it is answered in reply to all this, that precisely what I have now denounced is, in fact, guaranteed and sanctioned by the Constitution of the United States; that the right to hold and to hunt slaves is a part of that Constitution framed by the illustrious Fathers of this Republic.

Then, I dare to affirm, notwithstanding all I have said before, your fathers stooped, basely stooped "To palter with us in a double sense: And keep the word of promise to the ear, But break it to the heart."

And instead of being the honest men I have before declared them to be, they were the veriest imposters that ever practiced on mankind. This is the inevitable conclusion, and from it there is no escape. But I differ from those who charge this baseness on the framers of the Constitution of the United States. It is a slander upon their memory, at least, so I believe. There is not time now to argue the constitutional question at length—nor have I the ability to discuss it as it ought to be discussed. The subject has been handled with masterly power by Lysander Spooner, Esq., by William Goodell, by Samuel E. Sewall, Esq., and last, though not least, by Gerritt Smith, Esq. These gentlemen have, as I think, fully and clearly vindicated the Constitution from any design to support slavery for an hour.

[L]et me ask, if it be not somewhat singular that, if the Constitution were intended to be, by its framers and adopters, a slave-holding instrument, why neither slavery, slaveholding, nor slave can anywhere be found in it.

Fellow-citizens! there is no matter in respect to which, the people of the North have allowed themselves to be so ruinously imposed upon, as that of the pro-slavery character of the Constitution. In that instrument I hold there is neither warrant, license, nor sanction of the hateful thing; but, interpreted as it ought to be interpreted, the Constitution is a GLORIOUS LIBERTY DOCUMENT. Read its preamble, consider its purposes. Is slavery among them? Is it at the gateway? or is it in the temple? It is neither. While I do not intend to argue this question on the present occasion, let me ask, if it be not somewhat singular that, if the Constitution were intended to be, by its framers and adopters, a slave-holding instrument, why neither slavery, slaveholding, nor slave can anywhere be found in it. What would be thought of an instrument, drawn up, legally drawn up, for the purpose of entitling the city of Rochester to a tract of land, in which no mention of land was made? Now, there are certain rules of interpretation, for the proper understanding of all legal instruments. These rules are well established. They are plain, common-sense rules, such as you and I, and all of us, can understand and apply, without having passed years in the study of law. I scout the idea that the question of the constitutionality or unconstitutionality of slavery is not a question for the people. I hold that every American citizen has a right to form an opinion of the constitution, and to propagate that opinion, and to use all honorable means to make his opinion the prevailing one. Without this fight, the liberty of an American citizen would be as insecure as that of a Frenchman. Ex-Vice-President Dallas tells us that the constitution is an object to which no American mind can be too attentive, and no American heart too devoted. He further says, the constitution, in its words, is plain and intelligible, and is meant for the home-bred, unsophisticated understandings of our fellow-citizens. Senator Berrien tell us that the Constitution is the fundamental law, that which controls all others. The charter of our liberties, which every citizen has a personal interest in understanding thoroughly. The testimony of Senator Breese, Lewis Cass, and many others that might be named, who are everywhere esteemed as sound lawyers, so regard the constitution. I take it, therefore, that it is not presumption in a private citizen to form an opinion of that instrument.

Now, take the constitution according to its plain reading, and I defy the presentation of a single pro-slavery clause in it. On the other hand it will be found to contain principles and purposes, entirely hostile to the existence of slavery.

I have detained my audience entirely too long already. At some future period I will gladly avail myself of an opportunity to give this subject a full and fair discussion.

Allow me to say, in conclusion, notwithstanding the dark picture I have this day presented of the state of the nation, I do not despair of this country. There are forces in operation, which must inevitably work the downfall of slavery. "The arm of the Lord is not shortened," and the doom of slavery is certain. I, therefore, leave off where I began, with hope. While drawing encouragement from the Declaration of Independence, the great principles it contains, and the genius of American Institutions, my spirit is also cheered by the obvious tendencies of the age. Nations do not now stand in the same relation to each other that they did ages ago. No nation can now shut itself up from the surrounding world, and trot round in the same old path of its fathers without interference. The time was when such could be done. Long established customs of hurtful character could formerly fence themselves in, and do their evil work with social impunity. Knowledge was then confined and enjoyed by the privileged few, and the multitude walked on in mental darkness. But a change has now come over the affairs of mankind. Walled cities and empires have become unfashionable. The arm of commerce has borne away the gates of the strong city. Intelligence is penetrating the darkest corners of the globe. It makes its pathway over and under the sea, as well as on the earth. Wind, steam, and lightning are its chartered agents. Oceans no longer divide, but link nations together. From Boston to London is now a holiday excursion. Space is comparatively annihilated. Thoughts expressed on one side of the Atlantic are, distinctly heard on the other. The far off and almost fabulous Pacific rolls in grandeur at our feet. The Celestial Empire, the mystery of ages, is being solved. The fiat of the Almighty, "Let there be Light," has not yet spent its force. No abuse, no outrage whether in taste, sport or avarice, can now hide itself from the all-pervading light. The iron shoe, and crippled foot of China must be seen, in contrast with nature. Africa must rise and put on her yet unwoven garment. "Ethiopia shall stretch out her hand unto God." In the fervent aspirations of William Lloyd Garrison, I say, and let every heart join in saying it:

God speed the year of jubilee
The wide world o'er
When from their galling chains set free,
Th' oppress'd shall vilely bend the knee,
And wear the yoke of tyranny
Like brutes no more.
That year will come, and freedom's reign,
To man his plundered fights again
Restore.

God speed the day when human blood
Shall cease to flow!
In every clime be understood,
The claims of human brotherhood,
And each return for evil, good,
Not blow for blow;
That day will come all feuds to end.
And change into a faithful friend
Each foe.

God speed the hour, the glorious hour,
When none on earth
Shall exercise a lordly power,
Nor in a tyrant's presence cower;
But all to manhood's stature tower,
By equal birth!
THAT HOUR WILL COME, to each, to all,
And from his prison-house, the thrall
Go forth.

Until that year, day, hour, arrive,
With head, and heart, and hand I'll strive,
To break the rod, and rend the gyve,

The spoiler of his prey deprive—
So witness Heaven!
And never from my chosen post,
Whate'er the peril or the cost,
Be driven.

ABRAHAM LINCOLN

First Inaugural Address (March 4, 1861)

Abraham Lincoln (1809–1865) was inaugurated as president of the United States only two weeks after Jefferson Davis was inaugurated as president of the Confederacy. As the inauguration was to be held in the shadow of the South's secession, Lincoln had to travel by a secret route to Washington D.C., though on the day of the ceremony he paid little attention to safety when he rode in an open carriage with President Buchanan to the Capitol. Lincoln was given the oath of office on the East Portico of the Capitol by Chief Justice Roger Taney, after which he delivered the following address.

FELLOW-CITIZENS OF THE UNITED STATES: In compliance with a custom as old as the government itself, I appear before you to address you briefly, and to take in your presence the oath prescribed by the Constitution of the United States to be taken by the President "before he enters on the execution of his office."

I do not consider it necessary at present for me to discuss those matters of administration about which there is no special anxiety or excitement.

Apprehension seems to exist among the people of the Southern States that by the accession of a Republican administration their property and their peace and personal security are to be endangered. There has never been any reasonable cause for such apprehension. Indeed, the most ample evidence to the contrary has all the while existed and been open to their inspection. It is found in nearly all the published speeches of him who now addresses you. I do but quote from one of those speeches when I declare that "I have no purpose, directly or indirectly, to interfere with the institution of slavery in the States where it exists. I believe I have no lawful right to do so, and I have no inclination to do so." Those who nominated and elected me did so with full knowledge that I had made this and many similar declarations, and had never recanted them. And, more than this, they placed in the platform for my acceptance, and as a law to themselves and to me, the clear and emphatic resolution which I now read:

> *Resolved,* That the maintenance inviolate of the rights of the States, and especially the right of each State to order and control its own domestic institutions according to its own judgment exclusively, is essential to that balance of power on which the perfection and endurance of our political fabric depend, and we denounce the lawless invasion by armed force of the soil of any State or Territory, no matter under what pretext, as among the gravest of crimes.

I now reiterate these sentiments; and, in doing so, I only press upon the public attention the most conclusive evidence of which the case is susceptible, that the property, peace, and security of no section are to be in any wise endangered by the now incoming administration. I add, too, that all the protection which, consistently with the Constitution and the laws, can be given, will be cheerfully given to all the States when lawfully demanded, for whatever cause—as cheerfully to one section as to another.

There is much controversy about the delivering up of fugitives from service or labor. The clause I now read is as plainly written in the Constitution as any other of its provisions:

> No person held to service or labor in one State, under the laws thereof, escaping into another, shall in consequence of any law or regulation therein be discharged from such service or labor, but shall be delivered up on claim of the party to whom such service or labor may be due.

It is scarcely questioned that this provision was intended by those who made it for the reclaiming of what we call fugitive slaves; and the intention of the lawgiver is the law. All members of Congress swear their support to the whole Constitution—to this provision as much as to any other. To the proposition, then, that slaves whose cases come within the terms of this clause "shall be delivered up," their oaths are unanimous. Now, if they would make the effort in good temper, could they not with nearly equal unanimity frame and pass a law by means of which to keep good that unanimous oath?

There is some difference of opinion whether this clause should be enforced by national or by State authority; but surely that difference is not a very material one. If the slave is to be surrendered, it can be of but little consequence to him or to others by which authority it is done. And should any one in any case be content that his oath shall go unkept on a merely unsubstantial controversy as to how it shall be kept?

Again, in any law upon this subject, ought not all the safeguards of liberty known in civilized and humane jurisprudence to be introduced, so that a free man be not, in any case, surrendered as a slave? And might it not be well at the same time to provide by law for the enforcement of that clause in the Constitution which guarantees that "the citizen of each State shall be entitled to all privileges and immunities of citizens in the several States"?

I take the official oath to-day with no mental reservations, and with no purpose to construe the Constitution or laws by any hyper-critical rules. And while I do not choose now to specify particular acts of Congress as proper to be enforced, I do suggest that it will be much safer for all, both in official and private stations, to conform to and abide by all those acts which stand unrepealed, than to violate any of them, trusting to find impunity in having them held to be unconstitutional.

It is seventy-two years since the first inauguration of a President under our National Constitution. During that period fifteen different and greatly distinguished citizens have, in succession, administered the executive branch of the government. They have conducted it through many perils, and generally with great success. Yet, with all this scope of precedent, I now enter upon the same task for the brief constitutional term of four years under great and peculiar difficulty. A disruption of the Federal Union, heretofore only menaced, is now formidably attempted.

I hold that, in contemplation of universal law and of the Constitution, the Union of these States is perpetual. Perpetuity is implied, if not expressed, in the fundamental law of all national governments. It is safe to assert that no government proper ever had a provision in its organic law for its own termination. Continue to execute all the express provisions of our National Constitution, and the Union will endure forever—it being impossible to destroy it except by some action not provided for in the instrument itself.

Again, if the United States be not a government proper, but an association of States in the nature of contract merely, can it, as a contract, be peaceably unmade by less than all the parties who made it? One party to a contract may violate it—break it, so to speak; but does it not require all to lawfully rescind it?

Descending from these general principles, we find the proposition that, in legal contemplation the Union is perpetual confirmed by the history of the Union itself. The Union is much older than the Constitution. It was formed, in fact, by the Articles of Association in 1774. It was matured and continued by the Declaration of Independence in 1776. It was further matured, and the faith of all the then thirteen States expressly plighted and engaged that it should be perpetual, by the Articles of Confederation in 1778. And, finally, in 1787 one of the declared objects for ordaining and establishing the Constitution was "to form a more perfect Union."

But if the destruction of the Union by one or by a part only of the States be lawfully possible, the Union is less perfect than before the Constitution, having lost the vital element of perpetuity.

It follows from these views that no State upon its own mere motion can lawfully get out of the Union; that resolves and ordinances to that effect are legally void; and that acts of violence, within any State or States, against the authority of the United States, are insurrectionary or revolutionary, according to circumstances.

I therefore consider that, in view of the Constitution and the laws, the Union is unbroken; and to the extent of my ability I shall take care, as the Constitution itself expressly enjoins upon me, that the laws of the Union be faithfully executed in all the States. Doing this I deem to be only a simple duty on my part; and I shall perform it so far as practicable, unless my rightful masters, the American people, shall withhold the requisite means, or in some authoritative manner direct the contrary. I trust this will not be regarded as a menace, but only as the declared purpose of the Union that it will constitutionally defend and maintain itself.

In doing this there needs to be no bloodshed or violence; and there shall be none, unless it be forced upon the national authority. The power confided to me will be used to hold, occupy, and possess the property and places belonging to the government, and to collect the duties and imposts; but beyond what may be necessary for these objects, there will be no invasion, no using of force against or among the people anywhere. Where hostility to the United States, in any interior locality, shall be so great and universal as to prevent competent resident citizens from holding the Federal offices, there will be no attempt to force obnoxious strangers among the people for that object. While the strict legal right may exist in the government to enforce the exercise of these offices, the attempt to do so would be so irritating, and so nearly impracticable withal, that I deem it better to forego for the time the uses of such offices.

The mails, unless repelled, will continue to be furnished in all parts of the Union. So far as possible, the people everywhere shall have that sense of perfect security which is most favorable to calm thought and reflection. The course here indicated will be followed unless current events and experience shall show a modification or change to be proper, and in every case and exigency my best discretion will be exercised according to circumstances actually existing, and with a view and a hope of a peaceful solution of the national troubles and the restoration of fraternal sympathies and affections.

That there are persons in one section or another who seek to destroy the Union at all events, and are glad of any pretext to do it, I will neither affirm nor deny; but if there be such, I need address no word to them. To those, however, who really love the Union may I not speak?

Before entering upon so grave a matter as the destruction of our national fabric, with all its benefits, its memories, and its hopes, would it not be wise to ascertain precisely why we do it? Will you hazard so desperate a step while there is any possibility that any portion of the ills you fly from have no real existence? Will you, while the certain ills you fly to are greater than all the real ones you fly from—will you risk the commission of so fearful a mistake?

All profess to be content in the Union if all constitutional rights can be maintained. Is it true, then, that any right, plainly written in the Constitution, has been denied? I think not. Happily the human mind is so constituted that no party can reach to the audacity of doing this. Think, if you can, of a single instance in which a plainly written provision of the Constitution has ever been denied. If by the mere force of numbers a majority should deprive a minority of any clearly written constitutional right, it might, in a moral point of view, justify revolution—certainly would if such a right were a vital one. But such is not our case. All the vital rights of minorities and of individuals are so plainly assured to them by affirmations and negations, guarantees and prohibitions, in the Constitution, that controversies never arise concerning them. But no organic law can ever be framed with a provision specifically applicable to every question which may occur in practical administration. No foresight can anticipate, nor any document of reasonable length contain, express provisions for all possible questions. Shall fugitives from labor be surrendered by national or by State authority? The Constitution does not expressly say *May* Congress prohibit slavery in the Territories? The Constitution does not expressly say *Must* Congress protect slavery in the Territories? The Constitution does not expressly say.

From questions of this class spring all our constitutional controversies, and we divide upon then into majorities and minorities. If the minority will not acquiesce, the majority must, or the government must cease. There is no other alternative; for continuing the government is acquiescence on one side or the other.

If a minority in such case will secede rather than acquiesce, they make a precedent which in turn will divide and ruin them; for a minority of their own will secede from them whenever a majority refuses to be controlled by such minority. For instance, why may not any portion of a new confederacy a year or two hence arbitrarily secede again, precisely as portions of the present Union now claim to secede from it? All who cherish disunion sentiments are now being educated to the exact temper of doing this.

Is there such perfect identity of interest among the States to compose a new Union, as to produce harmony only, and prevent renewed secession?

Plainly, the central idea of secession is the essence of anarchy. A majority held in restraint by constitutional checks and limitations, and always changing easily with deliberate changes of popular opinions and sentiments, is the only true sovereign of a free people. Whoever rejects it does, of necessity, fly to anarchy or to despotism. Unanimity is impossible; the rule of a minority, as a permanent arrangement, is wholly inadmissible; so that, rejecting the majority principle, anarchy or despotism in some form is all that is left.

I do not forget the position, assumed by some, that constitutional questions are to be decided by the Supreme Court; nor do I deny that such decisions must be binding, in any case, upon the parties to a suit, as to the object of that suit, while they are also entitled to very high respect and consideration in all parallel cases by all other departments of the government. And while it is obviously possible that such decision may be erroneous in any given case, still the evil effect following it, being limited to that particular case, with the chance that it may be overruled and never become a precedent for other cases, can better be borne than could the evils of a different practice. At the same time, the candid citizen must confess that if the policy of the government, upon vital questions affecting the whole people, is to be irrevocably fixed by decisions of the Supreme Court, the instant they are made, in ordinary litigation between parties in personal actions, the people will have ceased to be their own rulers, having to that extent practically resigned their government into the hands of that eminent tribunal. Nor is there in this view any assault upon the court or the judges. It is a duty from which they may not shrink to decide cases properly brought before them, and it is no fault of theirs if others seek to turn their decisions to political purposes.

One section of our country believes slavery is right, and ought to be extended, while the other believes it is wrong, and ought not to be extended. This is the only substantial dispute. The fugitive-slave clause of the Constitution, and the law for the suppression of the foreign slave-trade, are each as well enforced, perhaps, as any law can ever be in a community where the moral sense of the people imperfectly supports the law itself. The great body of the people abide by the dry legal obligation in both cases, and a few break over in each. This, I think, cannot be perfectly cured; and it would be worse in both cases after the separation of the sections than before. The foreign slave-trade, now imperfectly suppressed, would be ultimately revived, without restriction, in one section, while fugitive slaves, now only partially surrendered, would not be surrendered at all by the other.

Physically speaking, we cannot separate. We cannot remove our respective sections from each other, nor build an impassable wall between them. A husband and wife may be divorced, and go out of the presence and beyond the reach of each other; but the different parts of our country cannot do this. They cannot but remain face to face, and intercourse, either amicable or hostile, must continue between them. Is it possible, then, to make that intercourse more advantageous or more satisfactory after separation than before? Can aliens make treaties easier than friends can make laws? Can treaties be more faithfully enforced between aliens than laws can among friends? Suppose you go to war, you cannot fight always; and when, after much loss on both sides, and no gain on either, you cease fighting, the identical old questions as to terms of intercourse are again upon you.

This country, with its institutions, belongs to the people who inhabit it. Whenever they shall grow weary of the existing government, they can exercise their constitutional right of amending it, or their revolutionary right to dismember or overthrow it. I cannot be ignorant of the fact that many worthy and patriotic citizens are desirous of having the National Constitution amended. While I make no recommendation of amendments, I fully recognize the rightful authority of the people over the whole subject, to be exercised in either of the modes prescribed in the instrument itself; and I should, under existing circumstances, favor rather than oppose a fair opportunity being afforded the people to act upon it. I will venture to add that to me the convention mode seems preferable, in that it allows amendments to originate with the people themselves, instead of only permitting them to take or reject propositions originated by others not especially chosen for the purpose, and which might not be precisely such as they would wish to either accept or refuse. I understand a proposed amendment to the Constitution—which amendment, however, I have not seen—has passed Congress, to the effect that the Federal Government shall never interfere with the domestic institutions of the States, including that of persons held to service. To avoid misconstruction of what I have said, I depart from my purpose not to speak of particular amendments so far as to say that, holding such a provision to now be implied constitutional law, I have no objection to its being made express and irrevocable.

The chief magistrate derives all his authority from the people, and they have conferred none upon him to fix terms for the separation of the States. The people themselves can do this also if they choose; but the executive, as such, has nothing to do with it. His duty is to administer the present government, as it came to his hands, and to transmit it, unimpaired by him, to his successor.

Why should there not be a patient confidence in the ultimate justice of the people? Is there any better or equal hope in the world?

In our present differences is either party without faith of being in the right? If the Almighty Ruler of Nations, with his eternal truth and justice, be on your side of the North, or on yours of the South, that truth and that justice will surely prevail by the judgment of this great tribunal of the American people.

By the frame of the government under which we live, this same people have wisely given their public servants but little power for mischief; and have, with equal wisdom, provided for the return of that little to their own hands at very short intervals. While the people retain their virtue and vigilance, no administration, by any extreme of wickedness or folly, can very seriously injure the government in the short space of four years.

My countrymen, one and all, think calmly and well upon this whole subject. Nothing valuable can be lost by taking time. If there be an object to hurry any of you in hot haste to a step which you would never take deliberately, that object will be frustrated by taking time; but no good object can be frustrated by it. Such of you as are now dissatisfied, still have the old Constitution unimpaired, and, on the sensitive point, the laws of your own framing under it; while the new administration will have no immediate power, if it would, to change either. If it were admitted that you who are dissatisfied hold the right side in the dispute, there still is no single good reason for precipitate action. Intelligence, patriotism, Christianity, and a firm reliance on Him who has never yet forsaken this favored land, are still competent to adjust in the best way all our present difficulty.

In your hands, my dissatisfied fellow-countrymen, and not in mine, is the momentous issue of civil war. The government will not assail you. You can have no conflict without being yourselves the aggressors. You have no oath registered in heaven to destroy the government, while I shall have the most solemn one to "preserve, protect, and defend it."

I am loath to close. We are not enemies, but friends. We must not be enemies. Though passion may have strained, it must not break our bonds of affection. The mystic chords of memory, stretching from every battle-field and patriot grave to every living heart and hearthstone all over this broad land, will yet swell the chorus of the Union when again touched, as surely they will be, by the better angels of our nature.

ABRAHAM LINCOLN

Gettysburg Address (November 19, 1863)

A few months after the Battle of Gettysburg, which led to more than 51,000 Confederate and Union casualties, Abraham Lincoln traveled to the site of the battle for the dedication of a cemetery honoring the Union's fallen soldiers. Although Lincoln was not intended to be the main speaker at the event, his extremely brief address—a mere 267 words—has come to be considered one of the most eloquent and important speeches in the history of the United States.

FOURSCORE AND SEVEN YEARS ago our fathers brought forth on this continent a new nation, conceived in liberty and dedicated to the proposition that all men are created equal. Now we are engaged in a great civil war, testing whether that nation or any nation so conceived and so dedicated can long endure. We are met on a great battlefield of that war. We have come to dedicate a portion of that field as a final resting-place for those who here gave their lives that that nation might live. It is altogether fitting and proper that we should do this. But in a larger sense, we cannot dedicate, we cannot consecrate, we cannot hallow this ground. The brave men, living and dead who struggled here have consecrated it far above our poor power to add or detract. The world will little note nor long remember what we say here, but it can never forget what they did here. It is for us the living rather to be dedicated here to the unfinished work which they who fought here have thus far so nobly advanced. It is rather for us to be here dedicated to the great task remaining before us–that from these honored dead we take increased devotion to that cause for which they gave the last full measure of devotion–that we here highly resolve that these dead shall not have died in vain, that this nation under God shall have a new birth of freedom, and that government of the people, by the people, for the people shall not perish from the earth.

SUSAN B. ANTHONY

"On Behalf of the Woman Suffrage Amendment" (January 23, 1880)

Susan Brownell Anthony (1820–1906) was one of the most prominent and well-known civil rights leaders of the nineteenth century. Remembered mostly as an outspoken crusader for women's suffrage, Susan B. Anthony was also an important abolitionist and a pioneering figure in the temperance movement. The following address, delivered before the Senate Select Committee on Woman Suffrage in 1884, is a passionate appeal for the adoption of a women's suffrage amendment.

FRIENDS AND FELLOW-CITIZENS:—I stand before you under indictment for the alleged crime of having voted at the last presidential election, without having a lawful right to vote. It shall be my work this evening to prove to you that in thus doing, I not only committed no crime, but instead simply exercised my citizen's right, guaranteed to me and all United States citizens by the National Constitution beyond the power of any State to deny.

Our democratic-republican government is based on the idea of the natural right of every individual member thereof to a voice and a vote in making and executing the laws. We assert the province of government to be to secure the people in the enjoyment of their inalienable rights. We throw to the winds the old dogma that government can give rights. No one denies that before governments were organized each individual possessed the right to protect his own life, liberty and property. When 100 or 1,000,000 people enter into a free government, they do not barter away their natural rights; they simply pledge themselves to protect each other in the enjoyment of them through prescribed judicial and legislative tribunals. They agree to abandon the methods of brute force in the adjustment of their differences and adopt those of civilization. Nor can you find a word in any of the grand documents left us by the fathers which assumes for government the power to create or to confer rights. The Declaration of Independence, the United States Constitution, the constitutions of the several States and the organic laws of the Territories, all alike propose to *protect* the people in the exercise of their God-given rights. Not one of them pretends to bestow rights.

> All men are created equal, and endowed by their Creator with certain inalienable rights. Among these are life, liberty and the pursuit of happiness. To secure these, governments are instituted among men, deriving their just powers from the consent of the governed.

Here is no shadow of government authority over rights, or exclusion of any class from their full and equal enjoyment. Here is pronounced the right of all men, and "consequently," as the Quaker preacher said, "of all women," to a voice in the government. And here, in this first paragraph of the Declaration, is the assertion of the natural right of all to the ballot; for how can "the consent of the governed" be given, if the right to vote be denied? Again:

> Whenever any form of government becomes destructive of these ends, it is the right of the people to alter or abolish it, and to institute a new government, laying its foundations on such principles, and organizing its powers in such form, as to them shall seem most likely to effect their safety and happiness.

Surely the right of the whole people to vote is here clearly implied; for however destructive to their happiness this government might become, a disfranchised class could neither alter nor abolish it, nor institute a new one, except by the old brute force method of insurrection and rebellion. One-half of the people of this nation today are utterly powerless to blot from the statute books an unjust law, or to write there a new and a just one. The women, dissatisfied as they are with this form of government, that enforces taxation without representation—that compels them to obey laws to which they never have given their consent—that imprisons and hangs them without a trial by a jury of their peers—that robs them, in marriage, of the custody of their own persons, wages and children—are this half of the people who are left wholly at the mercy of the other half, in direct violation of the spirit and letter of the declarations of the framers of this government, every one of which was based on the immutable principle of equal rights to all. By these declarations, kings, popes, priests, aristocrats, all were alike dethroned and placed on a common level, politically, with the lowliest born subject or serf. By them, too, men, as such, were deprived of their divine right to rule and placed on a political level with women. By the practice of these declarations all class and caste distinctions would be abolished, and slave, serf, plebeian, wife, woman, all alike rise from their subject position to the broader platform of equality.

The preamble of the Federal Constitution says:

> We, the people of the United States, in order to form a more perfect union, establish justice, insure domestic tranquillity, provide for the common defence, promote the general welfare and secure the blessings of liberty to ourselves and our posterity, do ordain and establish this Constitution for the United States of America.

It was we, the people, not we, the white male citizens, nor we, the male citizens; but we, the whole people, who formed this Union. We formed it not to give the blessings of liberty but to secure them; not to the half of ourselves and the half of our posterity, but to the whole people—women as well as men. It is downright mockery to talk to women of their enjoyment of the blessings of liberty while they are denied the only means of securing them provided by this democratic-republican government—the ballot.

The early journals of Congress show that, when the committee reported to that body the original articles of confederation, the very first one which became the subject of discussion was that respecting equality of suffrage. Article IV said:

> The better to secure and perpetuate mutual friendship and intercourse between the people of the different States of this Union, the free inhabitants of each of the States (paupers, vagabonds and fugitives from justice excepted) shall be entitled to all the privileges and immunities of the free citizens of the several States.

Thus, at the very beginning, did the fathers see the necessity of the universal application of the great principle of equal rights to all, in order to produce the desired result—a harmonious union and a homogeneous people.

Luther Martin, attorney-general of Maryland, in his report to the legislature of that State of the convention which framed the United States Constitution, said:

> Those who advocated the equality of suffrage took the matter up on the original principles of government: that the reason why each individual man in forming a State government should have an equal vote, is because each individual, before he enters into government, is equally free and equally independent.

James Madison said:

> Under every view of the subject, it seems indispensable that the mass of the citizens should not be without a voice in making the laws which they are to obey, and in choosing the magistrates who are to administer them.... Let it be remembered, finally, that it has ever been the pride and the boast of America that the rights for which she contended were the rights of human nature.

These assertions by the framers of the United States Constitution of the equal and natural right of all the people to a voice in the government, have been affirmed and reaffirmed by the leading statesmen of the nation throughout the entire history of our government. Thaddeus Stevens, of Pennsylvania, said in 1866: "I have made up my mind that the elective franchise is one of the inalienable rights meant to be secured by the Declaration of Independence." B. Gratz Brown, of Missouri, in the three days' discussion in the United States Senate in 1866, on Senator Cowan's motion to strike "male" from the District of Columbia suffrage bill, said:

> Mr. President, I say here on the floor of the American Senate, I stand for universal suffrage; and as a matter of fundamental principle, do not recognize the right of society to limit it on any ground of race or sex. I will go farther and say that I recognize the right of franchise as being intrinsically a natural right. I do not believe that society is authorized to impose any limitations upon it that do not spring out of the necessities of the social state itself. Sir, I have

> been shocked, in the course of this debate, to hear senators declare this right only a conventional and political arrangement, a privilege yielded to you and me and others; not a right in any sense, only a concession! Mr. President, I do not hold my liberties by any such tenure. On the contrary, I believe that whenever you establish that doctrine, whenever you crystallize that idea in the public mind of this country, you ring the death-knell of American liberties.

Charles Sumner, in his brave protests against the Fourteenth and Fifteenth Amendments, insisted that so soon as by the Thirteenth Amendment the slaves became free men, the original powers of the United States Constitution guaranteed to them equal rights—the right to vote and to be voted for. In closing one of his great speeches he said:

> I do not hesitate to say that when the slaves of our country became "citizens" they took their place in the body politic as a component part of the "people," entitled to equal rights and under the protection of these two guardian principles: First, that all just governments stand on the consent of the governed; and second, that taxation without representation is tyranny; and these rights it is the duty of Congress to guarantee as essential to the idea of a republic.

The preamble of the constitution of the State of New York declares the same purpose. It says: "We, the people of the State of New York, grateful to Almighty God for our freedom, in order to secure its blessings, do establish this constitution." Here is not the slightest intimation either of receiving freedom from the United States Constitution, or of the State's conferring the blessings of liberty upon the people; and the same is true of every other State constitution. Each and all declare rights God-given, and that to secure the people in the enjoyment of their inalienable rights is their one and only object in ordaining and establishing government. All of the State constitutions are equally emphatic in their recognition of the ballot as the means of securing the people in the enjoyment of these rights. Article I of the New York State constitution says:

> No member of this State shall be disfranchised or deprived of the rights or privileges secured to any citizen thereof, unless by the law of the land, or the judgment of his peers.

So carefully guarded is the citizen's right to vote, that the constitution makes special mention of all who may be excluded. It says: "Laws may be passed excluding from the right of suffrage all persons who have been or may be convicted of bribery, larceny or any infamous crime."

In naming the various employments which shall not affect the residence of voters, Section 3, Article II, says "that neither being kept in any almshouse, or other asylum, at public expense, nor being confined in any public prison, shall deprive a person of his residence," and hence of his vote. Thus is the right of voting most sacredly hedged about. The only seeming permission in the New York State constitution for the disfranchisement of women is in Section 1, Article II, which says: "Every male citizen of the age of twenty-one years, etc., shall be entitled to vote."

But I submit that in view of the explicit assertions of the equal right of the whole people, both in the preamble and previous article of the constitution, this omission of the adjective "female" should not be construed into a denial; but instead should be considered as of no effect. Mark the direct prohibition, "No member of this State shall be disfranchised, unless by the law of the land, or the judgment of his peers." "The law of the land" is the United States Constitution; and there is no provision in that document which can be fairly construed into a permission to the States to deprive any class of citizens of their right to vote. Hence New York can get no power from that source to disfranchise one entire half of her members. Nor has "the judgment of their peers" been pronounced against women exercising their right to vote; no disfranchised person is allowed to be judge or juror—and none but disfranchised persons can be women's peers. Nor has the legislature passed laws excluding women as a class on account of idiocy or lunacy; nor have the courts convicted them of bribery, larceny or any infamous crime. Clearly, then, there is no constitutional ground for the exclusion of women from the ballot-box in the State of New York. No barriers whatever stand today between women and the exercise of their right to vote save those of precedent and prejudice, which refuse to expunge the word "male" from the constitution.

The clauses of the United States Constitution cited by our opponents as giving power to the States to disfranchise any classes of citizens they please, are contained in Sections 2 and 4, Article I. The second says:

> The House of Representatives shall be composed of members chosen every second year by the people of the several States; and the electors in each State shall have the qualifications requisite for electors of the most numerous branch of the State legislature.

This can not be construed into a concession to the States of the power to destroy the right to become an elector, but simply to prescribe what shall be the qualifications, such as competency of intellect, maturity of age, length of residence, that shall be deemed necessary to enable them to make an intelligent choice of candidates. If, as our opponents assert, it is the duty of the United States to protect citizens in the several States against higher or different qualifications for electors for representatives in Congress than for members of the Assembly, then it must be equally imperative for the national government to interfere with the States, and forbid them from arbitrarily cutting off the right of one-half the people to become electors altogether. Section 4 says:

> The times, places and manner of holding elections for senators and representatives shall be prescribed in each State by the legislature thereof; but Congress may at any time, by law, make or alter such regulations, except as to the places of choosing senators.

Here is conceded to the States only the power to prescribe times, places and manner of holding the elections; and even with these Congress may interfere in all excepting the mere place of choosing senators. Thus, you see, there is not the slightest permission for the States to discriminate against the right of any class of citizens to vote. Surely, to regulate can not be to annihilate; to qualify can not be wholly to deprive. To this principle every true Democrat and Republican said amen, when applied to black men by Senator Sumner in his great speeches from 1865 to 1869 for equal rights to all; and when, in 1871, I asked that senator to declare the power of the United States Constitution to protect women in their right to vote—as he had done for black men—he handed me a copy of all his speeches during that reconstruction period, and said:

> Put "sex" where I have "race" or "color," and you have here the best and strongest argument I can make for woman. There is not a doubt but women have the constitutional right to vote, and I will never

> vote for a Sixteenth Amendment to guarantee it to them. I voted for both the Fourteenth and Fifteenth under protest; would never have done it but for the pressing emergency of that hour; would have insisted that the power of the original Constitution to protect all citizens in the equal enjoyment of their rights should have been vindicated through the courts. But the newly-made freedmen had neither the intelligence, wealth nor time to await that slow process. Women do possess all these in an eminent degree, and I insist that they shall appeal to the courts, and through them establish the powers of our American magna charta to protect every citizen of the republic.

But, friends, when in accordance with Senator Sumner's counsel I went to the ballot-box, last November, and exercised my citizen's right to vote, the courts did not wait for me to appeal to them—they appealed to me, and indicted me on the charge of having voted illegally. Putting sex where he did color, Senator Sumner would have said:

> Qualifications can not be in their nature permanent or insurmountable. Sex can not be a qualification any more than size, race, color or previous condition of servitude. A permanent or insurmountable qualification is equivalent to a deprivation of the suffrage. In other words, it is the tyranny of taxation without representation, against which our Revolutionary mothers, as well as fathers, rebelled.

For any State to make sex a qualification, which must ever result in the disfranchisement of one entire half of the people, is to pass a bill of attainder, an ex post facto law, and is therefore a violation of the supreme law of the land. By it the blessings of liberty are forever withheld from women and their female posterity. For them, this government has no just powers derived from the consent of the governed. For them this government is not a democracy; it is not a republic. It is the most odious aristocracy ever established on the face of the globe. An oligarchy of wealth, where the rich govern the poor; an oligarchy of learning, where the educated govern the ignorant; or even an oligarchy of race, where the Saxon rules the African, might be endured; but this oligarchy of sex which makes father, brothers, husband, sons, the oligarchs over the mother and sisters, the wife and daughters of every household; which ordains all men sovereigns, all women subjects—carries discord and rebellion into every home of the nation. This most odious aristocracy exists, too, in the face of Section 4, Article IV, which says: "The United States shall guarantee to every State in the Union a republican form of government."

What, I ask you, is the distinctive difference between the inhabitants of a monarchical and those of a republican form of government, save that in the monarchical the people are subjects, helpless, powerless, bound to obey laws made by political superiors; while in the republican the people are citizens, individual sovereigns, all clothed with equal power to make and unmake both their laws and law-makers? The moment you deprive a person of his right to a voice in the government, you degrade him from the status of a citizen of the republic to that of a subject. It matters very little to him whether his monarch be an individual tyrant, as is the Czar of Russia, or a 15,000,000 headed monster, as here in the United States; he is a powerless subject, serf or slave; not in any sense a free and independent citizen.

It is urged that the use of the masculine pronouns *he, his* and *him* in all the constitutions and laws, is proof that only men were meant to be included in their provisions. If you insist on this version of the letter of the law, we shall insist that you be consistent and accept the other horn of the dilemma, which would compel you to exempt women from taxation for the support of the government and from penalties for the violation of laws. There is no *she* or *her* or *hers* in the tax laws, and this is equally true of all the criminal laws.

Take for example the civil rights law which I am charged with having violated; not only are all the pronouns in it masculine, but everybody knows that it was intended expressly to hinder the rebel men from voting. It reads, "If any person shall knowingly vote without *his* having a lawful right." It was precisely so with all the papers served on me—the United States marshal's warrant, the bail-bond, the petition for habeas corpus, the bill of indictment—not one of them had a feminine pronoun; but to make them applicable to me, the clerk of the court prefixed an "s" to the "he" and made "her" out of "his" and "him;" and I insist if government officials may thus manipulate the pronouns to tax, fine, imprison and hang women, it is their duty to thus change them in order to protect us in our right to vote.

So long as any classes of men were denied this right, the government made a show of consistency by exempting them from taxation. When a property qualification of $250 was required of black men in New York, they were not compelled to pay taxes so long as they were content to report themselves worth less than that sum; but the moment the black man died and his property fell to his widow or daughter, the black woman's name was put on the assessor's list and she was compelled to pay taxes on this same property. This also is true of ministers in New York. So long as the minister lives, he is exempted from taxation on $1,500 of property, but the moment the breath leaves his body, his widow's name goes on the assessor's list and she has to pay taxes on the $1,500. So much for special legislation in favor of women!

In all the penalties and burdens of government (except the military) women are reckoned as citizens, equally with men. Also, in all the privileges and immunities, save those of the jury and the ballot-box, the foundation on which rest all the others. The United States government not only taxes, fines, imprisons and hangs women, but it allows them to pre-empt lands, register ships and take out passports and naturalization papers. Not only does the law permit single women and widows the right of naturalization, but Section 2 says, "A married woman may be naturalized without the concurrence of her husband;" (I wonder the fathers were not afraid of creating discord in the families of foreigners;) and again:

> When an alien, having complied with the law and declared his intention to become a citizen, dies before he is actually naturalized, his widow and children shall be considered citizens, entitled to all rights and privileges as such, on taking the required oath.

If a foreign born woman by becoming a naturalized citizen is entitled to all the rights and privileges of citizenship, do not these include the ballot which would have belonged to her husband? If this is true of a naturalized woman, is it not equally true of one who is native born?

The question of the masculine pronouns—yes, and nouns too—was settled by the United States Supreme Court, in the case of Silver *versus* Ladd, December, 1868. The court said:

> In construing a benevolent statute of the government, made for the benefit of its own citizens, inviting and encouraging them to settle on its distant public lands, the words "single man" and "unmarried man" may, especially if aided by the context and other parts

of the statute, be taken in a generic sense. Held, accordingly, that the Fourth Section of the Act of Congress, of September 27, 1850, granting by way of donation lands in Oregon Territory to every white settler or occupant, American half-breed Indians included, embraced within the term single man an unmarried woman.

Though the words persons, people, inhabitants, electors, citizens, are all used indiscriminately in the national and State constitutions, there was always a conflict of opinion, prior to the war, as to whether they were synonymous terms, but whatever room there was for doubt, under the old regime, the adoption of the Fourteenth Amendment settled that question forever in its first sentence:

> All persons born or naturalized in the United States, and subject to the jurisdiction thereof, are citizens of the United States, and of the State wherein they reside.

The second settles the equal status of all citizens:

> No State shall make or enforce any law which shall abridge the privileges or immunities of citizens of the United States; nor shall any State deprive any person of life, liberty or property without due process of law, or deny to any person within its jurisdiction the equal protection of the laws.

The only question left to be settled now is: Are women persons? I scarcely believe any of our opponents will have the hardihood to say they are not. Being persons, then, women are citizens, and no State has a right to make any new law, or to enforce any old law, which shall abridge their privileges or immunities. Hence, every discrimination against women in the constitutions and laws of the several States is today null and void, precisely as is every one against negroes.

Is the right to vote one of the privileges or immunities of citizens? I think the disfranchised ex-rebels and ex-State prisoners all will agree that it is not only one of them, but the one without which all the others are nothing. Seek first the kingdom of the ballot and all things else shall be added, is the political injunction.

Webster, Worcester and Bouvier all define citizen to be a person, in the United States, entitled to vote and hold office. Prior to the adoption of the Thirteenth Amendment, by which slavery was forever abolished and black men transformed from property to persons, the judicial opinions of the country had always been in harmony with this definition: In order to be a citizen one must be a voter. Associate-Justice Washington, in defining the privileges and immunities of the citizen, more than fifty years ago, said: "They include all such privileges as are fundamental in their nature; and among them is the right to exercise the elective franchise, and to hold office." Even the Dred Scott decision, pronounced by the Abolitionists and Republicans infamous because it virtually declared "black men had no rights white men were bound to respect," gave this true and logical conclusion, that to be one of the people was to be a citizen and a voter.

Chief-Justice Daniels said:

> There is not, it is believed, to be found in the theories of writers on government, or in any actual experiment heretofore made, an exposition of the term citizen which has not been considered as conferring the actual possession and enjoyment of an entire equality of privileges, civil and political.

Associate-Justice Taney said:

> The words "people of the United States" and "citizens" are synonymous terms, and mean the same thing. They both describe the political body, who, according to our republican institutions, form the sovereignty, and who hold the power and conduct the government through their representatives. They are what we familiarly call "the sovereign people," and every citizen is one of this people, and a constituent member of this sovereignty.

Thus does Judge Taney's decision, which was so terrible a ban to the black man while he was a slave, now that he is a person and no longer property, pronounce him a citizen, possessed of entire equality of privileges, civil and political; and not only the black man, but the black woman, and all women. It was not until after the abolition of slavery, by which the negroes became free men and hence citizens, that any contrary opinion was rendered. U.S. Attorney-General Bates then said:

> The Constitution uses the word "citizen" only to express the political quality, [not equality, mark,] of the individual in his relation

> to the nation; to declare that he is a member of the body politic, and bound to it by the reciprocal obligations of allegiance on the one side and protection on the other. The phrase, "a citizen of the United States," without addition or qualification, means neither more nor less than a member of the nation.

Then, to be a citizen of this republic is no more than to be a subject of an empire. You and I, and all true and patriotic citizens, must repudiate this base conclusion. We all know that American citizenship, without addition or qualification, means the possession of equal rights, civil and political. We all know that the crowning glory of every citizen of the United States is that he can either give or withhold his vote from every law and every legislator under the government.

Did "I am a Roman citizen" mean nothing more than that I am a "member" of the body politic of the republic of Rome, bound to it by the reciprocal obligations of allegiance on the one side and protection on the other? When you, young man, shall travel abroad, among the monarchies of the old world, and there proudly boast yourself an "American citizen," will you thereby declare yourself neither more nor less than a "member" of the American nation?

This opinion of Attorney-General Bates, that a black citizen was not a voter, given merely to suit the political exigency of the Republican party in that transition hour between emancipation and enfranchisement, was no less infamous, in spirit or purpose, than was the decision of Judge Taney, that a black man was not one of the people, rendered in the interest and at the behest of the old Democratic party in its darkest hour of subjection to the slave power. Nevertheless, all of the adverse arguments, congressional reports and judicial opinions, thus far, have been based on this purely partisan, timeserving decision of General Bates, that the normal condition of the citizen of the United States is that of disfranchisement; that only such classes of citizens as have had special legislative guarantee have a legal right to vote.

If this decision of Attorney-General Bates was infamous, as against black men, but yesterday plantation slaves, what shall we pronounce upon Judge Bingham, in the House of Representatives, and Carpenter, in the Senate of the United States, for citing it against the women of the entire nation, vast numbers of whom are the peers of those honorable gentlemen themselves in morals, intellect, culture, wealth,

family, paying taxes on large estates, and contributing equally with them and their sex, in every direction, to the growth, prosperity and well-being of the republic? And what shall be said of the judicial opinions of Judges Cartter, Jameson, McKay and Sharswood, all based upon this aristocratic, monarchial idea of the right of one class to govern another?

I am proud to mention the names of the two United States judges who have given opinions honorable to our republican idea, and honorable to themselves—Judge Howe, of Wyoming Territory, and Judge Underwood, of Virginia. The former gave it as his opinion a year ago, when the legislature seemed likely to revoke the law enfranchising the women of that Territory that, in case they succeeded, the women would still possess the right to vote under the Fourteenth Amendment. The latter, in noticing the recent decision of Judge Cartter, of the Supreme Court of the District of Columbia, denying to women the right to vote under the Fourteenth and Fifteenth Amendments, says:

> If the people of the United States, by amendment of their Constitution, could expunge, without any explanatory or assisting legislation, an adjective of five letters from all State and local constitutions, and thereby raise millions of our most ignorant fellow-citizens to all of the rights and privileges of electors, why should not the same people, by the same amendment, expunge an adjective of four letters from the same State and local constitutions, and thereby raise other millions of more educated and better informed citizens to equal rights and privileges, without explanatory or assisting legislation?

If the Fourteenth Amendment does not secure to all citizens the right to vote, for what purpose was that grand old charter of the fathers lumbered with its unwieldy proportions? The Republican party, and Judges Howard and Bingham, who drafted the document, pretended it was to do something for black men; and if that something were not to secure them in their right to vote and hold office, what could it have been? For by the Thirteenth Amendment black men had become people, and hence were entitled to all the privileges and immunities of the government, precisely as were the women of the country and foreign men not naturalized. According to Associate-Justice Washington, they already had:

> Protection of the government, the enjoyment of life and liberty, with the right to acquire and possess property of every kind, and to pursue and obtain happiness and safety, subject to such restraints as the government may justly prescribe for the general welfare of the whole; the right of a citizen of one State to pass through or to reside in any other State for the purpose of trade, agriculture, professional pursuit, or otherwise; to claim the benefit of the writ of habeas corpus, to institute and maintain actions of any kind in the courts of the State; to take, hold, and dispose of property, either real or personal, and an exemption from higher taxes or impositions than are paid by the other citizens of the State.

Thus, you see, those newly-freed men were in possession of every possible right, privilege and immunity of the government, except that of suffrage, and hence needed no constitutional amendment for any other purpose. What right in this country has the Irishman the day after he receives his naturalization papers that he did not possess the day before, save the right to vote and hold office? The Chinamen now crowding our Pacific coast are in precisely the same position. What privilege or immunity has California or Oregon the right to deny them, save that of the ballot? Clearly, then, if the Fourteenth Amendment was not to secure to black men their right to vote it did nothing for them, since they possessed everything else before. But if it was intended to prohibit the States from denying or abridging their right to vote, then it did the same for all persons, white women included, born or naturalized in the United States; for the amendment does not say that all male persons of African descent, but that all persons are citizens.

The second section is simply a threat to punish the States by reducing their representation on the floor of Congress, should they disfranchise any of their male citizens, and can not be construed into a sanction to disfranchise female citizens, nor does it in any wise weaken or invalidate the universal guarantee of the first section.

However much the doctors of the law may disagree as to whether people and citizens, in the original Constitution, were one and the same, or whether the privileges and immunities in the Fourteenth Amendment include the right of suffrage, the question of the citizen's right to vote is forever settled by the Fifteenth Amendment. "The right of citizens of the United States to vote shall not be denied or abridged by the United States, or by any State, on account of race, color or previous condition of servitude." How can the State deny or abridge the right of the citizen, if the citizen does not possess it? There is no escape from the conclusion that to vote is the citizen's right, and the specifications of race, color or previous condition of servitude can in no way impair the force of that emphatic assertion that the citizen's right to vote shall not be denied or abridged.

The political strategy of the second section of the Fourteenth Amendment failing to coerce the rebel States into enfranchising their negroes, and the necessities of the Republican party demanding their votes throughout the South to ensure the re-election of Grant in 1872, that party was compelled to place this positive prohibition of the Fifteenth Amendment upon the United States and all the States thereof.

If once we establish the false principle that United States citizenship does not carry with it the right to vote in every State in this Union, there is no end to the petty tricks and cunning devices which will be attempted to exclude one and another class of citizens from the right of suffrage. It will not always be the men combining to disfranchise all women; native born men combining to abridge the rights of all naturalized citizens, as in Rhode Island. It will not always be the rich and educated who may combine to cut off the poor and ignorant; but we may live to see the hard-working, uncultivated day laborers, foreign and native born, learning the power of the ballot and their vast majority of numbers, combine and amend State constitutions so as to disfranchise the Vanderbilts, the Stewarts, the Conklings and the Fentons. It is a poor rule that won't work more ways than one. Establish this precedent, admit the State's right to deny suffrage, and there is no limit to the confusion, discord and disruption that may await us. There is and can be but one safe principle of government—equal rights to all. Discrimination against any class on account of color, race, nativity, sex, property, culture, can but embitter and disaffect that class, and thereby endanger the safety of the whole people. Clearly, then, the national government not only must define the rights of citizens, but must stretch out its powerful hand and protect them in every State in this Union.

If, however, you will insist that the Fifteenth Amendment's emphatic interdiction against robbing United States citizens of their suffrage "on account of race, color or previous condition of servitude," is a recognition of the right of either the United States or any State to deprive them of the ballot for any or all other reasons, I will prove to you that the class of citizens for whom I now plead are, by all the principles of our government and many of the laws of the States, included under the term "previous condition of servitude."

Consider first married women and their legal status. What is servitude? "The condition of a slave." What is a slave? "A person who is robbed of the proceeds of his labor; a person who is subject to the will of another." By the laws of Georgia, South Carolina and all the States of the South, the negro had no right to the custody and control of his person. He belonged to his master. If he were disobedient, the master had the right to use correction. If the negro did not like the correction and ran away, the master had the right to use coercion to bring him back. By the laws of almost every State in this Union today, North as well as South, the married woman has no right to the custody and control of her person. The wife belongs to the husband; and if she refuse obedience he may use moderate correction, and if she do not like his moderate correction and leave his "bed and board," the husband may use moderate coercion to bring her back. The little word "moderate," you see, is the saving clause for the wife, and would doubtless be overstepped should her offended husband administer his correction with the "cat-o'-nine-tails," or accomplish his coercion with blood-hounds.

Again the slave had no right to the earnings of his hands, they belonged to his master; no right to the custody of his children, they belonged to his master; no right to sue or be sued, or to testify in the courts. If he committed a crime, it was the master who must sue or be sued. In many of the States there has been special legislation, giving married women the right to property inherited or received by bequest, or earned by the pursuit of any avocation outside the home; also giving them the right to sue and be sued in matters pertaining to such separate property; but not a single State of this Union has ever secured the wife in the enjoyment of her right to equal ownership of the joint earnings of the marriage copartnership. And since, in the nature of things, the vast majority of married women never earn a dollar by work outside their families, or inherit a dollar from their fathers, it follows that from the day of their marriage to the day of the death of their husbands not one of them ever has a dollar, except it shall please her husband to let her have it.

In some of the States, also, laws have been passed giving to the mother a joint right with the father in the guardianship of the children. Twenty-five years ago, when our woman's rights movement commenced, by the laws of all the States the father had the sole custody and control of the children. No matter if he were a brutal, drunken libertine, he had the legal right, without the mother's consent, to apprentice her sons to rumsellers or her daughters to brothel-keepers. He even could will away an unborn child from the mother. In most of the States this law still prevails, and the mothers are utterly powerless.

I doubt if there is, today, a State in this Union where a married woman can sue or be sued for slander of character, and until recently there was not one where she could sue or be sued for injury of person. However damaging to the wife's reputation any slander may be, she is wholly powerless to institute legal proceedings against her accuser unless her husband shall join with her; and how often have we heard of the husband conspiring with some outside barbarian to blast the good name of his wife? A married woman can not testify in courts in cases of joint interest with her husband.

A good farmer's wife in Illinois, who had all the rights she wanted, had had made for herself a full set of false teeth. The dentist pronounced them an admirable fit, and the wife declared it gave her fits to wear them. The dentist sued the husband for his bill; his counsel brought the wife as witness; the judge ruled her off the stand, saying, "A married woman can not be a witness in matters of joint interest between herself and her husband." Think of it, ye good wives, the false teeth in your mouths are a joint interest with your husbands, about which you are legally incompetent to speak! If a married woman is injured by accident, in nearly all of the States it is her husband who must sue, and it is to him that the damages will be awarded. In Massachusetts a married woman was severely injured by a defective sidewalk. Her husband sued the corporation and recovered $13,000 damages, which belong to him absolutely, and whenever that unfortunate wife wishes a dollar of that money she must ask her husband for it; and if he be of a niggardly nature, she will hear him say, every time, "What have you done with the twenty-five cents I gave you yesterday?" Isn't such a position humiliating enough to be called "servitude?" That husband sued and obtained damages for the loss of the services of his wife, precisely as he would have done had it been his ox, cow or horse; and exactly as the master, under the old regime, would have recovered for the services of his slave.

I submit the question, if the deprivation by law of the ownership of one's own person, wages, property, children, the denial of the right as an individual to sue and be sued and testify in the courts, is not a condition of servitude most bitter and absolute, even though under the sacred name of marriage? Does any lawyer doubt my statement of the legal status of married women? I will remind him of the fact that the common law of England prevails in every State but two in this Union, except where the legislature has enacted special laws annulling it. I am ashamed that not one of the States yet has blotted from its statute books the old law of marriage, which, summed up in the fewest words possible, is in effect "husband and wife are one, and that one the husband."

Thus may all married women and widows, by the laws of the several States, be technically included in the Fifteenth Amendment's specification of "condition of servitude," present or previous. The facts also prove that, by all the great fundamental principles of our free government, not only married women but the entire womanhood of the nation are in a "condition of servitude" as surely as were our Revolutionary fathers when they rebelled against King George. Women are taxed without representation, governed without their consent, tried, convicted and punished without a jury of their peers. Is all this tyranny any less humiliating and degrading to women under our democratic-republican government today than it was to men under their aristocratic, monarchial government one hundred years ago? There is not an utterance of John Adams, John Hancock or Patrick Henry, but finds a living response in the soul of every intelligent, patriotic woman of the nation. Show me a justice-loving woman property-holder, and I will show you one whose soul is fired with all the indignation of 1776 every time the tax-collector presents himself at her door. You will not find one such but feels her condition of servitude as galling as did James Otis when he said:

> The very act of taxing exercised over those who are not represented appears to me to be depriving them of one of their most essential rights, and if continued seems to be in effect an entire disfranchisement of every civil right. For what one civil right is worth a rush after a man's property is subject to be taken from him at pleasure without his consent? If a man is not his own assessor in person,

or by deputy, his liberty is gone, for he is wholly at the mercy of others.

What was the three-penny tax on tea or the paltry tax on paper and sugar to which our Revolutionary fathers were subjected, when compared with the taxation of the women of this republic? And again, to show that disfranchisement was precisely the slavery of which the fathers complained, allow me to cite Benjamin Franklin, who in those olden times was admitted to be good authority, not merely in domestic but also in political economy:

> Every man of the commonalty, except infants, insane persons and criminals, is, of common right and the law of God, a freeman and entitled to the free enjoyment of liberty. That liberty or freedom consists in having an actual share in the appointment of those who are to frame the laws, and who are to be the guardians of every man's life, property and peace. For the all of one man is as dear to him as the all of another; and the poor man has an equal right, but more need, to have representatives in the legislature than the rich one. They who have no voice or vote in the electing of representatives do not enjoy liberty, but are absolutely enslaved to those who have votes and to their representatives; for to be enslaved is to have governors whom other men have set over us, and to be subject to laws made by the representatives of others, without having had representatives of our own to give consent in our behalf.

Suppose I read it with the feminine gender:

> Women who have no voice or vote in the electing of representatives do not enjoy liberty, but are absolutely enslaved to men who have votes and to their representatives; for to be enslaved is to have governors whom men have set over us, and to be subject to the laws made by the representatives of men, without having representatives of our own to give consent in our behalf.

And yet one more authority, that of Thomas Paine, than whom not one of the Revolutionary patriots more ably vindicated the principles upon which our government is founded:

> The right of voting for representatives is the primary right by which other rights are protected. To take away this right is to reduce man to a state of slavery; for slavery consists in being subject to the will

> of another; and he that has not a vote in the election of representatives is in this case. The proposal, therefore, to disfranchise any class of men is as criminal as the proposal to take away property.

Is anything further needed to prove woman's condition of servitude sufficient to entitle her to the guarantees of the Fifteenth Amendment? Is there a man who will not agree with me that to talk of freedom without the ballot is mockery to the women of this republic, precisely as New England's orator, Wendell Phillips, at the close of the late war declared it to be to the newly emancipated black man? I admit that, prior to the rebellion, by common consent, the right to enslave, as well as to disfranchise both native and foreign born persons, was conceded to the States. But the one grand principle settled by the war and the reconstruction legislation, is the supremacy of the national government to protect the citizens of the United States in their right to freedom and the elective franchise, against any and every interference on the part of the several States; and again and again have the American people asserted the triumph of this principle by their overwhelming majorities for Lincoln and Grant.

The one issue of the last two presidential elections was whether the Fourteenth and Fifteenth Amendments should be considered the irrevocable will of the people; and the decision was that they should be, and that it is not only the right, but the duty of the national government to protect all United States citizens in the full enjoyment and free exercise of their privileges and immunities against the attempt of any State to deny or abridge. In this conclusion Republicans and Democrats alike agree. Senator Frelinghuysen said: "The heresy of State rights has been completely buried in these amendments, and as amended, the Constitution confers not only National but State citizenship upon all persons born or naturalized within our limits."

The call for the National Republican Convention of 1872 said: "Equal suffrage has been engrafted on the National Constitution; the privileges and immunities of American citizenship have become a part of the organic law." The National Republican platform said: "Complete liberty and exact equality in the enjoyment of all civil, political and public rights, should be established and maintained throughout the Union by efficient and appropriate State and Federal legislation."

If that means anything it is that Congress should pass a law to protect women in their equal political rights, and that the States should enact laws making it the duty of inspectors of elections to receive the votes of women on precisely the same conditions as they do those of men.

Judge Stanley Matthews, a substantial Ohio Democrat, in his preliminary speech at the Cincinnati Liberal Convention, said most emphatically: "The constitutional amendments have established the political equality of all citizens before the law."

President Grant, in his message to Congress, March 30, 1870, on the adoption of the Fifteenth Amendment, said, "A measure which makes at once four millions of people voters, is indeed a measure of greater importance than any act of the kind from the foundation of the government to the present time."

How could *four* million negroes be made voters if two million out of the four were women?

The California Republican platform of 1872 said:

> Among the many practical and substantial triumphs of the principles achieved by the Republican party during the past twelve years, it enumerates with pride and pleasure the prohibiting of any State from abridging the privileges of any citizen of the republic, the declaring the civil and political equality of every citizen, and the establishing all these principles in the Federal Constitution, by amendments thereto, as the permanent law.

Benjamin F. Butler, in a recent letter to me, said: "I do not believe anybody in Congress doubts that the Constitution authorizes the right of women to vote, precisely as it authorizes trial by jury and many other like rights guaranteed to citizens."

It is upon this just interpretation of the United States Constitution that our National Woman Suffrage Association, which celebrates the twenty-fifth anniversary of the woman's rights movement next May in New York City, has based all its arguments and action since the passage of these amendments. We no longer petition legislature or Congress to give us the right to vote, but appeal to women everywhere to exercise their too long neglected "citizen's right." We appeal to the inspectors of election to receive the votes of all United States citizens, as it is their duty to do. We appeal to United States commissioners and marshals to arrest, as is their duty, the inspectors who reject the votes of United States citizens, and leave alone those who perform their duties and accept these votes. We ask the juries to return verdicts of "not guilty" in the cases of law-abiding United States citizens who cast their votes, and inspectors of election who receive and count them.

We ask the judges to render unprejudiced opinions of the law, and whereever there is room for doubt to give the benefit to the side of liberty and equal rights for women, remembering that, as Sumner says, "The true rule of interpretation under our National Constitution, especially since its amendments, is that anything *for* human rights is constitutional, everything *against* human rights unconstitutional." It is on this line that we propose to fight our battle for the ballot—peaceably but nevertheless persistently—until we achieve complete triumph and all United States citizens, men and women alike, are recognized as equals in the government.

THEODORE ROOSEVELT

"Duties of American Citizenship" (January 26, 1883)

Nearly twenty years before becoming the 26th president of the United States, Theodore Roosevelt (1858–1919) was a young, first-term legislator in the New York State Assembly when he was invited to Buffalo to speak on the subject of American civic duty. In this speech, Roosevelt begins by chastising the men of his own generation for their passive approach to citizenship. He then goes on to argue that all American citizens, who enjoy their country's great freedoms and liberties, have a responsibility to devote a portion of their time and labor to maintaining a good government.

Of course, in one sense, the first essential for a man's being a good citizen is his possession of the home virtues of which we think when we call a man by the emphatic adjective of manly. No man can be a good citizen who is not a good husband and a good father, who is not honest in his dealings with other men and women, faithful to his friends and fearless in the presence of his foes, who has not got a sound heart, a sound mind, and a sound body; exactly as no amount of attention to civil duties will save a nation if the domestic life is undermined, or there is lack of the rude military virtues which alone can assure a country's position in the world. In a free republic the ideal citizen must be one willing and able to take arms for the defense of the flag, exactly as the ideal citizen must be the father of many healthy children. A race must be strong and vigorous; it must be a race of good fighters and good breeders, else its wisdom will come to naught and its virtue be ineffective;

and no sweetness and delicacy, no love for and appreciation of beauty in art or literature, no capacity for building up material prosperity can possibly atone for the lack of the great virile virtues.

But this is aside from my subject, for what I wish to talk of is the attitude of the American citizen in civic life. It ought to be axiomatic in this country that every man must devote a reasonable share of his time to doing his duty in the political life of the community. No man has a right to shirk his political duties under whatever plea of pleasure or business; and while such shirking may be pardoned in those of small means it is entirely unpardonable in those among whom it is most common—in the people whose circumstances give them freedom in the struggle for life. In so far as the community grows to think rightly, it will likewise grow to regard the young man of means who shirks his duty to the State in time of peace as being only one degree worse than the man who thus shirks it in time of war. A great many of our men in business, or of our young men who are bent on enjoying life (as they have a perfect right to do if only they do not sacrifice other things to enjoyment), rather plume themselves upon being good citizens if they even vote; yet voting is the very least of their duties. Nothing worth gaining is ever gained without effort. You can no more have freedom without striving and suffering for it than you can win success as a banker or a lawyer without labor and effort, without self-denial in youth and the display of a ready and alert intelligence in middle age. The people who say that they have not time to attend to politics are simply saying that they are unfit to live in a free community. Their place is under a despotism; or if they are content to do nothing but vote, you can take despotism tempered by an occasional plebiscite, like that of the second Napoleon. In one of Lowell's magnificent stanzas about the Civil War he speaks of the fact which his countrymen were then learning, that freedom is not a gift that tarries long in the hands of cowards: nor yet does it tarry long in the hands of the sluggard and the idler, in the hands of the man so much absorbed in the pursuit of pleasure or in the pursuit of gain, or so much wrapped up in his own easy home life as to be unable to take his part in the rough struggle with his fellow men for political supremacy. If freedom is worth having, if the right of self-government is a valuable right, then the one and the other must be retained exactly as our forefathers acquired them, by labor, and especially by labor in organization, that is in combination with our fellows who have the same interests and the same principles. We should not accept the excuse of the business man who attributed his failure to the fact that his social duties were so pleasant and engrossing that he had no time left for work in his office; nor would we pay much heed to his further statement that he did not like business anyhow because he thought the morals of the business community by no means what they should be, and saw that the great successes were most often won by men of the Jay Gould stamp. It is just the same way with politics. It makes one feel half angry and half amused, and wholly contemptuous, to find men of high business or social standing in the community saying that they really have not got time to go to ward meetings, to organize political clubs, and to take a personal share in all the important details of practical politics; men who further urge against their going the fact that they think the condition of political morality low, and are afraid that they may be required to do what is not right if they go into politics.

The first duty of an American citizen, then, is that he shall work in politics; his second duty is that he shall do that work in a practical manner; and his third is that it shall be done in accord with the highest principles of honor and justice. Of course, it is not possible to define rigidly just the way in which the work shall be made practical. Each man's individual temper and convictions must be taken into account. To a certain extent his work must be done in accordance with his individual beliefs and theories of right and wrong. To a yet greater extent it must be done in combination with others, he yielding or modifying certain of his own theories and beliefs so as to enable him to stand on a common ground with his fellows, who have likewise yielded or modified certain of their theories and beliefs. There is no need of dogmatizing about independence on the one hand or party allegiance on the other. There are occasions when it may be the highest duty of any man to act outside of parties and against the one with which he has himself been hitherto identified; and there may be many more occasions when his highest duty is to sacrifice some of his own cherished opinions for the sake of the success of the party which he on the whole believes to be right. I do not think that the average citizen, at least in one of our great cities, can very well manage to support his own party all the time on every issue, local and otherwise; at any rate if he can do so he has been more fortunately placed than I have been. On the other hand, I am fully convinced that to do the best work people must be organized; and of course an organization is really a party, whether it be a great organization covering the whole nation and numbering its millions of adherents, or an association of citizens in a particular locality, banded together to win a certain specific victory, as, for instance, that of municipal reform. Somebody has said that a racing-yacht, like a good rifle, is a bundle of incompatibilities; that you must get the utmost possible sail power without sacrificing some other quality if you really do get the utmost sail power, that, in short you have got to make more or less of a compromise on each in order to acquire the dozen things needful; but, of course, in making this compromise you must be very careful for the sake of something unimportant not to sacrifice any of the great principles of successful naval architecture. Well, it is about so with a man's political work. He has got to preserve his independence on the one hand; and on the other, unless he wishes to be a wholly ineffective crank, he has got to have some sense of party allegiance and party responsibility, and he has got to realize that in any given exigency it may be a matter of duty to sacrifice one quality, or it may be a matter of duty to sacrifice the other.

If it is difficult to lay down any fixed rules for party action in the abstract; it would, of course, be wholly impossible to lay them down for party action in the concrete, with reference to the organizations of the present day. I think that we ought to be broad-minded enough to recognize the fact that a good citizen, striving with fearlessness, honesty, and common sense to do his best for the nation, can render service to it in many different ways, and by connection with many different organizations. It is well for a man if he is able conscientiously to feel that his views on the great questions of the day, on such questions as the tariff, finance, immigration, the regulation of the liquor traffic, and others like them, are such as to put him in accord with the bulk of those of his fellow citizens who compose one of the greatest parties: but it is perfectly supposable that he may feel so strongly for or against certain principles held by one party, or certain principles held by the other, that he is unable to give his full adherence to either. In such a case I feel that he has no right to plead this lack of agreement with either party as an excuse for refraining from active political work prior to election. It will, of course, bar him from the primaries of the two leading parties, and preclude him from doing his share in organizing their management; but, unless he is very unfortunate, he can surely find a number of men who are in the same position as himself and who agree with him on some specific piece of political work, and they can turn in practically and effectively long before election to try to do this new piece of work in a practical manner.

One seemingly very necessary caution to utter is, that a man who goes into politics should not expect to reform everything right off, with a jump. I know many excellent young men who, when awakened to the fact that they have neglected their political duties, feel an immediate impulse to form themselves into an organization which shall forthwith purify politics everywhere, national, State, and city alike; and I know of a man who having gone round once to a primary, and having, of course, been unable to accomplish anything in a place where he knew no one and could not combine with anyone, returned saying it was quite useless for a good citizen to try to accomplish anything in such a manner. To these too hopeful or too easily discouraged people I always feel like reading Artemus Ward's article upon the people of his town who came together in a meeting to resolve that the town should support the Union and the Civil War, but were unwilling to take any part in putting down the rebellion unless they could go as brigadier-generals. After the battle of Bull Run there were a good many hundreds of thousands of young men in the North who felt it to be their duty to enter the Northern armies; but no one of them who possessed much intelligence expected to take high place at the outset, or anticipated that individual action would be of decisive importance in any given campaign. He went in as private or sergeant, lieutenant or captain, as the case might be, and did his duty in his company, in his regiment, after a while in his brigade. When Ball's Bluff and Bull Run succeeded the utter failure of the Peninsular campaign, when the terrible defeat of Fredericksburg was followed by the scarcely less disastrous day at Chancellorsville he did not announce (if he had any pluck or manliness about him) that he considered it quite useless for any self-respecting citizen to enter the Army of the Potomac, because he really was not of much weight in its councils, and did not approve of its management; he simply gritted his teeth and went doggedly on with his duty, grieving over, but not disheartened at the innumerable shortcomings and follies committed by those who helped to guide the destinies of the army, recognizing also the bravery, the patience, intelligence, and resolution with which other men in high places offset the follies and shortcomings and persevering with equal mind through triumph and defeat until finally he saw the tide of failure turn at Gettysburg and the full flood of victory come with Appomattox.

I do wish that more of our good citizens would go into politics, and would do it in the same spirit with which their fathers went into the Federal armies. Begin with the little thing, and do not expect to accomplish anything without an effort. Of course, if you go to a primary just once, never having taken the trouble to know any of the other people who go there you will find yourself wholly out of place; but if you keep on attending and try to form associations with other men whom you meet at the political gatherings, or whom you can persuade to attend them, you will very soon find yourself a weight. In the same way, if a man feels that the politics of his city, for instance, are very corrupt and wants to reform them, it would be an excellent idea for him to begin with his district. If he joins with other people, who think as he does, to form a club where abstract political virtue will be discussed he may do a great deal of good. We need such clubs; but he must also get to know his own ward or his own district, put himself in communication with the decent people in that district, of whom we may rest assured there will be many, willing and able to do something practical for the procurance of better government. Let him set to work to procure a better assemblyman or better alderman before he tries his hand at making a mayor, a governor, or a president. If he begins at the top he may make a brilliant temporary success, but the chances are a thousand to one that he will only be defeated eventually; and in no event will the good he does stand on the same broad and permanent foundation as if he had begun at the bottom. Of course, one or two of his efforts may be failures; but if he has the right stuff in him he will go ahead and do his duty irrespective of whether he meets with success or defeat. It is perfectly right to consider the question of failure while shaping one's efforts to succeed in the struggle for the right; but there should be no consideration of it whatsoever when the question is as to whether one should or should not make a struggle for the right. When once a band of one hundred and fifty or two hundred honest, intelligent men, who mean business and know their business, is found in any district, whether in one of the regular organizations or outside, you can guarantee that the local politicians of that district will begin to treat it with a combination of fear, hatred, and respect, and that its influence will be felt; and that while sometimes men will be elected to office in direct defiance of its wishes, more often the successful candidates will feel that they have to pay some regard to its demands for public decency and honesty.

But in advising you to be practical and to work hard, I must not for one moment be understood as advising you to abandon one iota of your self-respect and devotion to principle. It is a bad sign for the country to see one class of our citizens sneer at practical politicians, and another at Sunday-school politics. No man can do both effective and decent work in public life unless he is a practical politician on the one hand, and a sturdy believer in Sunday-school politics on the other. He must always strive manfully for the best, and yet, like Abraham Lincoln, must often resign himself to accept the best possible. Of course when a man verges on to the higher ground of statesmanship, when he becomes a leader, he must very often consult with others and defer to their opinion, and must be continually settling in his mind how far he can go in just deference to the wishes and prejudices of others while yet adhering to his own moral standards: but I speak not so much of men of this stamp as I do of the ordinary citizen, who wants to do his duty as a member of the commonwealth in its civic life; and for this man I feel that the one quality which he ought always to hold most essential is that of disinterestedness. If he once begins to feel that he wants office himself, with a willingness to get it at the cost of his convictions, or to keep it when gotten, at the cost of his convictions, his usefulness is gone. Let him make up his mind to do his duty in politics without regard to holding office at all, and let him know that often the men in this country who have done the best work for our public life have not been the men in office. If, on the other hand, he attains public position, let him not strive to plan out for himself a career. I do not think that any man should let himself regard his political career as a means of livelihood, or as his sole occupation in life; for if he does he immediately becomes most seriously handicapped. The moment that he begins to think how such and such an act will affect the voters in his district, or will affect some great political leader who will have an influence over his destiny, he is hampered and his hands are bound. Not only may it be his duty often to disregard the wishes of politicians, but it may be his clear duty at times to disregard the wishes of the people. The voice of the people is not always the voice of God; and when it happens to be the voice of the devil, then it is a man's clear duty to defy its behests. Different political conditions breed different dangers. The demagogue is as unlovely a creature as the courtier, though one is fostered under republican and the other under monarchical institutions. There is every reason why a man should have an honorable ambition to enter public life, and an honorable ambition to stay there when he is in; but he ought to make up his mind that he cares for it only as long as he can stay in it on his own terms, without sacrifice of his own principles; and if he does thus make up his mind he can really accomplish twice as much for the nation, and can reflect a hundredfold greater honor upon himself, in a short term of service, than can the man who grows gray in the public employment at the cost of sacrificing what he believes to be true and honest. And moreover, when a public servant has definitely made up his mind that he will pay no heed to his own future, but will do what he honestly deems best for the community, without regard to how his actions may affect his prospects, not only does he become infinitely more useful as a public servant, but he has a far better time. He is freed from the harassing care which is inevitably the portion of him who is trying to shape his sails to catch every gust of the wind of political favor.

But let me reiterate, that in being virtuous he must not become ineffective, and that he must not excuse himself for shirking his duties by any false plea that he cannot do his duties and retain his self-respect. This is nonsense, he can; and when he urges such a plea it is a mark of mere laziness and self-indulgence. And again, he should beware how he becomes a critic of the actions of others, rather than a doer of deeds himself; and in so far as he does act as a critic (and of course the critic has a great and necessary function) he must beware of indiscriminate censure even more than of indiscriminate praise. The screaming vulgarity of the foolish spread-eagle orator who is continually yelling defiance at Europe, praising everything American, good and bad, and resenting the introduction of any reform because it has previously been tried successfully abroad, is offensive and contemptible to the last degree; but after all it is scarcely as harmful as the peevish, fretful, sneering, and continual faultfinding of the refined, well-educated man, who is always attacking good and bad alike, who genuinely distrusts America, and in the true spirit of servile colonialism considers us inferior to the people across the water. It may be taken for granted that the man who is always sneering at our public life and our public men is a thoroughly bad citizen, and that what little influence he wields in the community is wielded for evil. The public speaker or the editorial writer who teaches men of education that their proper attitude toward American politics should be one of dislike or indifference is doing all he can to perpetuate and aggravate the very evils of which he is ostensibly complaining. Exactly as it is generally the case that when a man bewails the decadence of our civilization he is himself physically, mentally, and morally a first-class type of the decadent, so it is usually the case that when a man is perpetually sneering at American politicians, whether worthy or unworthy, he himself is a poor citizen and a friend of the very forces of evil against which he professes to contend. Too often these men seem to care less for attacking bad men, than for ruining the characters of good men with whom they disagree on some public question; and while their influence against the bad is almost nil, they are sometimes able to weaken the hands of the good by withdrawing from them support to which they are entitled, and they thus count in the sum total of forces that work for evil. They answer to the political prohibitionist, who, in a close contest between a temperance man and a liquor seller diverts enough votes from the former to elect the liquor seller. Occasionally it is necessary to beat a pretty good man, who is not quite good enough, even at the cost of electing a bad one—but it should be thoroughly recognized that this can be necessary only occasionally and indeed, I may say, only in very exceptional cases, and that as a rule where it is done the effect is thoroughly unwholesome in every way, and those taking part in it deserve the severest censure from all honest men.

Moreover, the very need of denouncing evil makes it all the more wicked to weaken the effect of such denunciations by denouncing also the good. It is the duty of all citizens, irrespective of party, to denounce, and, so far as may be, to punish crimes against the public on the part of politicians or officials. But exactly as the public man who commits a crime against the public is one of the worst of criminals, so, close on his heels in the race for iniquitous distinction, comes the man who falsely charges the public servant with outrageous wrongdoing; whether it is done with foul-mouthed and foolish directness in the vulgar and violent party organ, or with sarcasm, innuendo, and the half-truths that are worse than lies, in some professed organ of independence. Not only should criticism be honest, but it should be intelligent, in order to be effective. I recently read in a religious paper an article railing at the corruption of our public life, in which it stated incidentally that the lobby was recognized as all-powerful in Washington. This is untrue. There was a day when the lobby was very important at Washington, but its influence in Congress is now very small indeed; and from a pretty intimate acquaintance with several Congresses I am entirely satisfied that there is among the members a very small proportion indeed who are corruptible, in the sense that they will let their action be influenced by money or its equivalent. Congressmen are very often demagogues; they are very often blind partisans; they are often exceedingly short-sighted, narrow-minded, and bigoted; but they are not usually corrupt; and to accuse a narrow-minded demagogue of corruption when he is perfectly honest, is merely to set him more firmly in his evil course and to help him with his constituents, who recognize that the charge is entirely unjust, and in repelling it lose sight of the man's real shortcomings. I have known more than one State legislature, more than one board of aldermen against which the charge of corruption could perfectly legitimately be brought, but it cannot be brought against Congress. Moreover these sweeping charges really do very little good. When I was in the New York legislature, one of the things that I used to mind most was the fact that at the close of every session the papers that affect morality invariably said that particular legislature was the worst legislature since the days of Tweed. The statement was not true as a rule; and, in any event, to lump all the members, good and bad, in sweeping condemnation simply hurt the good and helped the bad. Criticism should be fearless, but I again reiterate that it should be honest and should be discriminating. When it is sweeping and unintelligent, and directed against good and bad alike, or against the good and bad qualities of any man alike, it is very harmful. It tends steadily to deteriorate the character of our public men; and it tends to produce a very unwholesome spirit among young men of education, and especially among the young men in our colleges.

Against nothing is fearless and specific criticism more urgently needed than against the "spoils system," which is the degradation of American politics. And nothing is more effective in thwarting the purposes of the spoilsmen than the civil service reform. To be sure, practical politicians sneer at it. One of them even went so far as to say that civil-service reform is asking a man irrelevant questions. What more irrelevant question could there be than that of the practical politician who asks the aspirant for his political favor—"Whom did you vote for in the last election?" There is certainly nothing more interesting, from a humorous point of view, than the heads of departments urging changes to be made in their underlings, "on the score of increased efficiency" they say; when as the result of such a change the old incumbent often spends six months teaching the new incumbent how to do the work almost as well as he did himself! Occasionally the civil-service reform has been abused, but not often. Certainly the reform is needed when you contemplate the spectacle of a New York City treasurer who acknowledges his annual fees to be eighty-five thousand dollars, and who pays a deputy one thousand five hundred dollars to do his work—when you note the corruptions in the New York legislature, where one man says he has a horror of the Constitution because it prevents active benevolence, and another says that you should never allow the Constitution to come between friends! All these corruptions and vices are what every good American citizen must fight against.

Finally, the man who wishes to do his duty as a citizen in our country must be imbued through and through with the spirit of Americanism. I am not saying this as a matter of spread-eagle rhetoric: I am saying it quite soberly as a piece of matter-of-fact, common-sense advice, derived from my own experience of others. Of course, the question of Americanism has several sides. If a man is an educated man, he must show his Americanism by not getting misled into following out and trying to apply all the theories of the political thinkers of other countries, such as Germany and France, to our own entirely different conditions. He must not get a fad, for instance, about responsible government; and above all things he must not, merely because he is intelligent, or a college professor well read in political literature, try to discuss our institutions when he has had no practical knowledge of how they are worked. Again, if he is a wealthy man, a man of means and standing, he must really feel, not merely affect to feel, that no social differences obtain save such as a man can in some way himself make by his own actions. People sometimes ask me if there is not a prejudice against a man of wealth and education in ward politics.

I do not think that there is, unless the man in turn shows that he regards the facts of his having wealth and education as giving him a claim to superiority aside from the merit he is able to prove himself to have in actual service. Of course, if he feels that he ought to have a little better treatment than a carpenter, a plumber, or a butcher, who happens to stand beside him, he is going to be thrown out of the race very quickly, and probably quite roughly; and if he starts in to patronize and elaborately condescend to these men he will find that they resent this attitude even more. Do not let him think about the matter at all. Let him go into the political contest with no more thought of such matters than a college boy gives to the social standing of the members of his own and rival teams in a hotly contested football match. As soon as he begins to take an interest in politics (and he will speedily not only get interested for the sake of politics, but also take a good healthy interest in playing the game itself—an interest which is perfectly normal and praise-worthy, and to which only a prig would object), he will begin to work up the organization in the way that will be most effective, and he won't care a rap about who is put to work with him, save in so far as he is a good fellow and an efficient worker. There was one time that a number of men who think as we do here to-night (one of the number being myself) got hold of one of the assembly districts of New York, and ran it in really an ideal way, better than any other assembly district has ever been run before or since by either party. We did it by hard work and good organization; by working practically, and yet by being honest and square in motive and method: especially did we do it by all turning in as straight-out Americans without any regard to distinctions of race origin. Among the many men who did a great deal in organizing our victories was the son of a Presbyterian clergyman, the nephew of a Hebrew rabbi, and two well-known Catholic gentlemen. We also had a Columbia College professor (the stroke-oar of a university crew), a noted retail butcher, and the editor of a local German paper, various brokers, bankers, lawyers, bricklayers and a stone-mason who was particularly useful to us, although on questions of theoretic rather than applied politics he had a decidedly socialistic turn of mind.

Again, questions of race origin, like questions of creed, must not be considered: we wish to do good work, and we are all Americans, pure and simple. In the New York legislature, when it fell to my lot to choose a committee—which I always esteemed my most important duty at Albany—no less than three out of the four men I chose were of Irish birth or parentage; and three abler and more fearless and disinterested men never sat in a legislative body; while among my especial political and personal friends in that body was a gentleman from the southern tier of counties, who was, I incidentally found out, a German by birth, but who was just as straight United States as if his ancestors had come over here in the Mayflower or in Henry Hudson's yacht. Of course, none of these men of Irish or German birth would have been worth their salt had they continued to act after coming here as Irishmen or Germans, or as anything but plain straight-out Americans. We have not any room here for a divided allegiance. A man has got to be an American and nothing else; and he has no business to be mixing us up with questions of foreign politics, British or Irish, German or French, and no business to try to perpetuate their language and customs in the land of complete religious toleration and equality. If, however, he does become honestly and in good faith an American, then he is entitled to stand precisely as all other Americans stand, and it is the height of un-Americanism to discriminate against him in any way because of creed or birthplace. No spirit can be more thoroughly alien to American institutions, than the spirit of the Know-Nothings.

In facing the future and in striving, each according to the measure of his individual capacity, to work out the salvation of our land, we should be neither timid pessimists nor foolish optimists. We should recognize the dangers that exist and that threaten us: we should neither overestimate them nor shrink from them, but steadily fronting them should set to work to overcome and beat them down. Grave perils are yet to be encountered in the stormy course of the Republic—perils from political corruption, perils from individual laziness, indolence and timidity, perils springing from the greed of the unscrupulous rich, and from the anarchic violence of the thriftless and turbulent poor. There is every reason why we should recognize them, but there is no reason why we should fear them or doubt our capacity to overcome them, if only each will, according to the measure of his ability, do his full duty, and endeavor so to live as to deserve the high praise of being called a good American citizen.

FRANKLIN DELANO ROOSEVELT

First Inaugural Address (March 4, 1933)

Franklin D. Roosevelt (1882–1945) served as the governor of New York before winning a landslide victory over President Hoover in the election of 1932. Facing a nation that had already struggled through three years of depression, Roosevelt used his inaugural address to speak directly to the people, telling them of his far-reaching plans for lifting America out of its great difficulties. He took the oath of office from Chief Justice Charles Evans Hughes on the East Portico of the Capitol.

I AM CERTAIN that my fellow Americans expect that on my induction into the Presidency I will address them with a candor and a decision which the present situation of our Nation impels. This is preeminently the time to speak the truth, the whole truth, frankly and boldly. Nor need we shrink from honestly facing conditions in our country today. This great Nation will endure as it has endured, will revive and will prosper. So, first of all, let me assert my firm belief that the only thing we have to fear is fear itself–nameless, unreasoning, unjustified terror which paralyzes needed efforts to convert retreat into advance. In every dark hour of our national life a leadership of frankness and vigor has met with that understanding and support of the people themselves which is essential to victory. I am convinced that you will again give that support to leadership in these critical days.

In such a spirit on my part and on yours we face our common difficulties. They concern, thank God, only material things. Values have shrunken to fantastic levels; taxes have risen; our ability to pay has fallen; government of all kinds is faced by serious curtailment of income; the means of exchange are frozen in the currents of trade; the withered leaves of industrial enterprise lie on every side; farmers find no markets for their produce; the savings of many years in thousands of families are gone.

More important, a host of unemployed citizens face the grim problem of existence, and an equally great number toil with little return. Only a foolish optimist can deny the dark realities of the moment.

Yet our distress comes from no failure of substance. We are stricken by no plague of locusts. Compared with the perils which our forefathers conquered because they believed and were not afraid, we have still much to be thankful for. Nature still offers her bounty and human efforts have multiplied it. Plenty is at our doorstep, but a generous use of it languishes in the very sight of the supply. Primarily this is because the rulers of the exchange of mankind's goods have failed, through their own stubbornness and their own incompetence, have admitted their failure, and abdicated. Practices of the unscrupulous money changers stand indicted in the court of public opinion, rejected by the hearts and minds of men.

True they have tried, but their efforts have been cast in the pattern of an outworn tradition. Faced by failure of credit they have proposed only the lending of more money. Stripped of the lure of profit by which to induce our people to follow their false leadership, they have resorted to exhortations, pleading tearfully for restored confidence. They know only the rules of a generation of self-seekers. They have no vision, and when there is no vision the people perish.

The money changers have fled from their high seats in the temple of our civilization. We may now restore that temple to the ancient truths. The measure of the restoration lies in the extent to which we apply social values more noble than mere monetary profit.

Happiness lies not in the mere possession of money; it lies in the joy of achievement, in the thrill of creative effort. The joy and moral stimulation of work no longer must be forgotten in the mad chase of evanescent profits. These dark days will be worth all they cost us if they teach us that our true destiny is not to be ministered unto but to minister to ourselves and to our fellow men.

Recognition of the falsity of material wealth as the standard of success goes hand in hand with the abandonment of the false belief that public office and high political position are to be valued only by the standards of pride of place and personal profit; and there must be an end to a conduct in banking and in business which too often has given to a sacred trust the likeness of callous and selfish wrongdoing. Small wonder that confidence languishes, for it thrives only on honesty, on honor, on the sacredness of obligations, on faithful protection, on unselfish performance; without them it cannot live.

Restoration calls, however, not for changes in ethics alone. This Nation asks for action, and action now.

Our greatest primary task is to put people to work. This is no unsolvable problem if we face it wisely and courageously. It can be accomplished in part by direct recruiting by the Government itself, treating the task as we would treat the emergency of a war, but at the same time, through this employment, accomplishing greatly needed projects to stimulate and reorganize the use of our natural resources.

Hand in hand with this we must frankly recognize the overbalance of population in our industrial centers and, by engaging on a national scale in a redistribution, endeavor to provide a better use of the land for those best fitted for the land. The task can be helped by definite efforts to raise the values of agricultural products and with this the power to purchase the output of our cities. It can be helped by preventing realistically the tragedy of the growing loss through foreclosure of our small homes and our farms. It can be helped by insistence that the Federal, State, and local governments act forthwith on the demand that their cost be drastically reduced. It can be helped by the unifying of relief activities which today are often scattered, uneconomical, and unequal. It can be helped by national planning for and supervision of all forms of transportation and of communications and other utilities which have a definitely public character. There are many ways in which it can be helped, but it can never be helped merely by talking about it. We must act and act quickly.

Finally, in our progress toward a resumption of work we require two safeguards against a return of the evils of the old order; there must be a strict supervision of all banking and credits and investments; there must be an end to speculation with other people's money, and there must be provision for an adequate but sound currency.

There are the lines of attack. I shall presently urge upon a new Congress in special session detailed measures for their fulfillment, and I shall seek the immediate assistance of the several States.

Through this program of action we address ourselves to putting our own national house in order and making income balance outgo. Our international trade relations, though vastly important, are in point of time and necessity secondary to the establishment of a sound national economy. I favor as a practical policy the putting of first things first. I shall spare no effort to restore world trade by international economic readjustment, but the emergency at home cannot wait on that accomplishment.

The basic thought that guides these specific means of national recovery is not narrowly nationalistic. It is the insistence, as a first consideration, upon the interdependence of the various elements in all parts of the United States—a recognition of the old and permanently important manifestation of the American spirit of the pioneer. It is the way to recovery. It is the immediate way. It is the strongest assurance that the recovery will endure.

In the field of world policy I would dedicate this Nation to the policy of the good neighbor—the neighbor who resolutely respects himself and, because he does so, respects the rights of others—the neighbor who respects his obligations and respects the sanctity of his agreements in and with a world of neighbors.

If I read the temper of our people correctly, we now realize as we have never realized before our interdependence on each other; that we can not merely take but we must give as well; that if we are to go forward, we must move as a trained and loyal army willing to sacrifice for the good of a common discipline, because without such discipline no progress is made, no leadership becomes effective. We are, I know, ready and willing to submit our lives and property to such discipline, because it makes possible a leadership which aims at a larger good. This I propose to offer, pledging that the larger purposes will bind upon us all as a sacred obligation with a unity of duty hitherto evoked only in time of armed strife.

With this pledge taken, I assume unhesitatingly the leadership of this great army of our people dedicated to a disciplined attack upon our common problems.

Action in this image and to this end is feasible under the form of government which we have inherited from our ancestors. Our Constitution is so simple and practical that it is possible always to meet extraordinary needs by changes in emphasis and arrangement without loss of essential form. That is why our constitutional system has proved itself the most superbly enduring political mechanism the modern world has produced. It has met every stress of vast expansion of territory, of foreign wars, of bitter internal strife, of world relations.

It is to be hoped that the normal balance of executive and legislative authority may be wholly adequate to meet the unprecedented task before us. But it may be that an unprecedented demand and need for undelayed action may call for temporary departure from that normal balance of public procedure.

I am prepared under my constitutional duty to recommend the measures that a stricken nation in the midst of a stricken world may require. These measures, or such other measures as the Congress may build out of its experience and wisdom, I shall seek, within my constitutional authority, to bring to speedy adoption.

But in the event that the Congress shall fail to take one of these two courses, and in the event that the national emergency is still critical, I shall not evade the clear course of duty that will then confront me. I shall ask the Congress for the one remaining instrument to meet the crisis—broad Executive power to wage a war against the emergency, as great as the power that would be given to me if we were in fact invaded by a foreign foe.

For the trust reposed in me I will return the courage and the devotion that befit the time. I can do no less.

We face the arduous days that lie before us in the warm courage of the national unity; with the clear consciousness of seeking old and precious moral values; with the clean satisfaction that comes from the stem performance of duty by old and young alike. We aim at the assurance of a rounded and permanent national life.

We do not distrust the future of essential democracy. The people of the United States have not failed. In their need they have registered a mandate that they want direct, vigorous action. They have asked for discipline and direction under leadership. They have made me the present instrument of their wishes. In the spirit of the gift I take it.

In this dedication of a Nation we humbly ask the blessing of God. May He protect each and every one of us. May He guide me in the days to come.

KING GEORGE VI

"The Outbreak of World War II" (September 3, 1939)

George VI (1895–1952) ascended to to the throne of England after the unexpected abdication of his older brother Edward in 1936. Although he never expected to be king, George VI reigned during one of England's most trying periods, seeing the nation through the Second World War and much of its transition from an Empire to a Commonwealth of Nations. After struggling for most of his life with a stammer, George VI disliked public speaking, though he rose to the occasion when England was drawn into war by the Nazis. In this moving address, broadcast from Buckingham Palace, George VI urges his countrymen to remain strong and resolute during the difficult days ahead.

IN THIS GRAVE HOUR, perhaps the most fateful in our history, I send to every household of my peoples, both at home and overseas, this message, spoken with the same depth of feeling for each one of you as if I were able to cross your threshold and speak to you myself.

For the second time in the lives of most of us we are at war. Over and over again we have tried to find a peaceful way out of the differences between ourselves and those who are now our enemies. But it has been in vain. We have been forced into a conflict. For we are called, with our allies, to meet the challenge of a principle which, if it were to prevail, would be fatal to any civilised order in the world.

It is the principle which permits a state, in the selfish pursuit of power, to disregard its treaties and its solemn pledges; which sanctions the use of force, or threat of force, against the sovereignty and independence of other states. Such a principle, stripped of all disguise, is surely the mere primitive doctrine that might is right; and if this principle were established throughout the world, the freedom of our own country and of the whole British Commonwealth of Nations would be in danger. But far more than this—the peoples of the world would be kept in the bondage of fear, and all hopes of settled peace and of the security of justice and liberty among nations would be ended.

This is the ultimate issue which confronts us. For the sake of all that we ourselves hold dear, and of the world's order and peace, it is unthinkable that we should refuse to meet the challenge.

It is to this high purpose that I now call my people at home and my peoples across the seas, who will make our cause their own. I ask them to stand calm, firm, and united in this time of trial. The task will be hard. There may be dark days ahead, and war can no longer be confined to the battlefield. But we can only do the right as we see the right, and reverently commit our cause to God. If one and all we keep resolutely faithful to it, ready for whatever service or sacrifice it may demand, then, with God's help, we shall prevail.

May He bless and keep us all.

WINSTON CHURCHILL

"We Shall Fight on the Beaches" (June 4, 1940)

Winston Churchill (1874–1965) became the British prime minister on May 10, 1940, just eight months after the beginning of World War II, and on the same day that Germany began its invasion of France. A few weeks later, Churchill addressed the House of Commons to report that more than 300,000 Allied troops had been evacuated from the French city of Dunkirk, and that the collapse of France had become a real possibility. In what is widely considered one of his finest oratories, Churchill went on to declare that despite what may happen in the days ahead, Britain would defend itself and attain victory against the Nazis, no matter what the cost.

FROM THE MOMENT that the French defenses at Sedan and on the Meuse were broken at the end of the second week of May, only a rapid retreat to Amiens and the south could have saved the British and French Armies who had entered Belgium at the appeal of the Belgian King; but this strategic fact was not immediately realized. The French High Command hoped they would be able to close the gap, and the Armies of the north were under their orders. Moreover, a retirement of this kind would have involved almost certainly the destruction of the fine Belgian Army of over 20 divisions and the abandonment of the whole of Belgium. Therefore, when the force and scope of the German penetration were realized and when a new French Generalissimo, General Weygand, assumed command in place of General Gamelin, an effort was made by the French and British Armies in Belgium to keep on holding the right hand of the Belgians and to give their own right hand to a newly created French Army which was to have advanced across the Somme in great strength to grasp it.

However, the German eruption swept like a sharp scythe around the right and rear of the Armies of the north. Eight or nine armored divisions, each of about four hundred armored vehicles of different kinds, but carefully assorted to be complementary and divisible into small self-contained units, cut off all communications between us and the main French Armies. It severed our own communications for food and ammunition, which ran first to Amiens and afterwards through Abbeville, and it shore its way up the coast to Boulogne and Calais, and almost to Dunkirk. Behind this armored and mechanized onslaught came a number of German divisions in lorries, and behind them again there plodded comparatively slowly the dull brute mass of the ordinary German Army and German people, always so ready to be led to the trampling down in other lands of liberties and comforts which they have never known in their own.

I have said this armored scythe-stroke almost reached Dunkirk—almost but not quite. Boulogne and Calais were the scenes of desperate fighting. The Guards defended Boulogne for a while and were then withdrawn by orders from this country. The Rifle Brigade, the 60th Rifles, and the Queen Victoria's Rifles, with a battalion of British tanks and 1,000 Frenchmen, in all about four thousand strong, defended Calais to the last. The British Brigadier was given an hour to surrender. He spurned the offer, and four days of intense street fighting passed before silence reigned over Calais, which marked the end of a memorable resistance. Only 30 unwounded survivors were brought off by the Navy, and we do not know the fate of their comrades. Their sacrifice, however, was not in vain. At least two armored divisions, which otherwise would have been turned against the British Expeditionary Force, had to be sent to overcome them. They have added another page to the glories of the light divisions, and the time gained enabled the Graveline water lines to be flooded and to be held by the French troops.

Thus it was that the port of Dunkirk was kept open. When it was found impossible for the Armies of the north to reopen their communications to Amiens with the main French Armies, only one choice remained. It seemed, indeed, forlorn. The Belgian, British and French Armies were almost surrounded. Their sole line of retreat was to a single port and to its neighboring beaches. They were pressed on every side by heavy attacks and far outnumbered in the air.

When, a week ago today, I asked the House to fix this afternoon as the occasion for a statement, I feared it would be my hard lot to announce the greatest military disaster in our long history. I thought—and some good judges agreed with me—that perhaps 20,000 or 30,000 men might be re-embarked. But it certainly seemed that the whole of the French First Army and the whole of the British Expeditionary Force north of the Amiens-Abbeville gap would be broken up in the open field or else would have to capitulate for lack of food and ammunition. These were the hard and heavy tidings for which I called upon the House and the nation to prepare themselves a week ago. The whole root and core and brain of the British Army, on which and around which we were to build, and are to build, the great British Armies in the later years of the war, seemed about to perish upon the field or to be led into an ignominious and starving captivity.

That was the prospect a week ago. But another blow which might well have proved final was yet to fall upon us. The King of the Belgians had called upon us to come to his aid. Had not this Ruler and his Government severed themselves from the Allies, who rescued their country from extinction in the late war, and had they not sought refuge in what was proved to be a fatal neutrality, the French and British Armies might well at the outset have saved not only Belgium but perhaps even Poland. Yet at the last moment, when Belgium was already invaded, King Leopold called upon us to come to his aid, and even at the last moment we came. He and his brave, efficient Army, nearly half a million strong, guarded our left flank and thus kept open our only line of retreat to the sea. Suddenly, without prior consultation, with the least possible notice, without the advice of his Ministers and upon his own personal act, he sent a plenipotentiary to the German Command, surrendered his Army, and exposed our whole flank and means of retreat.

I asked the House a week ago to suspend its judgment because the facts were not clear, but I do not feel that any reason now exists why we should not form our own opinions upon this pitiful episode. The surrender of the Belgian Army compelled the British at the shortest notice to cover a flank to the sea more than 30 miles in length. Otherwise all would have been cut off, and all would have shared the fate to which King Leopold had condemned the finest Army his country had ever formed. So in doing this and in exposing this flank, as anyone who followed the operations on the map will see, contact was lost between the British and two out of the three corps forming the First French Army, who were still farther from the coast than we were, and it seemed impossible that any large number of Allied troops could reach the coast.

The enemy attacked on all sides with great strength and fierceness, and their main power, the power of their far more numerous Air Force, was thrown into the battle or else concentrated upon Dunkirk and the beaches. Pressing in upon the narrow exit, both from the east and from the west, the enemy began to fire with cannon upon the beaches by which alone the shipping could approach or depart. They sowed magnetic mines in the channels and seas; they sent repeated waves of hostile aircraft, sometimes more than a hundred strong in one formation, to cast their bombs upon the single pier that remained, and upon the sand dunes upon which the troops had their eyes for shelter. Their U-boats, one of which was sunk, and their motor launches took their toll of the vast traffic which now began. For four or five days an intense struggle reigned. All their armored divisions—or what was left of them—together with great masses of infantry and artillery, hurled themselves in vain upon the ever-narrowing, ever-contracting appendix within which the British and French Armies fought.

Meanwhile, the Royal Navy, with the willing help of countless merchant seamen, strained every nerve to embark the British and Allied troops; 220 light warships and 650 other vessels were engaged. They had to operate upon the difficult coast, often in adverse weather, under an almost ceaseless hail of bombs and an increasing concentration of artillery fire. Nor were the seas, as I have said, themselves free from mines and torpedoes. It was in conditions such as these that our men carried on, with little or no rest, for days and nights on end, making trip after trip across the dangerous waters, bringing with them always men whom they had rescued. The numbers they have brought back are the measure of their devotion and their courage. The hospital ships, which brought off many thousands of British and French wounded, being so plainly marked were a special target for Nazi bombs; but the men and women on board them never faltered in their duty.

Meanwhile, the Royal Air Force, which had already been intervening in the battle, so far as its range would allow, from home bases, now used part of its main metropolitan fighter strength, and struck at the German bombers and at the fighters which in large numbers protected them. This struggle was protracted and fierce. Suddenly the scene has cleared, the crash and thunder has for the moment—but only for the moment—died away. A miracle of deliverance, achieved by valor, by perseverance, by perfect discipline, by faultless service, by resource, by skill, by unconquerable fidelity, is manifest to us all. The enemy was hurled back by the retreating British and French troops. He was so roughly handled that he did not hurry their departure seriously. The Royal Air Force engaged the main strength of the German Air Force, and inflicted upon them losses of at least four to one; and the Navy, using nearly 1,000 ships of all kinds, carried over 335,000 men, French and British, out of the jaws of death and shame, to their native land and to the tasks which lie immediately ahead. We must be very careful not to assign to this deliverance the attributes of a victory. Wars are not won by evacuations. But there was a victory inside this deliverance, which should be noted. It was gained by the Air Force. Many of our soldiers coming back have not seen the Air Force at work; they saw only the bombers which escaped its protective attack. They underrate its achievements. I have heard much talk of this; that is why I go out of my way to say this. I will tell you about it.

This was a great trial of strength between the British and German Air Forces. Can you conceive a greater objective for the Germans in the air than to make evacuation from these beaches impossible, and to sink all these ships which were displayed, almost to the extent of thousands? Could there have been an objective of greater military importance and significance for the whole purpose of the war than this? They tried hard, and they were beaten back; they were frustrated in their task. We got the Army away; and they have paid fourfold for any losses which they have inflicted. Very large formations of German aeroplanes—and we know that they are a very brave race—have turned on several occasions from the attack of one-quarter of their number of the Royal Air Force, and have dispersed in different directions. Twelve aeroplanes have been hunted by two. One aeroplane was driven into the water and cast away by the mere charge of a British aeroplane, which had no more ammunition. All of our types—the Hurricane, the Spitfire and the new Defiant—and all our pilots have been vindicated as superior to what they have at present to face.

When we consider how much greater would be our advantage in defending the air above this Island against an overseas attack, I must say that I find in these facts a sure basis upon which practical and reassuring thoughts may rest. I will pay my tribute to these young airmen. The great French Army was very largely, for the time being, cast back and disturbed by the onrush of a few thousands of armored vehicles. May it not also be that the cause of civilization itself will be defended by the skill and devotion of a few thousand airmen? There never has been, I suppose, in all the world, in all the history of war, such an opportunity for youth. The Knights of the Round Table, the Crusaders, all fall back into the past—not only distant but prosaic; these young men, going forth every morn to guard their native land and all that we stand for, holding in their hands these instruments of colossal and shattering power, of whom it may be said that

Every morn brought forth a noble chance
And every chance brought forth a noble knight,

deserve our gratitude, as do all the brave men who, in so many ways and on so many occasions, are ready, and continue ready to give life and all for their native land.

I return to the Army. In the long series of very fierce battles, now on this front, now on that, fighting on three fronts at once, battles fought by two or three divisions against an equal or somewhat larger number of the enemy, and fought fiercely on some of the old grounds that so many of us knew so well—in these battles our losses in men have exceeded 30,000 killed, wounded and missing. I take occasion to express the sympathy of the House to all who have suffered bereavement or who are still anxious. The President of the Board of Trade [Sir Andrew Duncan] is not here today. His son has been killed, and many in the House have felt the pangs of affliction in the sharpest form. But I will say this about the missing: We have had a large number of wounded come home safely to this country, but I would say about the missing that there may be very many reported missing who will come back home, some day, in one way or another. In the confusion of this fight it is inevitable that many have been left in positions where honor required no further resistance from them.

Against this loss of over 30,000 men, we can set a far heavier loss certainly inflicted upon the enemy. But our losses in material are enormous. We have perhaps lost one-third of the men we lost in the opening days of the battle of 21st March, 1918, but we have lost nearly as many guns—nearly one thousand—and all our transport, all the armored vehicles that were with the Army in the north. This loss will impose a further delay on the expansion of our military strength. That expansion had not been proceeding as far as we had hoped. The best of all we had to give had gone to the British Expeditionary Force, and although they had not the numbers of tanks and some articles of equipment which were desirable, they were a very well and finely equipped Army. They had the first-fruits of all that our industry had to give, and that is gone. And now here is this further delay. How long it will be, how long it will last, depends upon the exertions which we make in this Island. An effort the like of which has never been seen in our records is now being made. Work is proceeding everywhere, night and day, Sundays and week days. Capital and Labor have cast aside their interests, rights, and customs and put them into the common stock. Already the flow of munitions has leaped forward. There is no reason why we should not in a few months overtake the sudden and serious loss that has come upon us, without retarding the development of our general program.

Nevertheless, our thankfulness at the escape of our Army and so many men, whose loved ones have passed through an agonizing week, must not blind us to the fact that what has happened in France and Belgium is a colossal military disaster. The French Army has been weakened, the Belgian Army has been lost, a large part of those fortified lines upon which so much faith had been reposed is gone, many valuable mining districts and factories have passed into the enemy's possession, the whole of the Channel ports are in his hands, with all the tragic consequences that follow from that, and we must expect another blow to be struck almost immediately at us or at France. We are told that Herr Hitler has a plan for invading the British Isles. This has often been thought of before. When Napoleon lay at Boulogne for a year with his flat-bottomed boats and his Grand Army, he was told by someone: "There are bitter weeds in England." There are certainly a great many more of them since the British Expeditionary Force returned.

The whole question of home defense against invasion is, of course, powerfully affected by the fact that we have for the time being in this Island incomparably more powerful military forces than we have ever had at any moment in this war or the last. But this will not continue. We shall not be content with a defensive war. We have our duty to our Ally. We have to reconstitute and build up the British Expeditionary Force once again, under its gallant Commander-in-Chief, Lord Gort. All this is in train; but in the interval we must put our defenses in this Island into such a high state of organization that the fewest possible numbers will be required to give effective security and that the largest possible potential of offensive effort may be realized. On this we are now engaged. It will be very convenient, if it be the desire of the House, to enter upon this subject in a secret Session. Not that the government would necessarily be able to reveal in very great detail military secrets, but we like to have our discussions free, without the restraint imposed by the fact that they will be read the next day by the enemy; and the Government would benefit by views freely expressed in all parts of the House by Members with their knowledge of so many different parts of the country. I understand that some request is to be made upon this subject, which will be readily acceded to by His Majesty's Government.

We have found it necessary to take measures of increasing stringency, not only against enemy aliens and suspicious characters of other nationalities, but also against British subjects who may become a danger or a nuisance should the war be transported to the United Kingdom. I know there are a great many people affected by the orders which we have made who are the passionate enemies of Nazi Germany. I am very sorry for them, but we cannot, at the present time and under the present stress, draw all the distinctions which we should like to do. If parachute landings were attempted and fierce fighting attendant upon them followed, these unfortunate people would be far better out of the way, for their own sakes as well as for ours. There is, however, another class, for which I feel not the slightest sympathy. Parliament has given us the powers to put down Fifth Column activities with a strong hand, and we shall use those powers subject to the supervision and correction of the House, without the slightest hesitation until we are satisfied, and more than satisfied, that this malignancy in our midst has been effectively stamped out.

Turning once again, and this time more generally, to the question of invasion, I would observe that there has never been a period in all these long centuries of which we boast when an absolute guarantee against invasion, still less against serious raids, could have been given to our people. In the days of Napoleon the same wind which would have carried his transports across the Channel might have driven away the blockading fleet. There was always the chance, and it is that chance which has excited and befooled the imaginations of many Continental tyrants. Many are the tales that are told. We are assured that novel methods will be adopted, and when we see the originality of malice, the ingenuity of aggression, which our enemy displays, we may certainly prepare ourselves for every kind of novel stratagem and every kind of brutal and treacherous maneuver. I think that no idea is so outlandish that it should not be considered and viewed with a searching, but at the same time, I hope, with a steady eye. We must never forget the solid assurances of sea power and those which belong to air power if it can be locally exercised.

I have, myself, full confidence that if all do their duty, if nothing is neglected, and if the best arrangements are made, as they are being made, we shall prove ourselves once again able to defend our Island home, to ride out the storm of war, and to outlive the menace of tyranny, if necessary for years, if necessary alone. At any rate, that is what we are going to try to do. That is the resolve of His Majesty's Government—every man of them. That is the will of Parliament and the nation. The British Empire and the French Republic, linked together in their cause and in their need, will defend to the death their native soil, aiding each other like good comrades to the utmost of their strength. Even though large tracts of Europe and many old and famous States have fallen or may fall into the grip of the Gestapo and all the odious apparatus of Nazi rule, we shall not flag or fail. We shall go on to the end, we shall fight in France, we shall fight on the seas and oceans, we shall fight with growing confidence and growing strength in the air, we shall defend our Island, whatever the cost may be, we shall fight on the beaches, we shall fight on the landing grounds, we shall fight in the fields and in the streets, we shall fight in the hills; we shall never surrender, and even if, which I do not for a moment believe, this Island or a large part of it were subjugated and starving, then our Empire beyond the seas, armed and guarded by the British Fleet, would carry on the struggle, until, in God's good time, the New World, with all its power and might, steps forth to the rescue and the liberation of the old.

MAHATMA GANDHI

"Quit India"
(August 8, 1942)

Although Mahatma Gandhi (1869–1948) first began to work for India's freedom from British rule in 1915, it was not until Britain was embroiled in World War II that the goal of Indian independence finally came within reach. In August of 1942, the All India Congress Committee gathered in Gowalia Tank Maidan, a park in Bombay, to demonstrate against British rule and formally endorse the Quit India movement, which called for an immediate end to British Imperialism. Gandhi's powerful address to the assembled demonstrators called for determined passive resistance and would later become a powerful influence on the speeches and writings of Martin Luther King, Jr.

BEFORE YOU DISCUSS the resolution, let me place before you one or two things. I want you to understand two things very clearly and to consider them from the same point of view from which I am placing them before you. I ask you to consider it from my point of view, because if you approve of it, you will be enjoined to carry out all I say. It will be a great responsibility. There are people who ask me whether I am the same man that I was in 1920, or whether there has been any change in me. You are right in asking that question.

Let me, however, hasten to assure that I am the same Gandhi as I was in 1920. I have not changed in any fundamental respect. I attach the same importance to nonviolence that I did then. If at all, my emphasis on it has grown stronger. There is no real contradiction between the present resolution and my previous writings and utterances.

Occasions like the present do not occur in everybody's and, but rarely, in anybody's life. I want you to know and feel that there is nothing but purest Ahimsa in all that I am saying and doing today. The draft resolution of the working committee is based on Ahimsa. The contemplated struggle, similarly, has its roots in Ahimsa. If, therefore, there is any among you who has lost faith in Ahimsa or is wearied of it, let him not vote for this resolution.

Let me explain my position clearly. God has vouchsafed to me a priceless gift in the weapon of Ahimsa. I and my Ahimsa are on our trail today. If in the present crisis, when the earth is being scorched by the flames of Himsa and crying for deliverance, I failed to make use of the God-given talent, God will not forgive me and I shall be judged un-wrongly of the great gift. I must act now. I may not hesitate and merely look on when Russia and China are threatened.

Ours is not a drive for power, but purely a nonviolent fight for India's independence. In a violent struggle, a successful general has been often known to effect a military coup and to set up a dictatorship. But under the Congress scheme of things, essentially nonviolent as it is; there can be no room for dictatorship. A nonviolent soldier of freedom will covet nothing for himself; he fights only for the freedom of his country. The Congress is unconcerned as to who will rule when freedom is attained. The power, when it comes, will belong to the people of India, and it will be for them to decide to whom it placed in the entrusted. May be that the reins will be placed in the hands of the Parsis, for instance—as I would love to see happen—or they may be handed to some others whose names are not heard in the Congress today. It will not be for you then to object saying, "This community is microscopic. That party did not play its due part in the freedom's struggle; why should it have all the power?" Ever since its inception, the Congress has kept itself meticulously free of the communal taint. It has thought always in terms of the whole nation and has acted accordingly....

I know how imperfect our Ahimsa is and how far away we are still from the ideal, but in Ahimsa there is no final failure or defeat. I have faith, therefore, that if, in spite of our shortcomings, the big thing does happen, it will be because God wanted to help us by crowning with success our silent, unremitting Sadhana for the last twenty-two years.

I believe that in the history of the world, there has not been a more genuinely democratic struggle for freedom than ours. I read Carlyle's French Revolution while I was in prison, and Pandit Jawaharlal has told me something about the Russian revolution. But it is my conviction that inasmuch as these struggles were fought with the weapon of violence, they failed to realise the democratic ideal. In the democracy which I have envisaged—a democracy established by non-violence—there will be equal freedom for all. Everybody will be his own master. It is to join a struggle for such democracy that I invite you today. Once you realize this, you will forget the differences between the Hindus and Muslims, and think of yourselves as Indians only, engaged in the common struggle for independence.

Then, there is the question of your attitude towards the British. I have noticed that there is hatred towards the British among the people. The people say they are disgusted with their behaviour. The people make no distinction between British imperialism and the British people. To them, the two are one. This hatred would even make them welcome the Japanese. It is most dangerous. It means that they will exchange one slavery for another. We must get rid of this feeling. Our quarrel is not with the British people. We fight their imperialism. The proposal for the withdrawal of British power did not come out of anger. It came to enable India to play its due part at the present critical juncture. It is not a happy position for a big country like India to be merely helping with money and material obtained willy-nilly from her while the United Nations are conducting the war. We cannot evoke the true spirit of sacrifice and valour, so long as we are not free. I know the British Government will not be able to withhold freedom from us when we have made enough self-sacrifice. We must, therefore, purge ourselves of hatred. Speaking for myself, I can say that I have never felt any hatred. As a matter of fact, I feel myself to be a greater friend of the British now than ever before. One reason is that they are today in distress. My very friendship, therefore, demands that I should try to save them from their mistakes. As I view the situation—they are on the brink of an abyss. It, therefore, becomes my duty to warn them of their danger even though it may, for the time being, anger them to the point of cutting off the friendly hand that is stretched out to help them. People may laugh. Nevertheless, that is my claim. At a time when I may have to launch the biggest struggle of my life, I may not harbour hatred against anybody.

ELEANOR ROOSEVELT

"On the Adoption of the Universal Declaration of Human Rights" (December 9, 1948)

Anna Eleanor Roosevelt (1884–1962) served as First Lady of the United States from 1933–1945, during which time she used her influence to support her husband's New Deal policies, while advocating for civil rights and women's equality. Her great work for human rights around the world led Harry Truman to call her "First Lady of the World." This impassioned and historic speech was delivered before the United Nations General Assembly on December 9, 1948.

THE LONG AND METICULOUS study and debate of which this Universal Declaration of Human Rights is the product means that it reflects the composite views of the many men and governments who have contributed to its formulation. Not every man nor every government can have what he wants in a document of this kind. There are of course particular provisions in the Declaration before us with which we are not fully satisfied. I have no doubt this is true of other delegations, and it would still be true if we continued our labors over many years. Taken as a whole the Delegation of the United States believes that this is a good document—even a great document—and we propose to give it our full support. The position of the United States on the various parts of the Declaration is a matter of record in the Third Committee. I shall not burden the Assembly, and particularly my colleagues of the Third Committee, with a restatement of that position here.

I should like to comment briefly on the amendments proposed by the Soviet delegation. The language of these amendments has been dressed up somewhat, but the substance is the same as the amendments which were offered by the Soviet delegation in committee and rejected after exhaustive discussion. Substantially the same amendments have been previously considered and rejected in the Human Rights Commission. We in the United States admire those who fight for their convictions, and the Soviet delegation has fought for their convictions. But in the older democracies we have learned that sometimes we bow to the will of the majority. In doing that, we do not give up our convictions. We continue sometimes to persuade, and eventually we may be successful. But we know that we have to work together and we have to progress. So, we believe that when we have made a good fight, and the majority is against us, it is perhaps better tactics to try to cooperate.

I feel bound to say that I think perhaps it is somewhat of an imposition on this Assembly to have these amendments offered again here, and I am confident that they will be rejected without debate.

The first two paragraphs of the amendment to article 3 deal with the question of minorities, which committee 3 decided required further study, and has recommended, in a separate resolution, their reference to the Economic and Social Council and the Human Rights Commission. As set out in the Soviet amendment, this provision clearly states "group," and not "individual," rights.

The Soviet amendment to article 20 is obviously a very restrictive statement of the right to freedom of opinion and expression. It sets up standards which would enable any state practically to deny all freedom of opinion and expression without violating the article. It introduces the terms "democratic view," "democratic systems," "democratic state," and "fascism," which we know all too well from debates in this Assembly over the past two years on warmongering and related subjects are liable to the most flagrant abuse and diverse interpretations.

The statement of the Soviet delegate here tonight is a very good case in point on this. The Soviet amendment of article 22 introduces new elements into the article without improving the committed text and again introduces specific reference to "discrimination." As was repeatedly pointed out in committee 3, the question of discrimination is comprehensively covered in article 2 of the Declaration, so that its restatement elsewhere is completely unnecessary and also has the effect of weakening the comprehensive principles stated in article 2. The new article proposed by the Soviet delegation is but a restatement of State obligation, which the Soviet delegation attempted to introduce into practically every article in the Declaration. It would convert the Declaration into a document stating obligations on states, thereby changing completely its character as a statement of principles to serve as a common standard of achievement for the members of the United Nations.

The Soviet proposal for deferring consideration of the Declaration to the 4th session of the Assembly requires no comment. An identical text was rejected in committee 3 by a vote of 6 in favor and 26 against. We are all agreed, I am sure, that the Declaration, which has been worked on with such great effort and devotion, and over such a long period of time, must be approved by this Assembly at this session.

Certain provisions of the Declaration are stated in such broad terms as to be acceptable only because of the provisions in article 30 providing for limitation on the exercise of the rights for the purpose of meeting the requirements of morality, public order, and the general welfare. An example of this is the provision that everyone has the right to equal access to the public service in his country. The basic principle of equality and of nondiscrimination as to public employment is sound, but it cannot be accepted without limitation. My government, for example, would consider that this is unquestionably subject to limitation in the interest of public order and the general welfare. It would not consider that the exclusion from public employment of persons holding subversive political beliefs and not loyal to the basic principles and practices of the constitution and laws of the country would in any way infringe upon this right.

Likewise, my government has made it clear in the course of the development of the Declaration that it does not consider that the economic and social and cultural rights stated in the Declaration imply an obligation on governments to assure the enjoyment of these rights by direct governmental action. This was made quite clear in the Human Rights Commission text of article 23 which served as a so-called "umbrella" article to the articles on economic and social rights. We consider that the principle has not been affected by the fact that this article no longer contains a reference to the articles which follow it. This in no way affects our whole-hearted support for the basic principles of economic, social, and cultural rights set forth in these articles.

In giving our approval to the Declaration today it is of primary importance that we keep clearly in mind the basic character of the document. It is not a treaty; it is not an international agreement. It is not and does not purport to be a statement of law or of legal obligation. It is a Declaration of basic principles of human rights and freedoms, to be stamped with the approval of the General Assembly by formal vote of its members, and to serve as a common standard of achievement for all peoples of all nations.

We stand today at the threshold of a great event both in the life of the United Nations and in the life of mankind. This Universal Declaration of Human Rights may well become the international Magna Carta of all men everywhere. We hope its proclamation by the General Assembly will be an event comparable to the proclamation of the Declaration of the Rights of Man by the French people in 1789, the adoption of the Bill of Rights by the people of the United States, and the adoption of comparable declarations at different times in other countries.

At a time when there are so many issues on which we find it difficult to reach a common basis of agreement, it is a significant fact that 58 states have found such a large measure of agreement in the complex field of human rights. This must be taken as testimony of our common aspiration first voiced in the Charter of the United Nations to lift men everywhere to a higher standard of life and to a greater enjoyment of freedom. Man's desire for peace lies behind this Declaration. The realization that the flagrant violation of human rights by Nazi and Fascist countries sowed the seeds of the last world war has supplied the impetus for the work which brings us to the moment of achievement here today.

In a recent speech in Canada, Gladstone Murray said:

> *The central fact is that man is fundamentally a moral being, that the light we have is imperfect does not matter so long as we are always trying to improve it. . . we are equal in sharing the moral freedom that distinguishes us as men. Man's status makes each individual an end in himself. No man is by nature simply the servant of the state or of another man. . . the ideal and fact of freedom—and not technology—are the true distinguishing marks of our civilization.*

This Declaration is based upon the spiritual fact that man must have freedom in which to develop his full stature and through common effort to raise the level of human dignity. We have much to do to fully achieve and to assure the rights set forth in this Declaration. But having them put before us with the moral backing of 58 nations will be a great step forward.

As we here bring to fruition our labors on this Declaration of Human Rights, we must at the same time rededicate ourselves to the unfinished task which lies before us. We can now move on with new courage and inspiration to the completion of an international covenant on human rights and of measures for the implementation of human rights.

In conclusion, I feel that I cannot do better than to repeat the call to action by Secretary Marshall in his opening statement to this Assembly:

> *Let this third regular session of the General Assembly approve by an overwhelming majority the Declaration of Human Rights as a standard of conduct for all; and let us, as Members of the United Nations, conscious of our own shortcomings and imperfections, join our effort in good faith to live up to this high standard.*

JOHN F. KENNEDY

Inaugural Address
(January 20, 1961)

John Fitzgerald Kennedy (1917–1963) defeated Republican Vice President Richard M. Nixon in the 1960 election to become the United States' first Catholic president. The morning of his inauguration, Kennedy attended Holy Trinity Catholic Church in Georgetown before traveling with President Eisenhower to the Capitol. Delivered at the height of the Cold War and amidst a struggling economy, J.F.K.'s speech focused on how Americans needed to put their country before themselves in order to overcome the nation's foreign and domestic challenges. President Kennedy served for less than three years before his assassination in Dallas on November 23, 1963.

VICE PRESIDENT JOHNSON, Mr. Speaker, Mr. Chief Justice, President Eisenhower, Vice President Nixon, President Truman, Reverend Clergy, fellow citizens:

We observe today not a victory of party but a celebration of freedom—symbolizing an end as well as a beginning—signifying renewal as well as change. For I have sworn before you and Almighty God the same solemn oath our forebears prescribed nearly a century and three quarters ago.

The world is very different now. For man holds in his mortal hands the power to abolish all forms of human poverty and all forms of human life. And yet the same revolutionary beliefs for which our forebears fought are still at issue around the globe—the belief that the rights of man come not from the generosity of the state but from the hand of God.

We dare not forget today that we are the heirs of that first revolution. Let the word go forth from this time and place, to friend and foe alike, that the torch has been passed to a new generation of Americans—born in this century, tempered by war, disciplined by a hard and bitter peace, proud of our ancient heritage—and unwilling to witness or permit the slow undoing of those human rights to which this nation has always been committed, and to which we are committed today at home and around the world.

Let every nation know, whether it wishes us well or ill, that we shall pay any price, bear any burden, meet any hardship, support any friend, oppose any foe to assure the survival and the success of liberty.

This much we pledge—and more.

To those old allies whose cultural and spiritual origins we share, we pledge the loyalty of faithful friends. United, there is little we cannot do in a host of cooperative ventures. Divided, there is little we can do—for we dare not meet a powerful challenge at odds and split asunder.

To those new states whom we welcome to the ranks of the free, we pledge our word that one form of colonial control shall not have passed away merely to be replaced by a far more iron tyranny. We shall not always expect to find them supporting our view. But we shall always hope to find them strongly supporting their own freedom—and to remember that, in the past, those who foolishly sought power by riding the back of the tiger ended up inside.

To those peoples in the huts and villages of half the globe struggling to break the bonds of mass misery, we pledge our best efforts to help them help themselves, for whatever period is required—not because the communists may be doing it, not because we seek their votes, but because it is right. If a free society cannot help the many who are poor, it cannot save the few who are rich.

To our sister republics south of our border, we offer a special pledge—to convert our good words into good deeds—in a new alliance for progress—to assist free men and free governments in casting off the chains of poverty. But this peaceful revolution of hope cannot become the prey of hostile powers. Let all our neighbors know that we shall join with them to oppose aggression or subversion anywhere in the Americas. And let every other power know that this Hemisphere intends to remain the master of its own house.

To that world assembly of sovereign states, the United Nations, our last best hope in an age where the instruments of war have far outpaced the instruments of peace, we renew our pledge of support—to prevent it from becoming merely a forum for invective—to strengthen its shield of the new and the weak—and to enlarge the area in which its writ may run.

Finally, to those nations who would make themselves our adversary, we offer not a pledge but a request: that both sides begin anew the quest for peace, before the dark powers of destruction unleashed by science engulf all humanity in planned or accidental self-destruction.

We dare not tempt them with weakness. For only when our arms are sufficient beyond doubt can we be certain beyond doubt that they will never be employed.

But neither can two great and powerful groups of nations take comfort from our present course—both sides overburdened by the cost of modern weapons, both rightly alarmed by the steady spread of the deadly atom, yet both racing to alter that uncertain balance of terror that stays the hand of mankind's final war.

So let us begin anew—remembering on both sides that civility is not a sign of weakness, and sincerity is always subject to proof. Let us never negotiate out of fear. But let us never fear to negotiate.

Let both sides explore what problems unite us instead of belaboring those problems which divide us.

Let both sides, for the first time, formulate serious and precise proposals for the inspection and control of arms—and bring the absolute power to destroy other nations under the absolute control of all nations.

Let both sides seek to invoke the wonders of science instead of its terrors. Together let us explore the stars, conquer the deserts, eradicate disease, tap the ocean depths and encourage the arts and commerce.

Let both sides unite to heed in all corners of the earth the command of Isaiah—to "undo the heavy burdens... (and) let the oppressed go free."

And if a beach-head of cooperation may push back the jungle of suspicion, let both sides join in creating a new endeavor, not a new balance of power, but a new world of law, where the strong are just and the weak secure and the peace preserved.

All this will not be finished in the first one hundred days. Nor will it be finished in the first one thousand days, nor in the life of this Administration, nor even perhaps in our lifetime on this planet. But let us begin.

In your hands, my fellow citizens, more than mine, will rest the final success or failure of our course. Since this country was founded, each generation of Americans has been summoned to give testimony to its national loyalty. The graves of young Americans who answered the call to service surround the globe.

Now the trumpet summons us again—not as a call to bear arms, though arms we need—not as a call to battle, though embattled we are—but a call to bear the burden of a long twilight struggle, year in and year out, "rejoicing in hope, patient in tribulation"—a struggle against the common enemies of man: tyranny, poverty, disease and war itself.

Can we forge against these enemies a grand and global alliance, North and South, East and West, that can assure a more fruitful life for all mankind? Will you join in that historic effort?

In the long history of the world, only a few generations have been granted the role of defending freedom in its hour of maximum danger. I do not shrink from this responsibility—I welcome it. I do not believe that any of us would exchange places with any other people or any other generation. The energy, the faith, the devotion which we bring to this endeavor will light our country and all who serve it—and the glow from that fire can truly light the world.

And so, my fellow Americans: ask not what your country can do for you—ask what you can do for your country.

My fellow citizens of the world: ask not what America will do for you, but what together we can do for the freedom of man.

Finally, whether you are citizens of America or citizens of the world, ask of us here the same high standards of strength and sacrifice which we ask of you. With a good conscience our only sure reward, with history the final judge of our deeds, let us go forth to lead the land we love, asking His blessing and His help, but knowing that here on earth God's work must truly be our own.

MARTIN LUTHER KING, JR.

"I Have A Dream" (August 28, 1963)

Perhaps the most important civil rights leader in American history, Martin Luther King, Jr., (1929–1968) preached a message of nonviolence and passive resistance as the means for achieving social change. The son of a Baptist preacher, King went on to follow in his father's footsteps, becoming minister of the Dexter Avenue Baptist Church in Montgomery, Alabama. He devoted his life to the advancement of the principles set forth in the following speech, which he delivered from the steps of the Lincoln Memorial during the outdoor gathering of the 1963 Civil Rights March, in Washington, D.C. In 1964 King was awarded the Nobel Peace Prize; he was assassinated in 1968.

I AM HAPPY to join with you today in what will go down in history as the greatest demonstration for freedom in the history of our nation.

Five score years ago, a great American, in whose symbolic shadow we stand today, signed the Emancipation Proclamation. This momentous decree came as a great beacon light of hope to millions of Negro slaves who had been seared in the flames of withering injustice. It came as a joyous daybreak to end the long night of their captivity.

But one hundred years later, the Negro still is not free. One hundred years later, the life of the Negro is still sadly crippled by the manacles of segregation and the chains of discrimination. One hundred years later, the Negro lives on a lonely island of poverty in the midst of a vast ocean of material prosperity. One hundred years later, the Negro is still languished in the corners of American society and finds himself an exile in his own land. And so we've come here today to dramatize a shameful condition.

In a sense we've come to our nation's capital to cash a check. When the architects of our republic wrote the magnificent words of the Constitution and the Declaration of Independence, they were signing a promissory note to which every American was to fall heir. This note was a promise that all men, yes, black men as well as white men, would be guaranteed the "unalienable Rights" of "Life, Liberty and the pursuit of Happiness." It is obvious today that America has defaulted on this promissory note, insofar as her citizens of color are concerned. Instead of honoring this sacred obligation, America has given the Negro people a bad check, a check which has come back marked "insufficient funds."

But we refuse to believe that the bank of justice is bankrupt. We refuse to believe that there are insufficient funds in the great vaults of opportunity of this nation. And so, we've come to cash this check, a check that will give us upon demand the riches of freedom and the security of justice.

We have also come to this hallowed spot to remind America of the fierce urgency of Now. This is no time to engage in the luxury of cooling off or to take the tranquilizing drug of gradualism. Now is the time to make real the promises of democracy. Now is the time to rise from the dark and desolate valley of segregation to the sunlit path of racial justice. Now is the time to lift our nation from the quicksands of racial injustice to the solid rock of brotherhood. Now is the time to make justice a reality for all of God's children.

It would be fatal for the nation to overlook the urgency of the moment. This sweltering summer of the Negro's legitimate discontent will not pass until there is an invigorating autumn of freedom and equality. Nineteen sixty-three is not an end, but a beginning. And those who hope that the Negro needed to blow off steam and will now be content will have a rude awakening if the nation returns to business as usual. And there will be neither rest nor tranquility in America until the Negro is granted his citizenship rights. The whirlwinds of revolt will continue to shake the foundations of our nation until the bright day of justice emerges.

But there is something that I must say to my people, who stand on the warm threshold which leads into the palace of justice: In the process of gaining our rightful place, we must not be guilty of wrongful deeds. Let us not seek to satisfy our thirst for freedom by drinking from the cup of bitterness and hatred. We must forever conduct our struggle on the high plane of dignity and discipline. We must not allow our creative protest to degenerate into physical violence. Again and again, we must rise to the majestic heights of meeting physical force with soul force.

The marvelous new militancy which has engulfed the Negro community must not lead us to a distrust of all white people, for many of our white brothers, as evidenced by their presence here today, have come to realize that their destiny is tied up with our destiny. And they have come to realize that their freedom is inextricably bound to our freedom.

We cannot walk alone.

And as we walk, we must make the pledge that we shall always march ahead.

We cannot turn back.

There are those who are asking the devotees of civil rights, "When will you be satisfied?" We can never be satisfied as long as the Negro is the victim of the unspeakable horrors of police brutality. We can never be satisfied as long as our bodies, heavy with the fatigue of travel, cannot gain lodging in the motels of the highways and the hotels of the cities. We cannot be satisfied as long as the Negro's basic mobility is from a smaller ghetto to a larger one. We can never be satisfied as long as our children are stripped of their self-hood and robbed of their dignity by signs stating: "For Whites Only." We cannot be satisfied as long as a Negro in Mississippi cannot vote and a Negro in New York believes he has nothing for which to vote. No, no, we are not satisfied, and we will not be satisfied until "justice rolls down like waters, and righteousness like a mighty stream."

I am not unmindful that some of you have come here out of great trials and tribulations. Some of you have come fresh from narrow jail cells. And some of you have come from areas where your quest—quest for freedom left you battered by the storms of persecution and staggered by the winds of police brutality. You have been the veterans of creative suffering. Continue to work with the faith that unearned suffering is redemptive. Go back to Mississippi, go back to Alabama, go back to South Carolina, go back to Georgia, go back to Louisiana, go back to the slums and ghettos of our northern cities, knowing that somehow this situation can and will be changed.

Let us not wallow in the valley of despair, I say to you today, my friends.

And so even though we face the difficulties of today and tomorrow, I still have a dream. It is a dream deeply rooted in the American dream.

I have a dream that one day this nation will rise up and live out the true meaning of its creed: "We hold these truths to be self-evident, that all men are created equal."

I have a dream that one day on the red hills of Georgia, the sons of former slaves and the sons of former slave owners will be able to sit down together at the table of brotherhood.

I have a dream that one day even the state of Mississippi, a state sweltering with the heat of injustice, sweltering with the heat of oppression, will be transformed into an oasis of freedom and justice.

I have a dream that my four little children will one day live in a nation where they will not be judged by the color of their skin but by the content of their character.

I have a *dream* today!

I have a dream that one day, down in Alabama, with its vicious racists, with its governor having his lips dripping with the words of "interposition" and "nullification"—one day right there in Alabama little black boys and black girls will be able to join hands with little white boys and white girls as sisters and brothers.

I have a *dream* today!

I have a dream that one day every valley shall be exalted, and every hill and mountain shall be made low, the rough places will be made plain, and the crooked places will be made straight; "and the glory of the Lord shall be revealed and all flesh shall see it together."

This is our hope, and this is the faith that I go back to the South with.

With this faith, we will be able to hew out of the mountain of despair a stone of hope. With this faith, we will be able to transform the jangling discords of our nation into a beautiful symphony of brotherhood. With this faith, we will be able to work together, to pray together, to struggle together, to go to jail together, to stand up for freedom together, knowing that we will be free one day.

And this will be the day—this will be the day when all of God's children will be able to sing with new meaning: My country 'tis of thee, sweet land of liberty, of thee I sing. Land where my fathers died, land of the Pilgrim's pride, From every mountainside, let freedom ring!"

And if America is to be a great nation, this must become true.
And so let freedom ring from the prodigious hilltops of New Hampshire.
Let freedom ring from the mighty mountains of New York.
Let freedom ring from the heightening Alleghenies of Pennsylvania.
Let freedom ring from the snow-capped Rockies of Colorado.
Let freedom ring from the curvaceous slopes of California.

But not only that:

Let freedom ring from Stone Mountain of Georgia.
Let freedom ring from Lookout Mountain of Tennessee.
Let freedom ring from every hill and molehill of Mississippi.
From every mountainside, let freedom ring.

And when this happens, when we allow freedom ring, when we let it ring from every village and every hamlet, from every state and every city, we will be able to speed up that day when *all* of God's children, black men and white men, Jews and Gentiles, Protestants and Catholics, will be able to join hands and sing in the words of the old Negro spiritual:

Free at last! Free at last!
Thank God Almighty, we are free at last!

HARVEY MILK

"The Hope Speech" (March 10, 1978)

Harvey Milk [1930–1978] became the first openly gay man to hold public office in California when he was elected to the San Francisco Board of Supervisors in 1977. The following speech, which would only later come to be known as "The Hope Speech," was delivered at the 1978 San Francisco Gay Freedom Day Parade. Harvey Milk was assassinated by former San Francisco Supervisor Dan White on November 27, 1978, just five months after giving this speech.

My name is Harvey Milk and I'm here to recruit you.

I've been saying this one for years. It's a political joke. I can't help it—I've got to tell it. I've never been able to talk to this many political people before, so if I tell you nothing else you may be able to go home laughing a bit.

This ocean liner was going across the ocean and it sank. And there was one little piece of wood floating and three people swam to it and they realized only one person could hold on to it. So they had a little debate about which was the person. It so happened that the three people were the Pope, the President, and Mayor Daley. The Pope said he was titular head of one of the greatest religions of the world and he was spiritual adviser to many, many millions and he went on and pontificated and they thought it was a good argument. Then the President said he was leader of the largest and most powerful nation of the world. What takes place in this country affects the whole world and they thought that was a good argument. And Mayor Daley said he was mayor of the backbone of the United States and what took place in Chicago affected the world, and what took place in the archdiocese of Chicago affected Catholicism. And they thought that was a good argument. So they did it the democratic way and voted. And Daley won, seven to two.

About six months ago, Anita Bryant in her speaking to God said that the drought in California was because of the gay people. On November 9, the day after I got elected, it started to rain. On the day I got sworn in, we walked to City Hall and it was kinda nice, and as soon as I said the word "I do," it started to rain again. It's been raining since then and the people of San Francisco figure the only way to stop it is to do a recall petition. That's the local joke.

So much for that. Why are we here? Why are gay people here? And what's happening? What's happening to me is the antithesis of what you read about in the papers and what you hear about on the radio. You hear about and read about this movement to the right. That we must band together and fight back this movement to the right. And I'm here to go ahead and say that what you hear and read is what they want you to think because it's not happening. The major media in this country has talked about the movement to the right so the legislators think that there is indeed a movement to the right and that the Congress and the legislators and the city councils will start to move to the right the way the major media want them. So they keep on talking about this move to the right.

So let's look at 1977 and see if there was indeed a move to the right. In 1977, gay people had their rights taken away from them in Miami. But you must remember that in the week before Miami and the week after that, the word homosexual or gay appeared in every single newspaper in this nation in articles both pro and con. In every radio station, in every TV station and every household. For the first time in the history of the world, everybody was talking about it, good or bad. Unless you have dialogue, unless you open the walls of dialogue, you can never reach to change people's opinion. In those two weeks, more good and bad, but more about the word homosexual and gay was written than probably in the history of mankind. Once you have dialogue starting, you know you can break down prejudice. In 1977 we saw a dialogue start. In 1977, we saw a gay person elected in San Francisco. In 1977 we saw the state of Mississippi decriminalize marijuana. In 1977, we saw the convention of conventions in Houston. And I want to know where the movement to the right is happening.

What that is is a record of what happened last year. What we must do is make sure that 1978 continues the movement that is really happening that the media don't want you to know about. That is the movement to the left. It's up to CDC to put the pressures on Sacramento—but to break down the walls and the barriers so the movement to the left continues and progress continues in the nation. We have before us coming up several issues we must speak out on. Probably the most important issue outside the Briggs—which we will come to—but we do know what will take place this June. We know there's an issue on the ballot called Jarvis-Gann. We hear the taxpayers talk about it on both sides. But what you don't hear is that it's probably the most racist issue on the ballot in a long time. In the city and county of San Francisco, if it passes and we indeed have to lay off people, who will they be? The last in, and the first in, and who are the last in but the minorities? Jarvis-Gann is a racist issue. We must address that issue. We must not talk away from it. We must not allow them to talk about the money it's going to save, because look at who's going to save the money and who's going to get hurt.

We also have another issue that we've started in some of the north counties and I hope in some of the south counties it continues. In San Francisco elections we're asking—at least we hope to ask—that the U.S. government put pressure on the closing of the South African consulate. That must happen. There is a major difference between an embassy in Washington which is a diplomatic bureau and a consulate in major cities. A consulate is there for one reason only—to promote business, economic gains, tourism, investment. And every time you have business going to South Africa, you're promoting a regime that's offensive.

In the city of San Francisco, if every one of 51 percent of that city were to go to South Africa, they would be treated as second-class citizens. That is an offense to the people of San Francisco and I hope all my colleagues up there will take every step we can to close down that consulate and hope that people in other parts of the state follow us in that lead. The battles must be started some place and CDC is the greatest place to start the battles. I know we are pressed for time so I'm going to cover just one more little point. That is to understand why it is important that gay people run for office and that gay people get elected. I know there are many people in this room who are running for central committee who are gay. I encourage you. There's a major reason why. If my non-gay friends and supporters in this room understand it, they'll probably understand why I've run so often before I finally made it. Y'see right now, there's a controversy going on in this convention about the gay governor. Is he speaking out enough? Is he strong enough for gay rights? And there is controversy and for us to say it is not would be foolish. Some people are satisfied and some people are not.

You see there is a major difference—and it remains a vital difference—between a friend and a gay person, a friend in office and a gay person in office. Gay people have been slandered nationwide. We've been tarred and we've been brushed with the picture of pornography. In Dade County, we were accused of child molestation. It's not enough anymore just to have friends represent us. No matter how good that friend may be.

The black community made up its mind to that a long time ago. That the myths against blacks can only be dispelled by electing black leaders, so the black community could be judged by the leaders and not by the myths or black criminals. The Spanish community must not be judged by Latin criminals or myths. The Asian community must not be judged by Asian criminals or myths. The Italian community must not be judged by the mafia myths. And the time has come when the gay community must not be judged by our criminals and myths.

Like every other group, we must be judged by our leaders and by those who are themselves gay, those who are visible. For invisible, we remain in limbo—a myth, a person with no parents, no brothers, no sisters, no friends who are straight, no important positions in employment. A tenth of the nation supposedly composed of stereotypes and would-be seducers of children—and no offense meant to the stereotypes. But today, the black community is not judged by its friends, but by its black legislators and leaders. And we must give people the chance to judge us by our leaders and legislators. A gay person in office can set a tone, can command respect not only from the larger community, but from the young people in our own community who need both examples and hope.

The first gay people we elect must be strong. They must not be content to sit in the back of the bus. They must not be content to accept pablum. They must be above wheeling and dealing. They must be—for the good of all of us—independent, unbought. The anger and the frustrations that some of us feel is because we are misunderstood, and friends can't feel the anger and frustration. They can sense it in us, but they can't feel it. Because a friend has never gone through what is known as coming out. I will never forget what it was like coming out and having nobody to look up toward. I remember the lack of hope—and our friends can't fulfill it.

I can't forget the looks on faces of people who've lost hope. Be they gay, be they seniors, be they blacks looking for an almost-impossible job, be they Latins trying to explain their problems and aspirations in a tongue that's foreign to them. I personally will never forget that people are more important than buildings. I use the word "I" because I'm proud. I stand here tonight in front of my gay sisters, brothers and friends because I'm proud of you. I think it's time that we have many legislators who are gay and proud of that fact and do not have to remain in the closet. I think that a gay person, up-front, will not walk away from a responsibility and be afraid of being tossed out of office. After Dade County, I walked among the angry and the frustrated night after night and I looked at their faces. And in San Francisco, three days before Gay Pride Day, a person was killed just because he was gay. And that night, I walked among the sad and the frustrated at City Hall in San Francisco and later that night as they lit candles on Castro Street and stood in silence, reaching out for some symbolic thing that would give them hope. These were strong people, whose faces I knew from the shop, the streets, meetings and people who I never saw before but I knew. They were strong, but even they needed hope.

And the young gay people in the Altoona, Pennsylvanias and the Richmond, Minnesotas who are coming out and hear Anita Bryant on television and her story. The only thing they have to look forward to is hope. And you have to give them hope. Hope for a better world, hope for a better tomorrow, hope for a better place to come to if the pressures at home are too great. Hope that all will be all right. Without hope, not only gays, but the blacks, the seniors, the handicapped, the us'es, the us'es will give up. And if you help elect to the central committee and other offices, more gay people, that gives a green light to all who feel disenfranchised, a green light to move forward. It means hope to a nation that has given up, because if a gay person makes it, the doors are open to everyone.

So if there is a message I have to give, it is that I've found one overriding thing about my personal election, it's the fact that if a gay person can be elected, it's a green light. And you and you and you, you have to give people hope. Thank you very much.

MOTHER TERESA

Nobel Lecture (December 11, 1979)

Mother Teresa (1910–1997), born Agnes Gonxha Bojaxhiu, was a Roman Catholic nun who dedicated her life to helping the poor and needy in India. After feeling that God had called her to help the poor while traveling by train to Darjeeling, Mother Teresa began her missionary work in 1948. She went on to found the Missionaries of Charity, a Roman Catholic congregation whose members vow to give "Wholehearted and Free service to the poorest of the poor." She was awarded the Nobel Peace Prize in 1979, which she called a "gift for the poor." Her acceptance speech was delivered in Oslo, Norway, and focused on the need for everyone to help those less fortunate than themselves.

As WE HAVE GATHERED here together to thank God for the Nobel Peace Prize I think it will be beautiful that we pray the prayer of St. Francis of Assisi which always surprises me very much—we pray this prayer every day after Holy Communion, because it is very fitting for each one of us, and I always wonder that four to five hundred years ago as St. Francis of Assisi composed this prayer that they had the same difficulties that we have today, as we compose this prayer that fits very nicely for us also. I think some of you already have got it—so we will pray together.

Let us thank God for the opportunity that we all have together today, for this gift of peace that reminds us that we have been created to live that peace, and Jesus became man to bring that good news to the poor. He being God became man in all things like us except sin, and he proclaimed very clearly that he had come to give the good news. The news was peace to all of good will and this is something that we all want—the peace of heart—and God loved the world so much that he gave his son—it was a giving—it is as much as if to say it hurt God to give, because he loved the world so much that he gave his son, and he gave him to Virgin Mary, and what did she do with him?

As soon as he came in her life—immediately she went in haste to give that good news, and as she came into the house of her cousin, the child—the unborn child—the child in the womb of Elizabeth, leapt with joy. He was that little unborn child, was the first messenger of peace. He recognised the Prince of Peace, he recognised that Christ has come to bring the good news for you and for me. And as if that was not enough—it was not enough to become a man—he died on the cross to show that greater love, and he died for you and for me and for that leper and for that man dying of hunger and that naked person lying in the street not only of Calcutta, but of Africa, and New York, and London, and Oslo—and insisted that we love one another as he loves each one of us. And we read that in the Gospel very clearly—love as I have loved you—as I love you—as the Father has loved me, I love you—and the harder the Father loved him, he gave him to us, and how much we love one another, we, too, must give each other until it hurts. It is not enough for us to say: I love God, but I do not love my neighbour. St. John says you are a liar if you say you love God and you don't love your neighbour. How can you love God whom you do not see, if you do not love your neighbour whom you see, whom you touch, with whom you live. And so this is very important for us to realise that love, to be true, has to hurt. It hurt Jesus to love us, it hurt him. And to make sure we remember his great love he made himself the bread of life to satisfy our hunger for his love. Our hunger for God, because we have been created for that love. We have been created in his image. We have been created to love and be loved, and then he has become man to make it possible for us to love as he loved us. He makes himself the hungry one—the naked one—the homeless one—the sick one—the one in prison—the lonely one—the unwanted one—and he says: You did it to me. Hungry for our love, and this is the hunger of our poor people. This is the hunger that you and I must find, it may be in our own home.

I never forget an opportunity I had in visiting a home where they had all these old parents of sons and daughters who had just put them in an institution and forgotten maybe. And I went there, and I saw in that home they had everything, beautiful things, but everybody was looking towards the door. And I did not see a single one with their smile on their face. And I turned to the Sister and I asked: How is that? How is it that the people they have everything here, why are they all looking towards the door, why are they not smiling? I am so used to see the smile on our people, even the dying one smile, and she said: This is nearly every day, they are expecting, they are hoping that a son or daughter will come to visit them. They are hurt because they are forgotten, and see—this is where love comes. That poverty comes right there in our own home, even neglect to love. Maybe in our own family we have somebody who is feeling lonely, who is feeling sick, who is feeling worried, and these are difficult days for everybody. Are we there, are we there to receive them, is the mother there to receive the child?

I was surprised in the West to see so many young boys and girls given into drugs, and I tried to find out why—why is it like that, and the answer was: Because there is no one in the family to receive them. Father and mother are so busy they have no time. Young parents are in some institution and the child takes back to the street and gets involved in something. We are talking of peace. These are things that break peace, but I feel the greatest destroyer of peace today is abortion, because it is a direct war, a direct killing—direct murder by the mother herself. And we read in the Scripture, for God says very clearly: Even if a mother could forget her child—I will not forget you—I have carved you in the palm of my hand. We are carved in the palm of His hand, so close to Him that unborn child has been carved in the hand of God. And that is what strikes me most, the beginning of that sentence, that even if a mother could forget something impossible—but even if she could forget—I will not forget you. And today the greatest means—the greatest destroyer of peace is abortion. And we who are standing here—our parents wanted us. We would not be here if our parents would do that to us. Our children, we want them, we love them, but what of the millions. Many people are very, very concerned with the children in India, with the children in Africa where quite a number die, maybe of malnutrition, of hunger and so on, but millions are dying deliberately by the will of the mother. And this is what is the greatest destroyer of peace today. Because if a mother can kill her own child—what is left for me to kill you and you kill me—there is nothing between. And this I appeal in India, I appeal everywhere: Let us bring the child back, and this year being the child's year: What have we done for the child? At the beginning of the year I told, I spoke everywhere and I said: Let us make this year that we make every single child born, and unborn, wanted. And today is the end of the year, have we really made the children wanted? I will give you something terrifying. We are fighting abortion by adoption, we have saved thousands of lives, we have sent words to all the clinics, to the hospitals, police stations—please don't destroy the child, we will take the child. So every hour of the day and night it is always somebody, we have quite a number of unwedded mothers—tell them come, we will take care of you, we will take the child from you, and we will get a home for the child. And we have a tremendous demand from families who have no children, that is the blessing of God for us. And also, we are doing another thing which is very beautiful—we are teaching our beggars, our leprosy patients, our slum dwellers, our people of the street, natural family planning.

And in Calcutta alone in six years—it is all in Calcutta—we have had 61,273 babies less from the families who would have had, but because they practise this natural way of abstaining, of self-control, out of love for each other. We teach them the temperature meter which is very beautiful, very simple, and our poor people understand. And you know what they have told me? Our family is healthy, our family is united, and we can have a baby whenever we want. So clear—those people in the street, those beggars—and I think that if our people can do like that how much more you and all the others who can know the ways and means without destroying the life that God has created in us.

The poor people are very great people. They can teach us so many beautiful things. The other day one of them came to thank and said: You people who have vowed chastity you are the best people to teach us family planning. Because it is nothing more than self-control out of love for each other. And I think they said a beautiful sentence. And these are people who maybe have nothing to eat, maybe they have not a home where to live, but they are great people. The poor are very wonderful people. One evening we went out and we picked up four people from the street. And one of them was in a most terrible condition—and I told the Sisters: You take care of the other three, I take of this one that looked worse. So I did for her all that my love can do. I put her in bed, and there was such a beautiful smile on her face. She took hold of my hand, as she said one word only: Thank you—and she died.

I could not help but examine my conscience before her, and I asked what would I say if I was in her place. And my answer was very simple. I would have tried to draw a little attention to myself, I would have said I am hungry, that I am dying, I am cold, I am in pain, or something, but she gave me much more—she gave me her grateful love. And she died with a smile on her face. As that man whom we picked up from the drain, half eaten with worms, and we brought him to the home. I have lived like an animal in the street, but I am going to die like an angel, loved and cared for. And it was so wonderful to see the greatness of that man who could speak like that, who could die like that without blaming anybody, without cursing anybody, without comparing anything. Like an angel—this is the greatness of our people. And that is why we believe what Jesus had said: I was hungry—I was naked—I was homeless—I was unwanted, unloved, uncared for—and you did it to me.

I believe that we are not real social workers. We may be doing social work in the eyes of the people, but we are really contemplatives in the heart of the world. For we are touching the Body of Christ 24 hours. We have 24 hours in this presence, and so you and I. You too try to bring that presence of God in your family, for the family that prays together stays together. And I think that we in our family don't need bombs and guns, to destroy to bring peace—just get together, love one another, bring that peace, that joy, that strength of presence of each other in the home. And we will be able to overcome all the evil that is in the world.

There is so much suffering, so much hatred, so much misery, and we with our prayer, with our sacrifice are beginning at home. Love begins at home, and it is not how much we do, but how much love we put in the action that we do. It is to God Almighty—how much we do it does not matter, because He is infinite, but how much love we put in that action. How much we do to Him in the person that we are serving.

Some time ago in Calcutta we had great difficulty in getting sugar, and I don't know how the word got around to the children, and a little boy of four years old, Hindu boy, went home and told his parents: I will not eat sugar for three days, I will give my sugar to Mother Teresa for her children. After three days his father and mother brought him to our home. I had never met them before, and this little one could scarcely pronounce my name, but he knew exactly what he had come to do. He knew that he wanted to share his love.

And this is why I have received such a lot of love from you all. From the time that I have come here I have simply been surrounded with love, and with real, real understanding love. It could feel as if everyone in India, everyone in Africa is somebody very special to you. And I felt quite at home I was telling Sister today. I feel in the Convent with the Sisters as if I am in Calcutta with my own Sisters. So completely at home here, right here.

And so here I am talking with you—I want you to find the poor here, right in your own home first. And begin love there. Be that good news to your own people. And find out about your next-door neighbour—do you know who they are? I had the most extraordinary experience with a Hindu family who had eight children. A gentleman came to our house and said: Mother Teresa, there is a family with eight children, they had not eaten for so long—do something. So I took some rice and I went there immediately. And I saw the children—their eyes shining with hunger—I don't know if you have ever seen hunger. But I have seen it very often. And she took the rice, she divided the rice, and she went out. When she came back I asked her—where did you go, what did you do? And she gave me a very simple answer: They are hungry also. What struck me most was that she knew—and who are they, a Muslim family—and she knew. I didn't bring more rice that evening because I wanted them to enjoy the joy of sharing. But there were those children, radiating joy, sharing the joy with their mother because she had the love to give. And you see this is where love begins—at home. And I want you—and I am very grateful for what I have received. It has been a tremendous experience and I go back to India—I will be back by next week, the 15th I hope—and I will be able to bring your love.

And I know well that you have not given from your abundance, but you have given until it has hurt you. Today the little children they have—I was so surprised—there is so much joy for the children that are hungry. That the children like themselves will need love and care and tenderness, like they get so much from their parents. So let us thank God that we have had this opportunity to come to know each other, and this knowledge of each other has brought us very close. And we will be able to help not only the children of India and Africa, but will be able to help the children of the whole world, because as you know our Sisters are all over the world. And with this prize that I have received as a prize of peace, I am going to try to make the home for many people that have no home. Because I believe that love begins at home, and if we can create a home for the poor—I think that more and more love will spread. And we will be able through this understanding love to bring peace, be the good news to the poor. The poor in our own family first, in our country and in the world.

To be able to do this, our Sisters, our lives have to be woven with prayer. They have to be woven with Christ to be able to understand, to be able to share. Because today there is so much suffering—and I feel that the passion of Christ is being relived all over again—are we there to share that passion, to share that suffering of people. Around the world, not only in the poor countries, but I found the poverty of the West so much more difficult to remove. When I pick up a person from the street, hungry, I give him a plate of rice, a piece of bread, I have satisfied. I have removed that hunger. But a person that is shut out, that feels unwanted, unloved, terrified, the person that has been thrown out from society—that poverty is so hurtable and so much, and I find that very difficult. Our Sisters are working amongst that kind of people in the West. So you must pray for us that we may be able to be that good news, but we cannot do that without you, you have to do that here in your country. You must come to know the poor, maybe our people here have material things, everything, but I think that if we all look into our own homes, how difficult we find it sometimes to smile at each other, and that the smile is the beginning of love.

And so let us always meet each other with a smile, for the smile is the beginning of love, and once we begin to love each other naturally we want to do something. So you pray for our Sisters and for me and for our Brothers, and for our Co-Workers that are around the world. That we may remain faithful to the gift of God, to love Him and serve Him in the poor together with you. What we have done we should not have been able to do if you did not share with your prayers, with your gifts, this continual giving. But

I don't want you to give me from your abundance, I want that you give me until it hurts.

The other day I received 15 dollars from a man who has been on his back for twenty years, and the only part that he can move is his right hand. And the only companion that he enjoys is smoking. And he said to me: I do not smoke for one week, and I send you this money. It must have been a terrible sacrifice for him, but see how beautiful, how he shared, and with that money I bought bread and I gave to those who are hungry with a joy on both sides, he was giving and the poor were receiving. This is something that you and I—it is a gift of God to us to be able to share our love with others. And let it be as it was for Jesus. Let us love one another as he loved us. Let us love Him with undivided love. And the joy of loving Him and each other—let us give now—that Christmas is coming so close. Let us keep that joy of loving Jesus in our hearts. And share that joy with all that we come in touch with. And that radiating joy is real, for we have no reason not to be happy because we have no Christ with us. Christ in our hearts, Christ in the poor that we meet, Christ in the smile that we give and the smile that we receive. Let us make that one point: That no child will be unwanted, and also that we meet each other always with a smile, especially when it is difficult to smile.

I never forget some time ago about fourteen professors came from the United States from different universities. And they came to Calcutta to our house. Then we were talking about that they had been to the home for the dying. We have a home for the dying in Calcutta, where we have picked up more than 36,000 people only from the streets of Calcutta, and out of that big number more than 18,000 have died a beautiful death. They have just gone home to God; and they came to our house and we talked of love, of compassion, and then one of them asked me: Say, Mother, please tell us something that we will remember, and I said to them: Smile at each other, make time for each other in your family. Smile at each other. And then another one asked me: Are you married, and I said: Yes, and I find it sometimes very difficult to smile at Jesus because he can be very demanding sometimes. This is really something true, and there is where love comes—when it is demanding, and yet we can give it to Him with joy. Just as I have said today, I have said that if I don't go to Heaven for anything else I will be going to Heaven for all the publicity because it has purified me and sacrificed me and made me really ready to go to Heaven. I think that this is something, that we must live life beautifully, we have Jesus with us and He loves us. If we could only remember that God loves me, and I have an opportunity to love others as he loves me, not in big things, but in small things with great love, then Norway becomes a nest of love. And how beautiful it will be that from here a centre for peace has been given. That from here the joy of life of the unborn child comes out. If you become a burning light in the world of peace, then really the Nobel Peace Prize is a gift of the Norwegian people. God bless you!

RONALD REAGAN

"Tear Down This Wall"
(June 12, 1987)

In June of 1987, Ronald Reagan (1911–2004) was at the end of his tenure as president of the United States when he traveled to Berlin for the commemoration of the city's 750th anniversary. After viewing the Berlin Wall from a balcony at the Reichstag, Reagan delivered the following address at the Brandenburg Gate, protected from potential snipers by two layers of bulletproof glass. His speech called for the Soviet Union to remove the twelve-foot-high concrete wall that separated communist-controlled East Berlin from democratic West Berlin.

THANK YOU VERY MUCH. Chancellor Kohl, Governing Mayor Diepgen, ladies and gentlemen:

Twenty four years ago, President John F. Kennedy visited Berlin, speaking to the people of this city and the world at the city hall. Well, since then two other presidents have come, each in his turn, to Berlin. And today I, myself, make my second visit to your city.

We come to Berlin, we American Presidents, because it's our duty to speak, in this place, of freedom. But I must confess, we're drawn here by other things as well: by the feeling of history in this city, more than 500 years older than our own nation; by the beauty of the Grunewald and the Tiergarten; most of all, by your courage and determination. Perhaps the composer, Paul Lincke, understood something about American Presidents. You see, like so many Presidents before me, I come here today because wherever I go, whatever

I do: "Ich hab noch einen Koffer in Berlin." [I still have a suitcase in Berlin.]

Our gathering today is being broadcast throughout Western Europe and North America. I understand that it is being seen and heard as well in the East. To those listening throughout Eastern Europe, I extend my warmest greetings and the good will of the American people. To those listening in East Berlin, a special word: Although I cannot be with you, I address my remarks to you just as surely as to those standing here before me. For I join you, as I join your fellow countrymen in the West, in this firm, this unalterable belief: Es gibt nur ein Berlin. [There is only one Berlin.]

Behind me stands a wall that encircles the free sectors of this city, part of a vast system of barriers that divides the entire continent of Europe. From the Baltic, south, those barriers cut across Germany in a gash of barbed wire, concrete, dog runs, and guard-towers. Farther south, there may be no visible, no obvious wall. But there remain armed guards and checkpoints all the same—still a restriction on the right to travel, still an instrument to impose upon ordinary men and women the will of a totalitarian state. Yet it is here in Berlin where the wall emerges most clearly; here, cutting across your city, where the news photo and the television screen have imprinted this brutal division of a continent upon the mind of the world. Standing before the Brandenburg Gate, every man is a German, separated from his fellow men. Every man is a Berliner, forced to look upon a scar.

President von Weizsäcker has said: "The German question is open as long as the Brandenburg Gate is closed." Today I say: As long as this gate is closed, as long as this scar of a wall is permitted to stand, it is not the German question alone that remains open, but the question of freedom for all mankind. Yet I do not come here to lament. For I find in Berlin a message of hope, even in the shadow of this wall, a message of triumph.

In this season of spring in 1945, the people of Berlin emerged from their air raid shelters to find devastation. Thousands of miles away, the people of the United States reached out to help. And in 1947 Secretary of State—as you've been told—George Marshall announced the creation of what would become known as the Marshall plan. Speaking precisely 40 years ago this month, he said: "Our policy is directed not against any country or doctrine, but against hunger, poverty, desperation, and chaos."

In the Reichstag a few moments ago, I saw a display commemorating this 40th anniversary of the Marshall plan. I was struck by the sign on a burnt-out, gutted structure that was being rebuilt. I understand that Berliners of my own generation can remember seeing signs like it dotted throughout the Western sectors of the city. The sign read simply: "The Marshall plan is helping here to strengthen the free world." A strong, free world in the West, that dream became real. Japan rose from ruin to become an economic giant. Italy, France, Belgium–virtually every nation in Western Europe saw political and economic rebirth; the European Community was founded.

In West Germany and here in Berlin, there took place an economic miracle, the Wirtschaftswunder. Adenauer, Erhard, Reuter, and other leaders understood the practical importance of liberty—that just as truth can flourish only when the journalist is given freedom of speech, so prosperity can come about only when the farmer and businessman enjoy economic freedom. The German leaders reduced tariffs, expanded free trade, lowered taxes. From 1950 to 1960 alone, the standard of living in West Germany and Berlin doubled.

Where four decades ago there was rubble, today in West Berlin there is the greatest industrial output of any city in Germany—busy office blocks, fine homes and apartments, proud avenues, and the spreading lawns of park land. Where a city's culture seemed to have been destroyed, today there are two great universities, orchestras and an opera, countless theaters, and museums. Where there was want, today there's abundance—food, clothing, automobiles—the wonderful goods of the Ku'damm. From devastation, from utter ruin, you Berliners have, in freedom, rebuilt a city that once again ranks as one of the greatest on Earth. The Soviets may have had other plans. But, my friends, there were a few things the Soviets didn't count on: Berliner Herz, Berliner Humor, ja, und Berliner Schnauze. [Berliner heart, Berliner humor, yes, and a Berliner schnauze.] [Laughter]

In the 1950's, Khrushchev predicted: "We will bury you." But in the West today, we see a free world that has achieved a level of prosperity and well-being unprecedented in all human history. In the Communist world, we see failure, technological backwardness, declining standards of health, even want of the most basic kind—too little food. Even today, the Soviet Union still cannot feed itself. After these four decades, then, there stands before the entire world one great and inescapable conclusion: Freedom leads to prosperity. Freedom replaces the ancient hatreds among the nations with comity and peace. Freedom is the victor.

And now the Soviets themselves may, in a limited way, be coming to understand the importance of freedom. We hear much from Moscow about a new policy of reform and openness. Some political prisoners have been released. Certain foreign news broadcasts are no longer being jammed. Some economic enterprises have been permitted to operate with greater freedom from state control. Are these the beginnings of profound changes in the Soviet state? Or are they token gestures, intended to raise false hopes in the West, or to strengthen the Soviet system without changing it? We welcome change and openness; for we believe that freedom and security go together, that the advance of human liberty can only strengthen the cause of world peace.

There is one sign the Soviets can make that would be unmistakable, that would advance dramatically the cause of freedom and peace. General Secretary Gorbachev, if you seek peace, if you seek prosperity for the Soviet Union and Eastern Europe, if you seek liberalization: Come here to this gate! Mr. Gorbachev, open this gate! Mr. Gorbachev, tear down this wall!

I understand the fear of war and the pain of division that afflict this continent—and I pledge to you my country's efforts to help overcome these burdens. To be sure, we in the West must resist Soviet expansion. So we must maintain defenses of unassailable strength. Yet we seek peace; so we must strive to reduce arms on both sides. Beginning 10 years ago, the Soviets challenged the Western alliance with a grave new threat, hundreds of new and more deadly SS-20 nuclear missiles, capable of striking every capital in Europe. The Western alliance responded by committing itself to a counterdeployment unless the Soviets agreed to negotiate a better solution; namely, the elimination of such weapons on both sides. For many months, the Soviets refused to bargain in earnestness. As the alliance, in turn, prepared to go forward with its counterdeployment, there were difficult days—days of protests like those during my 1982 visit to this city—and the Soviets later walked away from the table.

But through it all, the alliance held firm. And I invite those who protested then—I invite those who protest today—to mark this fact: Because we remained strong, the Soviets came back to the table. And because we remained strong, today we have within reach the possibility, not merely of limiting the growth of arms, but of eliminating, for the first time, an entire class of nuclear weapons from the face of the Earth. As I speak, NATO ministers are meeting in Iceland to review the progress of our proposals for eliminating these weapons. At the talks in Geneva, we have also proposed deep cuts in strategic offensive weapons. And the Western allies have likewise made far-reaching proposals to reduce the danger of conventional war and to place a total ban on chemical weapons.

While we pursue these arms reductions, I pledge to you that we will maintain the capacity to deter Soviet aggression at any level at which it might occur. And in cooperation with many of our allies, the United States is pursuing the Strategic Defense Initiative—research to base deterrence not on the threat of offensive retaliation, but on defenses that truly defend; on systems, in short, that will not target populations, but shield them. By these means we seek to increase the safety of Europe and all the world. But we must remember a crucial fact: East and West do not mistrust each other because we are armed; we are armed because we mistrust each other. And our differences are not about weapons but about liberty. When President Kennedy spoke at the City Hall those 24 years ago, freedom was encircled, Berlin was under siege. And today, despite all the pressures upon this city, Berlin stands secure in its liberty. And freedom itself is transforming the globe.

In the Philippines, in South and Central America, democracy has been given a rebirth. Throughout the Pacific, free markets are working miracle after miracle of economic growth. In the industrialized nations, a technological revolution is taking place—a revolution marked by rapid, dramatic advances in computers and telecommunications.

In Europe, only one nation and those it controls refuse to join the community of freedom. Yet in this age of redoubled economic growth, of information and innovation, the Soviet Union faces a choice: It must make fundamental changes, or it will become obsolete. Today thus represents a moment of hope. We in the West stand ready to cooperate with the East to promote true openness, to break down barriers that separate people, to create a safer, freer world.

And surely there is no better place than Berlin, the meeting place of East and West, to make a start. Free people of Berlin: Today, as in the past, the United States stands for the strict observance and full implementation of all parts of the Four Power Agreement of 1971. Let us use this occasion, the 750th anniversary of this city, to usher in a new era, to seek a still fuller, richer life for the Berlin of the future. Together, let us maintain and develop the ties between the Federal Republic and the Western sectors of Berlin, which is permitted by the 1971 agreement.

And I invite Mr. Gorbachev: Let us work to bring the Eastern and Western parts of the city closer together, so that all the inhabitants of all Berlin can enjoy the benefits that come with life in one of the great cities of the world. To open Berlin still further to all Europe, East and West, let us expand the vital air access to this city, finding ways of making commercial air service to Berlin more convenient, more comfortable, and more economical. We look to the day when West Berlin can become one of the chief aviation hubs in all central Europe.

With our French and British partners, the United States is prepared to help bring international meetings to Berlin. It would be only fitting for Berlin to serve as the site of United Nations meetings, or world conferences on human rights and arms control or other issues that call for international cooperation. There is no better way to establish hope for the future than to enlighten young minds, and we would be honored to sponsor summer youth exchanges, cultural events, and other programs for young Berliners from the East. Our French and British friends, I'm certain, will do the same. And it's my hope that an authority can be found in East Berlin to sponsor visits from young people of the Western sectors.

One final proposal, one close to my heart: Sport represents a source of enjoyment and ennoblement, and you may have noted that the Republic of Korea—South Korea—has offered to permit certain events of the 1988 Olympics to take place in the North. International sports competitions of all kinds could take place in both parts of this city. And what better way to demonstrate to the world the openness of this city than to offer in some future year to hold the Olympic games here in Berlin, East and West?

In these four decades, as I have said, you Berliners have built a great city. You've done so in spite of threats—the Soviet attempts to impose the East-mark, the blockade. Today the city thrives in spite of the challenges implicit in the very presence of this wall. What keeps you here? Certainly there's a great deal to be said for your fortitude, for your defiant courage. But I believe there's something deeper, something that involves Berlin's whole look and feel and way of life—not mere sentiment. No one could live long in Berlin without being completely disabused of illusions. Something instead, that has seen the difficulties of life in Berlin but chose to accept them, that continues to build this good and proud city in contrast to a surrounding totalitarian presence that refuses to release human energies or aspirations. Something that speaks with a powerful voice of affirmation, that says yes to this city, yes to the future, yes to freedom. In a word, I would submit that what keeps you in Berlin is love—love both profound and abiding.

Perhaps this gets to the root of the matter, to the most fundamental distinction of all between East and West. The totalitarian world produces backwardness because it does such violence to the spirit, thwarting the human impulse to create, to enjoy, to worship. The totalitarian world finds even symbols of love and of worship an affront. Years ago, before the East Germans began rebuilding their churches, they erected a secular structure: the television tower at Alexander Platz. Virtually ever since, the authorities have been working to correct what they view as the tower's one major flaw, treating the glass sphere at the top with paints and chemicals of every kind. Yet even today when the Sun strikes that sphere—that sphere that towers over all Berlin—the light makes the sign of the cross. There in Berlin, like the city itself, symbols of love, symbols of worship, cannot be suppressed.

As I looked out a moment ago from the Reichstag, that embodiment of German unity, I noticed words crudely spray-painted upon the wall, perhaps by a young Berliner, "This wall will fall. Beliefs become reality." Yes, across Europe, this wall will fall. For it cannot withstand faith; it cannot withstand truth. The wall cannot withstand freedom.

And I would like, before I close, to say one word. I have read, and I have been questioned since I've been here about certain demonstrations against my coming. And I would like to say just one thing, and to those who demonstrate so. I wonder if they have ever asked themselves that if they should have the kind of government they apparently seek, no one would ever be able to do what they're doing again.

Thank you and God bless you all.

NELSON MANDELA

Inaugural Address
(May 10, 1994)

Nelson Mandela (b. 1918) was elected as the first black president of South Africa in the country's first multi-racial elections in 1994. After spending much of his early career as a leader in the struggle to end white minority rule, Mandela was imprisoned for 28 years before his release in 1990. Upon regaining his freedom, Mandela resumed his work to end South African Apartheid, culminating in the many social changes he was able to enact as president. His inaugural address is noted for its forward-looking, optimistic tone that celebrates South Africa's progress instead of dwelling on the injustices of the past.

YOUR MAJESTIES, Your Royal Highnesses, distinguished guests, comrades and friends,

Today, all of us do, by our presence here, and by our celebrations in other parts of our country and the world, confer glory and hope to newborn liberty.

Out of the experience of an extraordinary human disaster that lasted too long, must be born a society of which all humanity will be proud.

Our daily deeds as ordinary South Africans must produce an actual South African reality that will reinforce humanity's belief in justice, strengthen its confidence in the nobility of the human soul and sustain all our hopes for a glorious life for all.

All this we owe both to ourselves and to the peoples of the world who are so well represented here today.

To my compatriots, I have no hesitation in saying that each one of us is as intimately attached to the soil of this beautiful country as are the famous jacaranda trees of Pretoria and the mimosa trees of the bushveld.

Each time one of us touches the soil of this land, we feel a sense of personal renewal. The national mood changes as the seasons change.

We are moved by a sense of joy and exhilaration when the grass turns green and the flowers bloom.

That spiritual and physical oneness we all share with this common homeland explains the depth of the pain we all carried in our hearts as we saw our country tear itself apart in terrible conflict, and as we saw it spurned, outlawed and isolated by the peoples of the world, precisely because it had become the universal base of the pernicious ideology and practice of racism and racial oppression.

We, the people of South Africa, feel fulfilled that humanity has taken us back into its bosom, that we, who were outlaws not so long ago, have today been given the rare privilege to be host to the nations of the world on our own soil.

We thank all our distinguished international guests for having come to take possession with the people of our country what is, after all, a common victory for justice, for peace, for human dignity.

We trust that you will continue to stand by us as we tackle the challenges of building peace, prosperity, non-sexism, non-racialism and democracy.

We deeply appreciate the role that the masses of our people and their political mass, democratic, religious, women, youth, business, traditional and other leaders have played to bring about this conclusion. Not least amongst them is my Second Deputy President, the Honourable F. W. de Klerk.

We would also like to pay tribute to our security forces, in all their ranks, for the distinguished role they have played in securing our first democratic elections and the transition to democracy, from bloodthirsty forces which still refuse to see the light.

The time for the healing of the wounds has come.

The moment to bridge the chasms that divide us has come.

The time to build is upon us.

We have, at last, achieved our political emancipation. We pledge ourselves to liberate all our people from the continuing bondage of poverty, deprivation, suffering, gender and other discrimination.

We succeeded to take our last steps to freedom in conditions of relative peace. We commit ourselves to the construction of a complete, just and lasting peace.

We have triumphed in the effort to implant hope in the breasts of the millions of our people. We enter into a covenant that we shall build the society in which all South Africans, both black and white, will be able to walk tall, without any fear in their hearts, assured of their inalienable right to human dignity—a rainbow nation at peace with itself and the world.

As a token of its commitment to the renewal of our country, the new Interim Government of National Unity will, as a matter of urgency, address the issue of amnesty for various categories of our people who are currently serving terms of imprisonment.

We dedicate this day to all the heroes and heroines in this country and the rest of the world who sacrificed in many ways and surrendered their lives so that we could be free.

Their dreams have become reality. Freedom is their reward.

We are both humbled and elevated by the honour and privilege that you, the people of South Africa, have bestowed on us, as the first president of a united, democratic, non-racial and non-sexist South Africa, to lead our country out of the valley of darkness.

We understand it still that there is no easy road to freedom.

We know it well that none of us acting alone can achieve success.

We must therefore act together as a united people, for national reconciliation, for nation building, for the birth of a new world.

Let there be justice for all.

Let there be peace for all.

Let there be work, bread, water and salt for all.

Let each know that for each the body, the mind and the soul have been freed to fulfil themselves.

Never, never and never again shall it be that this beautiful land will again experience the oppression of one by another and suffer the indignity of being the skunk of the world.

Let freedom reign!

The sun shall never set on so glorious a human achievement!

Let freedom reign. God bless Africa!

ELIE WIESEL

"The Perils of Indifference" (April 12, 1999)

Elie Wiesel (b. 1928) is a writer and political activist, best known as the author of Night, *a memoir about the time he spent in the Nazi concentration camps of Auschwitz and Buchenwald. After the publication of* Night *in 1955, Wiesel continued to write and speak about the importance of human dignity, receiving the Nobel Peace Prize for his work in 1986. In the following speech, delivered as part of the Millennium Lecture Series in the East Room of the White House, Wiesel discusses how it is the duty of every person to speak out against injustice, and how indifference to suffering is at the root of all evil.*

MR. PRESIDENT, Mrs. Clinton, members of Congress, Ambassador Holbrooke, Excellencies, friends:

Fifty-four years ago to the day, a young Jewish boy from a small town in the Carpathian Mountains woke up, not far from Goethe's beloved Weimar, in a place of eternal infamy called Buchenwald. He was finally free, but there was no joy in his heart. He thought there never would be again.

Liberated a day earlier by American soldiers, he remembers their rage at what they saw. And even if he lives to be a very old man, he will always be grateful to them for that rage, and also for their compassion. Though he did not understand their language, their eyes told him what he needed to know—that they, too, would remember, and bear witness.

And now, I stand before you, Mr. President—

Commander-in-Chief of the army that freed me, and tens of thousands of others—and I am filled with a profound and abiding gratitude to the American people.

Gratitude is a word that I cherish. Gratitude is what defines the humanity of the human being. And I am grateful to you, Hillary—or Mrs. Clinton—for what you said, and for what you are doing for children in the world, for the homeless, for the victims of injustice, the victims of destiny and society. And I thank all of you for being here.

We are on the threshold of a new century, a new millennium. What will the legacy of this vanishing century be? How will it be remembered in the new millennium? Surely it will be judged, and judged severely, in both moral and metaphysical terms. These failures have cast a dark shadow over humanity: two World Wars, countless civil wars, the senseless chain of assassinations—Gandhi, the Kennedys, Martin Luther King, Sadat, Rabin—bloodbaths in Cambodia and Nigeria, India and Pakistan, Ireland and Rwanda, Eritrea and Ethiopia, Sarajevo and Kosovo; the inhumanity in the gulag and the tragedy of Hiroshima. And, on a different level, of course, Auschwitz and Treblinka.

So much violence, so much indifference.

What is indifference? Etymologically, the word means "no difference." A strange and unnatural state in which the lines blur between light and darkness, dusk and dawn, crime and punishment, cruelty and compassion, good and evil.

What are its courses and inescapable consequences? Is it a philosophy? Is there a philosophy of indifference conceivable? Can one possibly view indifference as a virtue? Is it necessary at times to practice it simply to keep one's sanity, live normally, enjoy a fine meal and a glass of wine, as the world around us experiences harrowing upheavals?

Of course, indifference can be tempting—more than that, seductive. It is so much easier to look away from victims. It is so much easier to avoid such rude interruptions to our work, our dreams, our hopes. It is, after all, awkward, troublesome, to be involved in another person's pain and despair. Yet, for the person who is indifferent, his or her neighbor are of no consequence. And, therefore, their lives are meaningless. Their hidden or even visible anguish is of no interest.

Indifference reduces the other to an abstraction.

Over there, behind the black gates of Auschwitz, the most tragic of all prisoners were the "Muselmänner," as they were called. Wrapped in their torn blankets, they would sit or lie on the ground, staring vacantly into space, unaware of who or where they were, strangers to their surroundings. They no longer felt pain, hunger, thirst. They feared nothing. They felt nothing. They were dead and did not know it.

Rooted in our tradition, some of us felt that to be abandoned by humanity then was not the ultimate. We felt that to be abandoned by God was worse than to be punished by Him. Better an unjust God than an indifferent one. For us to be ignored by God was a harsher punishment than to be a victim of His anger. Man can live far from God—not outside God. God is wherever we are. Even in suffering? Even in suffering.

In a way, to be indifferent to that suffering is what makes the human being inhuman. Indifference, after all, is more dangerous than anger and hatred. Anger can at times be creative. One writes a great poem, a great symphony, has done something special for the sake of humanity because one is angry at the injustice that one witnesses. But indifference is never creative. Even hatred at times may elicit a response. You fight it. You denounce it. You disarm it. Indifference elicits no response. Indifference is not a response.

Indifference is not a beginning, it is an end. And, therefore, indifference is always the friend of the enemy, for it benefits the aggressor—never his victim, whose pain is magnified when he or she feels forgotten. The political prisoner in his cell, the hungry children, the homeless refugees—not to respond to their plight, not to relieve their solitude by offering them a spark of hope is to exile them from human memory. And in denying their humanity we betray our own.

Indifference, then, is not only a sin, it is a punishment. And this is one of the most important lessons of this outgoing century's wide-ranging experiments in good and evil.

In the place that I come from, society was composed of three simple categories: the killers, the victims, and the bystanders. During the darkest of times, inside the ghettoes and death camps—and I'm glad that Mrs. Clinton mentioned that we are now commemorating that event, that period, that we are now in the Days of Remembrance—but then, we felt abandoned, forgotten. All of us did.

And our only miserable consolation was that we believed that Auschwitz and Treblinka were closely guarded secrets; that the leaders of the free world did not know what was going on behind those black gates and barbed wire; that they had no knowledge of the war against the Jews that Hitler's armies and their accomplices waged as part of the war against the Allies.

If they knew, we thought, surely those leaders would have moved heaven and earth to intervene. They would have spoken out with great outrage and conviction. They would have bombed the railways leading to Birkenau, just the railways, just once.

And now we knew, we learned, we discovered that the Pentagon knew, the State Department knew. And the illustrious occupant of the White House then, who was a great leader—and I say it with some anguish and pain, because, today is exactly 54 years marking his death—Franklin Delano Roosevelt died on April the 12th, 1945, so he is very much present to me and to us.

No doubt, he was a great leader. He mobilized the American people and the world, going into battle, bringing hundreds and thousands of valiant and brave soldiers in America to fight fascism, to fight dictatorship, to fight Hitler. And so many of the young people fell in battle. And, nevertheless, his image in Jewish history—I must say it—his image in Jewish history is flawed.

The depressing tale of the *St. Louis* is a case in point. Sixty years ago, its human cargo—maybe 1,000 Jews—was turned back to Nazi Germany. And that happened after the Kristallnacht, after the first state sponsored pogrom, with hundreds of Jewish shops destroyed, synagogues burned, thousands of people put in concentration camps. And that ship, which was already on the shores of the United States, was sent back.

I don't understand. Roosevelt was a good man, with a heart. He understood those who needed help. Why didn't he allow these refugees to disembark? A thousand people—in America, a great country, the greatest democracy, the most generous of all new nations in modern history. What happened? I don't understand. Why the indifference, on the highest level, to the suffering of the victims?

But then, there were human beings who were sensitive to our tragedy. Those non-Jews, those Christians, that we called the "Righteous Gentiles," whose selfless acts of heroism saved the honor of their faith. Why were they so few? Why was there a greater effort to save SS murderers after the war than to save their victims during the war?

Why did some of America's largest corporations continue to do business with Hitler's Germany until 1942? It has been suggested, and it was documented, that the Wehrmacht could not have conducted its invasion of France without oil obtained from American sources. How is one to explain their indifference?

And yet, my friends, good things have also happened in this traumatic century: the defeat of Nazism, the collapse of communism, the rebirth of Israel on its ancestral soil, the demise of apartheid, Israel's peace treaty with Egypt, the peace accord in Ireland. And let us remember the meeting, filled with drama and emotion, between Rabin and Arafat that you, Mr. President, convened in this very place. I was here and I will never forget it.

And then, of course, the joint decision of the United States and NATO to intervene in Kosovo and save those victims, those refugees, those who were uprooted by a man whom I believe that because of his crimes, should be charged with crimes against humanity. But this time, the world was not silent. This time, we do respond. This time, we intervene.

Does it mean that we have learned from the past? Does it mean that society has changed? Has the human being become less indifferent and more human? Have we really learned from our experiences? Are we less insensitive to the plight of victims of ethnic cleansing and other forms of injustices in places near and far? Is today's justified intervention in Kosovo, led by you, Mr. President, a lasting warning that never again will the deportation, the terrorization of children and their parents be allowed anywhere in the world? Will it discourage other dictators in other lands to do the same?

What about the children? Oh, we see them on television, we read about them in the papers, and we do so with a broken heart. Their fate is always the most tragic, inevitably. When adults wage war, children perish. We see their faces, their eyes. Do we hear their pleas? Do we feel their pain, their agony? Every minute one of them dies of disease, violence, famine. Some of them—so many of them—could be saved.

And so, once again, I think of the young Jewish boy from the

Carpathian Mountains. He has accompanied the old man I have become throughout these years of quest and struggle. And together we walk towards the new millennium, carried by profound fear and extraordinary hope. [Applause.]

I conclude on that.

BARACK OBAMA

Inaugural Address (January 20, 2009)

After a campaign largely framed by the unpopular policies of George W. Bush, Illinois Senator Barack Obama (b. 1961) made history when he defeated Arizona Senator John McCain to become the nation's first African American president. Attended by an estimated 1.8 million people, this inauguration had the largest attendance of any event in the history of Washington, D.C. Chief Justice John G. Roberts, Jr. administered the oath of office on the West Front of the Capitol, using the same Bible sworn on by Abraham Lincoln.

My fellow citizens: I stand here today humbled by the task before us, grateful for the trust you've bestowed, mindful of the sacrifices borne by our ancestors.

I thank President Bush for his service to our nation—as well as the generosity and cooperation he has shown throughout this transition.

Forty-four Americans have now taken the presidential oath. The words have been spoken during rising tides of prosperity and the still waters of peace. Yet, every so often, the oath is taken amidst gathering clouds and raging storms. At these moments, America has carried on not simply because of the skill or vision of those in high office, but because we, the people, have remained faithful to the ideals of our forebears and true to our founding documents.

So it has been; so it must be with this generation of Americans.

That we are in the midst of crisis is now well understood. Our nation is at war against a far-reaching network of violence and hatred. Our economy is badly weakened, a consequence of greed and irresponsibility on the part of some, but also our collective failure to make hard choices and prepare the nation for a new age. Homes have been lost, jobs shed, businesses shuttered. Our health care is too costly, our schools fail too many—and each day brings further evidence that the ways we use energy strengthen our adversaries and threaten our planet.

These are the indicators of crisis, subject to data and statistics. Less measurable, but no less profound, is a sapping of confidence across our land; a nagging fear that America's decline is inevitable, that the next generation must lower its sights.

Today I say to you that the challenges we face are real. They are serious and they are many. They will not be met easily or in a short span of time. But know this America: They will be met.

On this day, we gather because we have chosen hope over fear, unity of purpose over conflict and discord. On this day, we come to proclaim an end to the petty grievances and false promises, the recriminations and worn-out dogmas that for far too long have strangled our politics. We remain a young nation. But in the words of Scripture, the time has come to set aside childish things. The time has come to reaffirm our enduring spirit; to choose our better history; to carry forward that precious gift, that noble idea passed on from generation to generation: the God-given promise that all are equal, all are free, and all deserve a chance to pursue their full measure of happiness.

In reaffirming the greatness of our nation we understand that greatness is never a given. It must be earned. Our journey has never been one of short-cuts or settling for less. It has not been the path for the faint-hearted, for those that prefer leisure over work, or seek only the pleasures of riches and fame. Rather, it has been the risk-takers, the doers, the makers of things—some celebrated, but more often men and women obscure in their labor—who have carried us up the long rugged path towards prosperity and freedom.

For us, they packed up their few worldly possessions and traveled across oceans in search of a new life. For us, they toiled in sweatshops, and settled the West, endured the lash of the whip, and plowed the hard earth. For us, they fought and died in places like Concord and Gettysburg, Normandy and Khe Sahn.

Time and again these men and women struggled and sacrificed and worked till their hands were raw so that we might live a better life. They saw America as bigger than the sum of our individual ambitions, greater than all the differences of birth or wealth or faction.

This is the journey we continue today. We remain the most prosperous, powerful nation on Earth. Our workers are no less productive than when this crisis began. Our minds are no less inventive, our goods and services no less needed than they were last week, or last month, or last year. Our capacity remains undiminished. But our time of standing pat, of protecting narrow interests and putting off unpleasant decisions—that time has surely passed. Starting today, we must pick ourselves up, dust ourselves off, and begin again the work of remaking America.

For everywhere we look, there is work to be done. The state of our economy calls for action, bold and swift. And we will act, not only to create new jobs, but to lay a new foundation for growth. We will build the roads and bridges, the electric grids and digital lines that feed our commerce and bind us together. We'll restore science to its rightful place, and wield technology's wonders to raise health care's quality and lower its cost. We will harness the sun and the winds and the soil to fuel our cars and run our factories. And we will transform our schools and colleges and universities to meet the demands of a new age. All this we can do. All this we will do.

Now, there are some who question the scale of our ambitions, who suggest that our system cannot tolerate too many big plans. Their memories are short, for they have forgotten what this country has already done, what free men and women can achieve when imagination is joined to common purpose, and necessity to courage. What the cynics fail to understand is that the ground has shifted beneath them, that the stale political arguments that have consumed us for so long no longer apply.

The question we ask today is not whether our government is too big or too small, but whether it works—whether it helps families find jobs at a decent wage, care they can afford, a retirement that is dignified. Where the answer is yes, we intend to move forward. Where the answer is no, programs will end. And those of us who manage the public's dollars will be held to account, to spend wisely, reform bad habits, and do our business in the light of day, because only then can we restore the vital trust between a people and their government.

Nor is the question before us whether the market is a force for good or ill. Its power to generate wealth and expand freedom is unmatched. But this crisis has reminded us that without a watchful eye, the market can spin out of control. The nation cannot prosper long when it favors only the prosperous. The success of our economy has always depended not just on the size of our gross domestic product, but on the reach of our prosperity, on the ability to extend opportunity to every willing heart—not out of charity, but because it is the surest route to our common good.

As for our common defense, we reject as false the choice between our safety and our ideals. Our Founding Fathers—our Founding Fathers, faced with perils that we can scarcely imagine, drafted a charter to assure the rule of law and the rights of man—a charter expanded by the blood of generations. Those ideals still light the world, and we will not give them up for expedience sake.

And so, to all the other peoples and governments who are watching today, from the grandest capitals to the small village where my father was born, know that America is a friend of each nation, and every man, woman and child who seeks a future of peace and dignity. And we are ready to lead once more.

Recall that earlier generations faced down fascism and communism not just with missiles and tanks, but with the sturdy alliances and enduring convictions. They understood that our power alone cannot protect us, nor does it entitle us to do as we please. Instead they knew that our power grows through its prudent use; our security emanates from the justness of our cause, the force of our example, the tempering qualities of humility and restraint.

We are the keepers of this legacy. Guided by these principles once more we can meet those new threats that demand even greater effort, even greater cooperation and understanding between nations. We will begin to responsibly leave Iraq to its people and forge a hard-earned peace in Afghanistan. With old friends and former foes, we'll work tirelessly to lessen the nuclear threat, and roll back the specter of a warming planet.

We will not apologize for our way of life, nor will we waver in its defense. And for those who seek to advance their aims by inducing terror and slaughtering innocents, we say to you now that our spirit is stronger and cannot be broken—you cannot outlast us, and we will defeat you.

For we know that our patchwork heritage is a strength, not a weakness. We are a nation of Christians and Muslims, Jews and Hindus, and non-believers. We are shaped by every language and culture, drawn from every end of this Earth; and because we have tasted the bitter swill of civil war and segregation, and emerged from that dark chapter stronger and more united, we cannot help but believe that the old hatreds shall someday pass; that the lines of tribe shall soon dissolve; that as the world grows smaller, our common humanity shall reveal itself; and that America must play its role in ushering in a new era of peace.

To the Muslim world, we seek a new way forward, based on mutual interest and mutual respect. To those leaders around the globe who seek to sow conflict, or blame their society's ills on the West, know that your people will judge you on what you can build, not what you destroy.

To those who cling to power through corruption and deceit and the silencing of dissent, know that you are on the wrong side of history, but that we will extend a hand if you are willing to unclench your fist.

To the people of poor nations, we pledge to work alongside you to make your farms flourish and let clean waters flow; to nourish starved bodies and feed hungry minds. And to those nations like ours that enjoy relative plenty, we say we can no longer afford indifference to the suffering outside our borders, nor can we consume the world's resources without regard to effect. For the world has changed, and we must change with it.

As we consider the role that unfolds before us, we remember with humble gratitude those brave Americans who at this very hour patrol far-off deserts and distant mountains. They have something to tell us, just as the fallen heroes who lie in Arlington whisper through the ages.

We honor them not only because they are the guardians of our liberty, but because they embody the spirit of service—a willingness to find meaning in something greater than themselves.

And yet at this moment, a moment that will define a generation, it is precisely this spirit that must inhabit us all. For as much as government can do, and must do, it is ultimately the faith and determination of the American people upon which this nation relies. It is the kindness to take in a stranger when the levees break, the selflessness of workers who would rather cut their hours than see a friend lose their job which sees us through our darkest hours. It is the firefighter's courage to storm a stairway filled with smoke, but also a parent's willingness to nurture a child that finally decides our fate.

Our challenges may be new. The instruments with which we meet them may be new. But those values upon which our success depends—honesty and hard work, courage and fair play, tolerance and curiosity, loyalty and patriotism—these things are old. These things are true. They have been the quiet force of progress throughout our history.

What is demanded, then, is a return to these truths. What is required of us now is a new era of responsibility—a recognition on the part of every American that we have duties to ourselves, our nation and the world; duties that we do not grudgingly accept, but rather seize gladly, firm in the knowledge that there is nothing so satisfying to the spirit, so defining of our character than giving our all to a difficult task.

This is the price and the promise of citizenship. This is the source of our confidence—the knowledge that God calls on us to shape an uncertain destiny. This is the meaning of our liberty and our creed, why men and women and children of every race and every faith can join in celebration across this magnificent mall; and why a man whose father less than 60 years ago might not have been served in a local restaurant can now stand before you to take a most sacred oath.

So let us mark this day with remembrance of who we are and how far we have traveled. In the year of America's birth, in the coldest of months, a small band of patriots huddled by dying campfires on the shores of an icy river. The capital was abandoned. The enemy was advancing. The snow was stained with blood. At the moment when the outcome of our revolution was most in doubt, the father of our nation ordered these words to be read to the people:

"Let it be told to the future world...that in the depth of winter, when nothing but hope and virtue could survive...that the city and the country, alarmed at one common danger, came forth to meet [it]."

America: In the face of our common dangers, in this winter of our hardship, let us remember these timeless words. With hope and virtue, let us brave once more the icy currents, and endure what storms may come. Let it be said by our children's children that when we were tested we refused to let this journey end, that we did not turn back nor did we falter; and with eyes fixed on the horizon and God's grace upon us, we carried forth that great gift of freedom and delivered it safely to future generations.

Thank you. God bless you. And God bless the United States of America.